Sport, Technology and the Body

What is the nature of athletic performance? This book offers an answer to this fascinating question by considering the relationship between sport, technology and the body. Specifically, it examines cultural resistance to the enhancement of athletes and explores the ways in which performance technologies complicate and confound our conception of the sporting body.

The book addresses concerns about the technological 'invasion' of the 'natural' body to investigate expectations that athletic performances reflect nothing more than the actual capacity of the untainted athlete. By examining a series of case studies, including Paralympic sprinter Oscar Pistorius, Fastskin swimsuits, hypoxic chambers and an array of illicit substances and methods, the book distinguishes between internal and external technologies to highlight the ways that performance enhancement, and public reaction to it, can be read.

Sport, Technology and the Body offers a powerful challenge to conventional views of athletic performance that stand authenticity against artifice, integrity against corruption, and athletic purity against technological intrusion. It is essential reading for all serious students of the sociology, culture or ethics of sport.

Tara Magdalinski is the Academic Director of the Centre for Sports Studies at University College Dublin. Her research focuses on the construction of social identities and the production of historical narratives through sport. She co-edited *With God on Their Side: Sport in the Service of Religion* (Routledge, 2002).

Sport, Technology and the Body

The nature of performance

Tara Magdalinski

LONDON AND NEW YORK

First published 2009
by Routledge
2 Park Square, Milton Park, Abingdon, Oxon, OX14 4RN

Simultaneously published in the USA and Canada
by Routledge
711 Third Avenue, New York, NY 10017

Routledge is an imprint of the Taylor & Francis Group, an informa business

© 2009 Tara Magdalinski

Typeset in Goudy by
Taylor & Francis Books

All rights reserved. No part of this book may be reprinted or reproduced
or utilised in any form or by any electronic, mechanical, or other means,
now known or hereafter invented, including photocopying and recording,
or in any information storage or retrieval system, without permission in
writing from the publishers.

British Library Cataloguing in Publication Data
A catalogue record for this book is available from the British Library

Library of Congress Cataloging in Publication Data
Magdalinski, Tara.
   Sport, technology and the body / by Tara Magdalinski.
      p. cm.
   Includes bibliographical references.
   1. Sports–Sociological aspects. 2. Sports–Physiological aspects. 3.
   Sports–Moral and ethical aspects. 4. Sports sciences. 5. Athletes–
   Training of. 6. Performance technology. 7. Body image. 8. Body,
   Human–Social aspects. I. Title.
   GV706.5.M33 2009
   796.01–dc22
                                          2008016085

ISBN13 978-0-415-37877-2 (hbk)
ISBN13 978-0-415-37876-5 (pbk)
ISBN13 978-0-203-09938-4 (ebk)

For Mummy,
for your strength,
for your courage,
for your wisdom,
for your love.
I miss you desperately.

Contents

	Acknowledgments	viii
	List of abbreviations	x
1	Introduction: sport, the body and performance technology	1
2	The nature of sport	14
3	The nature of the body	31
4	The nature of performance	54
5	The nature of health	71
6	'Those girls with sideburns': enhancing the female body	91
7	Enhancing the body from without: artificial skins and other prosthetics	109
8	Drugs, sport and Australian identity	128
9	The performance of nature at the Sydney 2000 Olympic Games	145
10	Conclusion	157
	Bibliography	163
	Index	181

Acknowledgments

Although writing can be a solitary, even lonely, experience, a book is never produced in isolation, and there are so many friends, family and colleagues who have supported me with ideas, encouragement and advice over the years. First, I would like to acknowledge the institutions that provided the requisite time, space and intellectual stimulation to see this project through to completion. The School of Human Movement Studies at the University of Queensland was my home during a long overdue sabbatical in 2005, and it was a wonderful opportunity to renew old acquaintances and make new friends. Despite the distractions of rugby, sheep and castles, I spent the second part of my research semester in the Department of Psychology and Education at the University of Glamorgan; thank you for making a 'ring in' feel so welcome. I would like to especially thank the Centre for Critical and Cultural Studies at the University of Queensland for offering 'asylum' when I needed it; your generosity was much appreciated. I would also like to express my sincerest gratitude to my understanding colleagues in the Centre for Sports Studies and the School of Public Health and Population Science at University College Dublin for indulging me the time and space, during a hectic restructure, to finish this manuscript. Finally, I have appreciated the backing of a terrific publisher, and several editors, and so would like to extend my thanks to Samantha Grant and Simon Whitmore for their guidance and, most importantly, their patience.

I am incredibly fortunate that the field of sports studies includes so many inspiring and accomplished individuals, who have been exceptionally generous with their time, advice and ideas. I would particularly like to recognise the support, encouragement and, most importantly, friendship I have received over the years from Patricia Vertinsky, Doug Booth, Murray Phillips, Malcolm MacLean, Mike Cronin, Allen Guttmann, Richard Cashman, Wray Vamplew, Doug Brown, Jim McKay, John Bale, Mel Adelman, Colin Tatz and John Hughson. Finally, I would like to acknowledge my friends and colleagues in both the Australian Society for Sports History and the North American Society for Sport History who have listened to, and offered constructive feedback on, versions of these chapters, despite my brief forays into tales of wombats and arses.

Acknowledgments ix

On a personal note, my friends and family know how difficult the last three years have been, and I hope you know that it is only your love and strength that has seen me through. I would especially like to acknowledge the talented Karen Brooks: you have provided invaluable love and advice for over a decade, and you cannot know how much your friendship has meant to me; darling Jane Prince, who gave me a bed (finally!), endless cups of tea and a good deal of wine during those sunny Cardiffian months. You made my stay in that quaint, green city particularly, well, quaint (say, is that the Millennium Stadium again?); my various 'families' (and crashpads) around the world include my honorary 'feral parents' Bobby and Pauline Simm, thank you for your love, the wine and the obligatory *Bold*; to Torsten, Diana and Eyleen Kothe for the years of love, friendship and my Neuenbrunslar home; and to Caley and Max Madden for being two of the brightest stars in my life.

Finally, to my family: what on earth could I ever say to thank you enough. To my gorgeous cousins, Rachel Vowles and Dale Williams, how can I ever tell you what you mean to me? You are my sisters. To my wonderful Daddy, Lloyd, if not for you, my journey through the world of sport would never have started, and for your love, belief in me and the coaching (!) I will forever thank the heavens. To my beautiful and brilliant sister, Anna. Moon, I love you very much and am so enormously proud of you – now it is your turn to write the 'Great [insert nation of choice] Novel'. And finally to Marcus Wehr, your love and constant support on the emotional rollercoaster that is my life means everything to me, as do you … oh, and thanks for the occasional insight into the crazy train!

Abbreviations

AIS	Australian Institute of Sport
ASC	Australian Sports Commission
FINA	Federation Internationale de Natation
IAAF	International Association of Athletics Federations
IFBB	International Federation of Bodybuilders
IOC	International Olympic Committee
rEPO	recombinant Erythropoietin
SOCOG	Sydney Organising Committee for the Olympic Games
TUE	Therapeutic Use Exemption
USOT	United States Olympic Team
WADA	World Anti-Doping Agency
WHO	World Health Organisation

1 Introduction

Sport, the body and performance technology

In 1995, Zoe Warwick committed suicide. A dedicated bodybuilder and former European champion, a career of abusing steroids had culminated in the disintegration of her once flawless body. The medications pumped into her to keep her alive could not prevent system after system from shutting down, and, unable to cope with the pain, she took her own life. In 1988, Ben Johnson was celebrated as the fastest human being to propel his body down a one hundred-metre track. He then became the most infamous drug cheat in the history of modern sport, testing positive to stanozolol. In 2000, after trialling a 'fastskin' for Adidas, Ian Thorpe announced to a press conference that the new full-length swimsuit certainly 'optimised' his performance but carefully pointed out that it did not 'enhance' it. A body destroyed, a world record negated, and a performance improved; each reveals the difficult relationship between the 'natural' body and technology to be central to contemporary constructions of elite sport.

Modern sport is a paradox. On the one hand, the quest for outstanding performances, encapsulated in the Olympic motto of *Citius, Altius, Fortius*, requires increasing scientific intrusion into the sporting body. Athletes, coaches and sports scientists rigorously search for techniques, supplements or modifications that will deliver the elusive 'edge', whilst the public crave world records each time an athlete steps onto the track, dives into the pool or tumbles across the mat. The promised commercial benefits that accompany international sporting success mean securing the slightest of advantages over a competitor is paramount. Not only the momentary glory of a gold medal, but financial security and a post-sport career rest on the split second or fraction of a centimetre found in a biomechanically adjusted gait or a nutritionally superior diet. Yet, modifying the body through physical culture is not confined to the elite athlete. Even casual participants are encouraged to submit their bodies to the tyranny of exercise equipment. A brief wander through a local fitness centre reveals a profusion of machinery and an excess of programmes to adjust a body's size, shape or capacity. At home, the latest dietary fads blare out from the television set or gaze up from the pages of glossy magazines. Pedometers, heart monitors and iPods, which accompany even the most lay of athletes on their daily constitutionals,

2 Introduction

are further evidence of the increasingly technologised exercising body. In the twenty-first century, exercise and sport are not simply amusing diversions but are conducted with the expectation of physical modification and augmentation achieved through discipline, hard work and, in many ways, the body's capitulation to the rigours of the machine.

The sports performance industry has grown exponentially over the latter part of the twentieth century for both recreational participants and professional athletes. It is now not uncommon to find physiologists, biomechanists and psychologists amongst a growing cadre of support personnel for elite athletes. Olympic, representative and professional teams travel with almost as many auxiliary staff as they do team members, and these adjuncts poke, prod, test and taunt the athletic body, trying to nudge it closer towards its limits, encouraged by the glittering prize just beyond their grasp. The athletic body itself is no longer worked on in its entirety, but, in a gesture towards the Cartesian body, is dissected into smaller and smaller pieces with each scientific discipline that emerges. Teams of specialists are assigned to these bits of the body, which are then honed until they increase their capacity and realise their potential. As such, sporting bodies are externally and internally crafted into a form that will both visually and functionally fulfil their athletic roles and expectations.

Whilst sports science has flourished in recent decades, for many, the single-minded pursuit of achievement rests uneasily on the traditional foundations of modern sport. Popularly predicated on notions of 'fair play', physical rejuvenation and a balance between body and mind, sport is thought to be an activity performed as an antidote to the rational modern world. It is constructed as more than mere physical activity and is believed to embody a philosophy that offers participants the opportunity to learn positive and desirable characteristics that can be adapted to 'real life' (Shields and Bredemeier 1995). For this reason, athletes are supposed to exemplify qualities that include honesty, patience, diligence, hard work, dedication, integrity and sacrifice, for which they are admired by the public and regarded as role models for the young. In essence, the sporting experience, regardless whether at the elite, junior or casual level, is thought to reflect a 'spirit' that privileges participation over winning, friendship over competition, and, for many, the value of sporting performance lies not in the quantitative result but in its qualitative meanings (Loland 2002; Voy 1991). The Olympic movement's 'Celebrate Humanity' advertisements, the Canadian 'Spirit of Sport' campaign and a range of similarly devised international programmes confirm that, although modern sport may seem to be on a wayward path, the philosophical and ethical precepts remain the ideological basis, even essence, of the sporting experience.

The discord between elite achievement sport and the traditional model of physical recreations as character building, or between the 'essence' or 'spirit' of sport (Møller 2003), is evident in concerns about increased technologisation. As sport is supposed to generate desirable human qualities and restore the healthy body, the scientific-based incursion of technology into the sports realm seems to threaten these fundamental principles. Rather than being a naturalistic activity that allows for freedom of movement and the bodily expression of physical potential, under the shadow of technology sport becomes a highly disciplined, rationalised endeavour that rewards performances for their measurable outcomes rather than any kind of inherent virtues. In response, administrators, athletes and the public alike try to promote sport's 'intrinsic' worth by reclaiming it as an authentic activity that is impervious to the damaging effects of technology, reflected in a range of proclamations and statements that privilege, even sanctify, the ideology of natural sport over its technological assault.

The perception that the meaning, value or spirit of sport is diminished by the presence of technology is, of course, only reasonable if sport and technology are juxtaposed against one another, where the former represents a natural activity in which the human body is the central concern, and the latter is an artificial product that corrupts the body. Such a binary construction relies on a broader cultural 'technophobia' that contends 'natural' products and methods to be superior to anything created by the human hand (Barilan and Weintraub 2001). The interaction between technology and human subjects in these hierarchies reveals a shifting relationship between nature, the body and technology, in which fears about the meaning and future of humanity have long been manifest. Whilst technology may now be accepted as an indispensable part of contemporary life, it is not all too long ago that the emergence of industrial technologies was accompanied by fears that the intrusion of, and a reliance on, technology would materially alter our conception of humanity (Stern 1998).

From working bodies coupled with machines through to genetic engineering, the ease with which bodies can be manipulated, as well as the emergence of organic/inorganic hybrids, has threatened to obscure clear boundaries between human and technology. With the recent publication of the map of the human genome, a decades-long endeavour that has opened up countless opportunities for a range of gene therapies, there have been renewed misgivings about our ability to manipulate or even design bodies. Fears about an emerging Frankensteinian world, where body parts are reduced to interchangeable commodities, are revived when news reports show mice growing transplantable human ears on their backs, and the revival of eugenicist tendencies is presaged when babies can be selected by desirable physical characteristic or even sexual orientation. It seems we prefer to regard technology as an adjunct to our daily lives, a tool, rather than an end in and of itself, one that identifies and confirms difference, rather than one that imperils the very conception of who we are as a species. This is particularly apparent within the context of contemporary sport where authorities are rushing to ensure that genetic therapies cannot be employed for athletic gain (Miah 2004), confirming that artifice and authenticity are categorically juxtaposed in an activity that is represented as a natural expression of humanity designed to refresh the working body and renew the dispirited soul.

4   *Introduction*

Yet, the conflicted relationship between sport and technology is far more complex than casual analyses might suggest, and it would certainly be naïve to regard, or even to prefer, sport and technology to be independent categories with little overlap. Modern sport is itself a thoroughly technological product that first emerged during an era of escalating scientific, industrial and technological advances. With the development of mechanised production processes, the informality of rural games was abandoned as the pressures of the time clock and other industrial techniques influenced the structure and conduct of physical activity. These emergent leisure pursuits came to closely mirror the new regulation of time, space and the body. Sport has thus been complicit in the regulation and surveillance of the body and has contributed to the creation of docile bodies (Foucault 1977). Participants are taught to start and stop at the sound of a whistle, remain within the strict confines of the pitch and play in specialised positions, each member of a team working together like cogs in a machine, just like the new factory regimes to which working bodies had been subjugated. The technological innovations in the workplace and on the sportsfield were symptomatic of both an increasingly regulated life and the physical and emotional alienation that resulted from industrial labour (Shilling 2005). The codification of modern sports replicated, in essence, the mechanised and rule-bound structure of the workplace and, rather than embodying freedom, was explicitly a 'prison of measured time' (Brohm 1978).

By the late nineteenth century, many leisure activities incorporated new mechanised forms and, rather than offering the promised escape from work, served to demystify industrial technology, 'redefining that source of stress as a means for pleasure' (de la Peña 2003: 87). Carolyn de la Peña (2003) notes how early amusement parks, such as Coney Island, converted the technology of the workplace into technologies of leisure, whilst the application of machines to the relaxing body, even within 'natural' settings, was thought to be healthful and rejuvenating. Similarly, new transport technologies allowed urban dwellers to recreate in wilderness or seaside precincts at the same time that these technologies were themselves transformed into sporting pursuits. Clearly, technology has been seamlessly incorporated into many aspects of sport without generating anxiety.

Despite the uneasiness it may provoke, technology is firmly embedded in contemporary sport. The production of improved equipment, such as larger tennis racquets, more flexible poles for vaulting, sprung floors in gymnastics, synthetic tracks or fields for athletics or team sports, and aerodynamic skis, as well as clothing that variously decreases drag, removes sweat or regulates body temperature, has relied on complex innovation in engineering and product and material design. Technological advances have also been instrumental in improving the safety of many sports. The development of sophisticated helmets, mouthguards and padding, for example, has ensured the health and well-being of participants. There is some evidence to suggest, however, that such complex protective equipment may have actually led to greater rates and degrees of injuries, as athletes feel more invincible and thus are prepared to take more risks or even may use their safety equipment as weapons on the sportsfield (Stoner and Keating 1993). Furthermore, the disciplinary regulation of time and space results from the application of technology to physical activity, and even the locations where sport is played are the consequence of the deliberate technological modification or reproduction of the landscape. Whilst technology is clearly central to the organisation and conduct of modern sport, perhaps the most explicit expression of the sport/technology nexus lies within exercise science, where the development of body technologies is designed to produce improved performances (Pronger 2002).

Modern sport emerged in an era where scientific enquiry into the body had lost its heretical connotations, and where the triumph of reason during the Enlightenment had ushered in new rational paradigms that were increasingly employed to map the human organism. The body was reconceived as a legitimate object of study, and new scientific disciplines tried to identify, categorise and determine its properties. The development of complex production processes influenced scientific representations of the body, which was increasingly conceived in the mechanistic terms of the new industrial landscape. Bodies were thought to be fixed entities that, like machines, could be improved upon to elicit a greater level of efficiency.

Establishing the limits of human capacity was part of a broader nineteenth-century concern with measuring and recording all kinds of bodies, particularly those encountered through various colonising missions (Gould 1981), and it was not until later in the nineteenth century that scientists began to conceive of bodies as a kind of 'raw material' that could be manipulated and enhanced through human intervention (de la Peña 2003). The idea that the body could be stretched beyond what existed challenged the notion of fixed, 'natural limits' (Hoberman 1992: 9), and as physical capacity was no longer thought to be predetermined, the body was reconceived as malleable and responsive to external stressors. Yet, these scientific advances were not initially applied to sport to improve athletic performances, for, although it was growing in popularity and significance, sport was not the global industry it is today, and applying scientific research to the small sector of the population who indulged in athletic pursuits was not a high priority for scientists. Furthermore, the dominant amateur philosophy at the time eschewed behaviours that took sport too seriously, and so, as was to become evident across the twentieth century, a rigorous scientific preparation of athletes conflicted with the gentlemanly approach to physical recreations.

It was not until the early twentieth century that the discipline of exercise science gradually emerged in its own right to chart the exercising body, using a range of biochemical and physical subdisciplines to predict and augment athletes' physical performances (Hoberman 1992). Stretching biological limits and increasing physiological capacities thus became a legitimate scientific pursuit, and the exercising body provided the ideal site where these

6 Introduction

new theories could be tested. Since the Second World War, there has been a significant 'paradigm shift' in the way that scientific results have been applied to training techniques, resulting in impressive performances and previously unimagined achievements (Beamish and Ritchie 2005).

Despite its critical appeal to both coaches and athletes, the intrusive presence of technology has provoked anxiety that the spirit of sport, the nature of performance and humanity itself are being irreparably harmed. Yet, given that chemical concoctions, radical training techniques and innumerable advances have been ingested, followed or applied to generate a greater physical output from the exercising body, it is clear that the notion of performance enhancement *per se* is not the issue, indeed, the single-minded pursuit of athletic glory is revered amongst the sports-loving public. In reality, the *manner* in which athletes augment their performance remains of greatest concern (Gardner 1989). For many, sporting performances are only considered of value if they represent an expression of a body's natural capacity and are the visible result of hard work, discipline and sacrifice (Reid 1998). Technological enhancements, by contrast, are typically rejected as 'shortcuts' that negate the need for toil and commitment, suggesting that, within sport, choosing what is regarded as a 'passive' means to an end does not engender as much respect as the hearty physical exertion that generates a good sweat. Physiological changes in the body thus have to be 'earned', so technologies such as hypoxic chambers in which athletes might simply sit or sleep are thought to violate the spirit of sport because there is no requirement to *do* anything to receive its benefits (Levine 2006). This is certainly not to suggest there is a simple Orwellian dichotomy in sport whereby 'nature is good' and 'technology is bad'. There are, indeed, many technologies that are wholeheartedly embraced by the sports fraternity, particularly those that are required as part of the actual activity itself. Without cycles or stopwatches, for example, the Tour de France would be reduced to a lengthy foot race; dispensing with yachts or surfboards would leave competitors treading water in the ocean; or prohibiting racquets, bats, clubs and balls would find tennis players, baseballers and golfers standing around, essentially unoccupied and perhaps more than a little confused.

Although some technologies find a comfortable place in sport, those that are categorically rejected as inappropriately intrusive include any that threaten to fundamentally alter the body and its capacity. Despite the emerging belief in the malleability of biological capacity, bodies nevertheless are subject to the basic laws of physics, such that, regardless of their preparation, a sprinter will never be able to complete one hundred metres in no time at all. Thus, increasingly smaller performance increments have exerted additional pressure on coaches, administrators and, above all, exercise scientists to discover methods or elixirs that will generate a winning margin. Nevertheless, the concept of 'performance enhancement' is marginalised within sport, conjuring up images of steroid-fuelled, Amazonian women with deep voices, facial hair and bulging muscles, or freakish bodybuilders, furtively injecting veterinary drugs into their thighs. Suspected drug abusers are exposed in the sports media even before their guilt is determined, whilst confirmed dopers are paraded publicly as monstrous warnings to those who dare transgress acceptable bodily limits (Magdalinski and Brooks 2002). Using illicit technologies to provide an 'unfair advantage', for many, represents the antithesis of all that is considered meaningful about organised physical activity, and conceiving elite performance as nothing more than the consequence of extreme technological intervention is similarly unthinkable. As such, training methods, supplements and other applications are targeted for particular criticism if they are determined to be an 'unnatural' or 'artificial' way of enhancing performance. Not only do these substances personify the extremes of technological intrusion, they are believed to negate sport's basic 'natural' or 'human' tenets. In fact, there appears to be almost no greater evil in sport than to supplement the body artificially in the pursuit of victory, despite the fact that the competitive structure of sport unashamedly compels competitors to consider any and every means possible to secure their victory. 'Performance enhancement', particularly chemical intervention, is rejected unreservedly, for it represents the inevitable consequence of the uneasy relationship between sport and technology.

Despite an ostensibly clear distinction between accepted technologies and those determined to be 'performance enhancing', the line between the two is ever shifting and there is remarkably little consistency in determining which innovations acceptably assist the body and which are considered thoroughly inappropriate. Numerous scientifically designed supplements and techniques are deemed to be legitimate means to realise biological potential, which, for many, suggests that the decision to ban particular technologies appears somewhat arbitrary. The list of banned substances is amended regularly as new substances are included and, at times, others are removed. Prohibited substances vary between sports; sports science textbooks not even a decade old recommend techniques that have been subsequently discredited; and coaches and athletes who once experimented with substances and training methods often become the most vocal supporters of sport's own 'war on drugs'. Whilst administrators blithely dream of the day when sport will be 'drug-free', none clarify that they are only working towards liberating sport from banned, not all, chemical interventions. Elite sporting bodies, it seems, still require a plethora of legal enhancements to perform at the levels expected of them.

Although the complex reasons why some technologies are disqualified and others are permitted in sport have been discussed at length, these tend to fall into one of two broad categories: morality and health (Miah 2006; Noakes 2004; Schneider and Butcher 2000; Gardner 1989). On the one hand, performance-enhancing technologies are banned because they are thought to provide an unfair advantage to those utilising them; on the other, they

8   *Introduction*

are proscribed because of an assumed risk to the health and well-being of the athlete. What is pertinent about these justifications is that whilst 'health' and 'morality' seem to be disparate reasons for regulating performance technologies in sport, both crucially reveal entrenched concerns about not just the nature of sport, but about nature *in* sport. Despite a never-ending thirst for new records and an elite sport culture that adheres to the tenet of *Citius, Altius, Fortius,* in the twenty-first century much of the anxiety about illicit performance enhancement centres on fears that an athlete and her/his authentic, natural performance are being irreparably disrupted, and potentially harmed, by artificial, external means. This assumes, of course, that sport represents a natural endeavour in the first place and that the athletic body similarly exists in a pure, unblemished state. Such assumptions about the nature of sport and about nature in sport must be interrogated to appreciate how particular performance technologies signify the uncomfortable dissolution of boundaries between nature and technology.

Whilst it is certainly true that many have studied the complex relationship between technology and the body in relation to sport (Miah 2004; Hoberman 1992), what has been missing is a careful analysis of the nature of performance, which considers in detail the relationship between nature, the body, sport and technology. As such, this volume offers an insight into the cultural significance of performance technologies and their place within traditional ideologies of sport to identify the impact these have on not just the athlete's body but on their performance. 'Performance technologies' is a collective term that encompasses a range of mechanical and chemical interventions designed to alter the body and improve the physical performance of an athlete. These include equipment, dietary and physical manipulations, drugs, supplements and other substances, as well as training methods and techniques. The main focus is, however, on illicit performance enhancement such as drugs, blood doping and other prohibited substances and methods, to determine the ways that technology and the body intersect within a discursive construction of the nature/artifice binary. The book begins by analysing the significance of nature for sport, the body and performance, as nature clearly represents the critical juncture where these intersect. The analysis traces the juxtaposition of nature/sport on the one hand against culture/technology on the other, each representing discrete categories that appear to come undone through the presence of illicitly enhanced athletic bodies. Further, this volume explores how this neat binary couplet is disrupted by the elite athletic body, an entity that is neither wholly natural nor completely technological. Rather than trying to re-establish these boundaries by pleading for a return to the 'natural athlete', this book examines the liminality of the elite athletic body and looks at the way that the ambivalence of this body is central to concerns about illicit or unnatural performance enhancement.

At the crux of the performance enhancement debate are fears about the disruption of the established categories of 'nature' and 'technology' within sport, and the despair that this destabilised relationship causes. As such, this study provides a cultural analysis of performance technologies, focusing on the ways that controversies surrounding banned substances and techniques reveal tensions within a range of social identities. In short, it argues that performance enhancement in sport has cultural and social implications and meanings beyond simply improving athletic output. It identifies and explores myriad ideologies that are inscribed onto sporting bodies and analyses the ways in which performance technologies complicate and confound our conception of the athletic body. The volume also addresses concerns about the technological 'invasion' of the 'natural' body and draws upon a number of case studies to examine the relationship between sport, bodies, health, the nation, landscape and gender to highlight the multifaceted ways that performance enhancement, and public reaction to it, can be read. The body is thus a central focus in this book, for it is here that the application of technologies is realised, and concerns about its vulnerability and permeability are revealed within the context of its enhancement. At the same time, the body becomes visual evidence for illicit performance enhancement, as the public are taught how to read athletic forms. Bodies that transgress expected gendered or national dimensions, for example, are recognised as unnaturally and illegally enhanced, revealing that physical contours must not exceed standard bodily proportions (Magdalinski and Brooks 2002). As individual athletic bodies represent broader collectivities, this book explores the way in which national identities, using the specific case study of Australian identity, are reinforced through athletic performance, and how accusations of illicit technological enhancement serve to undermine national standing and claims to authenticity. Thus, the issue of boundary maintenance is of concern in this monograph, both in terms of protecting the body from 'unnatural' technological intrusion, but also in terms of maintaining cogent territorial borders.

Before specifically examining the relationship between the body and technology in sport, a brief overview of the nature of sport is necessary. Chapter 2 reveals deeply held beliefs about sport and its intrinsic nature, and interrogates the popular conception of sport as natural, immutable and enduring. In doing so, this chapter focuses on the social construction of an athletic philosophy that was entrenched in the rhetoric of nineteenth-century Muscular Christianity, and which remains central to contemporary interpretations of sport as character-building. This 'spirit' of sport was aligned to Romantic ideas of nature as joyous and unrestrained, which were posited against the 'destructive' forces of industrial culture. Nature itself became a site of moral inspiration, and physical recreations within its space were similarly understood to generate worthy characters. Yet sport is revealed to be a technological concept, one in which neither the body nor the sportscape can be effectively regarded as authentically natural. As such, the relationship between sport and nature, whilst historically grounded, is difficult to sustain. Nevertheless, understanding the significance of each is

10 *Introduction*

critical, as it reveals the essentialised premises upon which many performance technologies are proscribed.

It is clear that within sport, there is an assumption that the body is natural, and the apprehension that performance enhancing technologies provoke derives from a primary fear of contaminating its purity. Chapter 3 examines conceptions of the body within sport and interrogates its 'natural' state with reference to the discord generated by the inappropriate introduction of synthetic and other corrupting agents. The horror inspired by the intrusion of technology into the body and the application of other artificial or 'unnatural' methods is, nevertheless, explicable if the body is regarded, not of nature, but rather as a social construct that is variously imagined as fluid, mechanical, abject and liminal. Rather than fixed, the body is flexible, the boundaries of the 'natural' stretching as easily as the skin that encases the corpus. Further, the body is theorised as a landscape, a kind of 'perfected nature', that resembles the tamed wilderness of the garden, more than the unrestrained freedom that nature is thought to represent. These interpretations offer a useful framework to explore not just how performance technologies operate within and upon the body, but how the body itself stands in for collective identities. The body, thus, symbolises broader social relations, whereby the construction of a national physical terrain can be mirrored in the landscape of the athletic body, intensifying the relationship between personal and national borders. The body's skin and the margins of the nation each present a threshold that has had a varied function, at times porous, at times a clear demarcation between inside and out. The 'unnatural' penetration of these borders is a significant concern, and an exploration of performance enhancing drugs and its relationship to the 'natural' body, as well as the mechanisms employed to surveil, monitor and discipline these bodies, is critical.

'Performance enhancement' is central to monitoring and regulating sporting practices and athletes' bodies, and although it is clear what 'enhancement' in this context means, there has, to date, been few discussions of the significance of 'performance', even though, essentially, the purpose of training is to improve it and the purpose of sport is to display it. Chapter 4 draws from the theory of performance, theatre and dance studies to develop an understanding of the nature of performance within sport. The various forms of performance share notable characteristics, including the essential presence of an audience as well as the limited time and space in which a performance is conducted. Yet, unlike theatrical or other artistic presentations, where the audience is aware that the actors in front of them are merely reciting a predetermined script, sports performances are thought to be more 'real' or 'authentic', an accurate reflection of the personal motivations and objectives of each participant. This chapter concludes with an overview of 'enhancement' strategies that have been applied to sports performance.

Given that sport is popularly agreed to benefit well-being, it seems fitting then, that performance technologies that jeopardise an athlete's health should be prohibited. Yet, given the dangerous nature of sport and the number of injuries that are reported each year, such measures appear contradictory, and Chapter 5 considers this proposition by examining the inconsistencies and assumptions in discourses of health within elite and professional sport. 'Health', in this context, is revealed to be a complex social and cultural construct that does not easily serve the interests of the anti-doping lobby. Whilst athletes are prohibited from taking only those substances that appear on the banned list, there are a range of other authorised supplements and additives that athletes rely on to restore their health. Only a fine line differentiates between 'restoration' and 'enhancement', and the distinction between the two relies to a large degree on an athlete's intent. Furthermore, health cannot be reduced to mere personal biology and is situated within a broader medico-moral discourse. Within this paradigm individual well-being is aligned with social stability, such that health becomes a moral duty to better not just oneself but one's society. Thus, concerns about health are invested in not just the body, but also the nation, and debates about boundary maintenance on a national level are replicated in desires to secure the integrity of individual bodies. As individual athletes are representative of the national body, the invasion of the nation by undesirable 'Others' is evident in fears about the corruption of the athletic body by unnatural substances.

The theme of bodily purity is particularly pertinent for female athletes, who typically have been denigrated for entering the 'masculine arena' of sport, and this chapter identifies fears that the presence of androgenising drugs in women will automatically lead to digressions from bodily norms. It is well established that sport is a patriarchal institution that delineates gender through the dress, body and activity of male and female athletes respectively. Whilst the participation of female athletes was first tolerated and now accepted, performance technologies nevertheless pose a significant threat to essentialised gender categories, and no more so than when women begin to resemble the size and shape of their male counterparts. As female athletes are discursively and visually presented as attractive, heterosexually desirable and, above all, feminine, the use of performance enhancing substances jeopardises these strictly monitored boundaries. Transgressing against the accepted female form is rejected as an unnatural or even monstrous manipulation and is understood as evidence of the ingestion of male hormones, which itself disrupts the very essence of 'femaleness'. Thus, the threat of the monstrous feminine resides in the bulked up bodies of those athletes who dare challenge the physical limits of femininity. Chapter 6 examines the construction of these 'monsters' that exceed their bodily expectations, focusing on bodybuilder Zoe Warwick to demonstrate how sports consumers are educated to 'read' illegal performance enhancement on the contours of the female body, at the same time that feminine and desirable bodies are understood as 'natural' and untainted.

Concerns about the unnatural penetration of female bodily borders by performance enhancing, and masculinising, substances seem to be assuaged by non-invasive alternatives, as an athlete may don an external device,

12   Introduction

which will assist her performance, but which will not disrupt her inherent femininity. In the case of swimming, the development of swimsuits to 'optimise', but not 'enhance', an athlete's performance provides a suitable reprieve from concerns about bodily transgression, for these costumes represent merely a temporary physical modification that does not contaminate the natural body, nor require a permanent rejection of the ideal female form. Similarly, prosthetic devices that are attached to bodies do not, despite their cyborgian nature, provoke fears that the human body is being 'unnaturally' enhanced, merely returned to a level of 'normal' functioning. Yet, the development of athletic prostheses that no longer resemble the limbs that they replace, and the threat that some athletes may, as a result of their redesigned body parts, actually eclipse able-bodied athletes is a debate that has only recently emerged. Chapter 7 examines the application of external technologies to the surface of athletes, locating these devices within the context of appropriate, 'natural' performance enhancement that does not inherently or irreparably alter the human organism.

The eighth chapter examines the processes by which performance technologies, specifically drugs, assist in the construction of social identities, and focuses on debates about illicit enhancement in Australia, which, in part, secure and promulgate an ideal vision of the nation's integrity. The Australian sports community is forcefully presented as a world leader in the fight against drugs in sport, an image that offers the nation a position of international prominence. Reinforcing the perception of a nation dedicated to eradicating drugs from sport, prior to major sporting events, the media, athletes and officials often cast aspersions on their competitors, suggesting performances are 'unexpected' and the result of illicit drug taking. At the same time, Australian athletes are reaffirmed as incontrovertibly 'clean'. This chapter argues that the establishment of a binary between a clean 'us' against a cheating 'them' may be viewed as part of a broader process to develop an agreed sense of 'Australianness'.

The representation of 'natural' bodies, competing in 'natural' activities in a 'natural' landscape was primary to the Sydney 2000 Olympic Games. Chapter 9 analyses the way in which the construction of an uncontaminated athletic body was mirrored in the manufactured 'nature' of Homebush Bay, which in turn was represented as a microcosm of the national environment. It examines how the conception of the natural athlete was replicated in the Olympic site, and discusses the relationships between the national landscape and athletic bodies in the production of Australian identities. Finally, this chapter focuses on the topography and terrain of environmental and bodily surfaces, relating the threat of disruption to the body to the nation as a whole, and looks at the significance of the 'green' environmentally restorative Olympics within the framework of elite performance enhancement. The performance of nature through the bodies and site of the Sydney 2000 Olympics is explored to determine the way that the body, sport, technology and nature intersect in a single sporting event.

Importantly, this book takes no particular stance in relation to performance enhancement, illicit or otherwise, and instead explores the cultural resistance to the application of technology to the athletic body. It examines the fluid nature of concepts of the body, technology and performance within the context of sporting practices that are agreed as 'natural', and questions the validity of fixed binary positions that posit authenticity against artifice, integrity against corruption and athletic purity against technological intrusion. In essence, then, this book interrogates those external and internal technologies that threaten to dismantle the carefully constructed athletic body and reinterpret the nature of sporting performance.

2 The nature of sport

Introduction

The thwack of leather on willow, the crunch as a body is tackled, the crowd's roar reverberating around a stadium, the joy, emotion, feeling, wonderment, glory of sport. A billion people slavishly follow every kick, goal and red card of a World Cup, passionate supporters take to the streets to celebrate their national team's victory, the non-victorious mourn 'their' loss until the next opportunity to avenge defeat. Philosophers, poets, fans and academics have each tried to explain the intrinsic appeal of sport, to distil its essence, yet it remains seductively elusive, beyond lyrical and analytical efforts to define its 'true' nature. On a base level, sport is no more than a banal physical pastime, where bodies are set against one another to secure territory, take possession or outperform each other, or they compete only against themselves, challenging and conquering nature in the pursuit of increasingly extreme and amazing feats. But none who have known the highs and lows of competition would ever agree that sport is little more than actively passing the time. For many, sport means so much more.

Although definitions of the nature of sport remain tantalisingly beyond reach, an extensive set of ideologies circulates in contemporary society that nevertheless professes to explain inherent truths about sport. Young children are inducted into the concept of fair play, adolescents are encouraged to play not just by the rules but according to the spirit of the game, elite athletes are reminded that they are role models who offer moral guidance to the public, and the Olympic Games marks itself as an avenue for achieving international peace and understanding. Sport is thought to offer a range of lessons that can be transferred to other aspects of a participant's life. It is supposed to teach social and moral behaviours, to impart a sense of commitment, discipline, dedication and sacrifice, and to strengthen character and fortitude in the face of adversity (Verroken 2003; Jenkins 2002; Butcher and Schneider 2001; Reid 1998). These noble characteristics remain largely uncontested outside the hallowed halls of the academy, and certainly in the public eye, attempts to interrogate and expose the ideological foundations of sport are met with scepticism. It is, however, important to acknowledge that the physical act of, for example, hitting a ball, tackling a player or riding a wave are not intrinsically meaningful beyond the confines of the game or activity, and any effort to solicit meaning explicitly reveals the ideological precepts that are inscribed onto sport from without. Yet modern sport has, in essence, come to signify more than mere recreation, and the philosophical significance attributed to sport differentiates it from other physical activities.

Whilst the idealised version of sport seems to be well entrenched, there are, nevertheless, concerns that the essence of sport is constantly under threat in a world where victory and financial gain seem to be more highly prized than playing fairly for the love of the game. Although commercialism and professionalism have influenced sport markedly, the influence of various technologies is often held responsible for chipping away at the spirit of sport and undermining its philosophical foundations. These anxieties are provoked by a 'technophobia' that values 'natural' products more than human-made or artificial exemplars (Barilan and Weintraub 2001), and are reinforced by the mythology of sport as a purely natural enterprise. Physical recreations are imbued with moral and social meanings that derived, in part, from Romantic conceptions of nature and its restorative potential. Furthermore, the Victorian virtues of 'fair play' and an emerging scientific belief in the 'natural' body as an immutable biological category served to entrench hostilities towards technological interventions, particularly those that sought to enhance athletic capacity. For this reason, the 'unnatural', scientised or serious pursuit of athletic glory has traditionally sat uncomfortably with those who insist that sport celebrates the 'natural' athlete and his or her potential. Incorporating technological remedies into sport, to any degree, is thought to violate this 'natural' order and reveal that the 'true spirit' of sport is slowly dissipating in favour of an emphasis on the unabashed pursuit of performance objectives.

The ingestion of performance enhancing drugs is regarded as perhaps the clearest evidence that the spirit of sport is at risk, and is passionately labelled a 'crime' that 'undermin[es] the very essence of sport' (O'Leary 2001: 29). Doping, it is reasoned, disrupts the level playing field upon which sport is predicated and offers 'unfair' advantages to those who partake. It is thought to reduce the element of chance and uncertainty that is fundamental to sport, creating an 'inevitable' outcome where the doped competitor is assured of victory (Reid 1998). This, in turn, seemingly lessens the value of the contest as an accurate measure of the capacities of individual competitors. Those who take a 'chemical shortcut' have their characters and morality questioned, are thought to lack discipline and courage, and are regarded as incapable of respecting 'natural capacities and limitations' (Reid 1998). It is apparent that not only the health and well-being of athletes are jeopardised by the presence of illicit performance technologies, but the very moral fibre of sport itself is at risk.

Sport is, of course, replete with technological advancements, as evidenced in the booming sports technology industry that designs everything from cutting-

16 *The nature of sport*

edge apparel and equipment through to high tech playing surfaces and improved safety items. Each of these advances are designed, in part, to offer an athletic environment that allows the athlete to perform unimpeded. Yet, the introduction of new technologies is closely monitored to ensure the integrity of sport is protected. Training regimes, improved equipment and nutritional substances, for example, are scrutinised to ensure they do no more than merely facilitate performance by reducing external influences that may obscure or hinder the true capacity of an athlete. In this sense, the competitor's physical ability should be reflected in, and measured by, their final result; however, assessing whether or not technologies inappropriately enhance performance is difficult, and the merits of various innovations are contested by sporting authorities, athletes, coaches and the public at large. The current controversy that surrounds the athletic application of hypoxic, or altitude, chambers attests to the fact that debates about technologies are never straightforward (Levine 2006; Kutt 2005).

To understand why technology is conceived as a threat to the sanctity of sport and its philosophical foundations, this chapter initially examines the 'spirit' of sport, locating its origins in nineteenth-century constructions of Muscular Christianity and amateurism. As a 'carefree' and 'joyous' expression of humanity, sport was regarded as an antidote to the twin threats of industrialisation and urbanisation, which were thought to jeopardise the health and hygiene of not only individuals but of society at large. Sport, in theory, offered a direct link to the natural realm, away from the confines of the city and the filth in the streets, and was inscribed with many of the Romantic qualities that were attributed to nature, particularly freedom and redemption. Nature, it was supposed, offered not only a site of rejuvenation but possessed an inherent morality that could inspire and instruct human society, and through its close association with this 'untouched' realm, sport was consequently imbued with a similar purpose. This chapter thus locates the origins of the ethical and moral precepts that underpin sport within broader constructions of nature as a moral touchstone. Nature represented an uncorrupted site against which the technological advances of human society could be measured, and sport was similarly regarded as part of an authentic realm into which technology could, and should, not intrude. As such, this chapter suggests that the social construction of nature as immutable and ahistorical has considerable implications for the place and reputation of sport in contemporary society and particularly its relationship to technology.

The spirit of sport

In light of increasing commercialisation and professionalisation, sport is still imaged as a natural, carefree activity that offers joy and freedom whilst imparting a sense of morality to its participants. Whilst it may seem endangered by commercial influences, purists are comforted in the nostalgic memory of various 'golden ages' where sport is alleged to have found its true expression, celebrated not for winning and the financial gain that comes with it, but for the spirit of community and camaraderie that such games engendered. Although many still gesture towards the 'true' spirit of sport and avow to protect it, there is little consensus on what that spirit may actually be. For some, sport represents the playful expression of the human condition, a feature endemic in all societies. For others, sport is 'amusement solely' and its essence is 'relaxation', a moment 'when we disport ourselves from labour and our usual daily work' (Allison 2001: 1), or a 'challenge', a quality that is closely associated with 'courage' (Reid 1998). Sport can be understood as 'a physical competition between opponents', the outcome of which is determined by 'ability, strategy, and chance' (Eitzen 2006: 1), or the 'recreation of the human spirit through the sheer joy of play' (Wigglesworth 1996: 152). Furthermore, sport is often regarded as reflective of traits that are favoured in society, including 'character building, health promotion, the pursuit of competitive excellence, and enjoyment' (Jenkins 2002: 99). What each of these descriptions has in common is the fundamental assumption that embedded in sport are positive or even redemptive qualities that are absent from other recreations.

The construction of sport as an activity with cultural significance beyond the playing field occurred in the mid-to-late nineteenth century, as the unregulated games of the countryside were gradually formalised and incorporated in the English public school system. The provision of games for the boys enrolled in these institutions was initially designed to control errant behaviour and to instil qualities such as teamwork and leadership into the future political and civic elite. The subsequent elevation of games to a formal part of the education system raised its status as a valuable pedagogical tool. Significantly, it was not only the body that was trained on the games field. According to physical educators at the time, the systematic participation in organised physical activity offered both a physical and moral education that could build 'muscular Christians', who were strong in body, mind and spirit (Chandler 1996; Mangan 1981). Sport was thus conceived as a meaningful activity that provided social and civic training for participants in preparation for the leadership roles that they were certain to acquire.

The spirit of Muscular Christianity provided the ideological basis for the concept of amateurism, which emerged during the formal processes of codification in the mid-to-late nineteenth century. Middle-class sportsmen sought ways to differentiate their 'noble' endeavours from those of the common folk, and the intrinsic qualities of sport were tendered as an important point of distinction (Allison 2001). Amateur athletes insisted that sport ought to be played with observance to its spirit, whilst the manner in which one played was to embody and convey desirable social and political character traits. An amateur, it was held, would never deliberately infringe against another player, for this would demonstrate an inappropriate degree

18   *The nature of sport*

of seriousness that was contrary to the effortless manner in which amateur sport should be played (Butcher and Schneider 2001). The presumed greater ethical and intellectual capacity of the gentleman amateur meant that they alone could appreciate and cultivate the higher moral purpose of sport.

Although represented as the natural condition of sport, amateurism functioned as little more than a class weapon, a 'crude exclusive device', that maintained class distinctions (Hutchinson 1996: 144). Prior to industrialisation, nobles and peasants were, for the most part, both proximally and socially segregated, typically interacting only in service situations, where the class hierarchy was strictly preserved. The rapid growth of the industrial city and the confined residential areas meant that the spatial divisions between these groups were acutely diminished, and the development of sporting and other exclusive spaces became a means to reinforce social, if not physical distance, from the working classes. The emerging middle class was particularly concerned with ensuring their position and power within the rapidly changing social, economic and political landscape, and the development of amateur sport ensured that a philosophical, if not spatial, territory could be claimed as their own. Adherence to the amateur ideal as a means to fortify class divisions confirms the political function of sport during the late nineteenth century. Introduced in its amateur form to the rowdy masses, this middle-class version of sport also had an important civilising mission, designed to teach refinement, manners and respect for authority and to counteract the increasingly politicised physical recreations of the working classes. But it was also an effortless, carefree expression of movement that restored 'man' to the pastoral settings of the landed gentry, away from the strictures of the industrial world (Holt 1989). Within the amateurist ideology, sport offered a return to a more organic humanity and was conceived as a spectacle designed to celebrate the human body, recalling the triumph of 'man' over 'nature' and machine. Sport was much more than mere amusement, and, entrusted to the gentleman amateur, its purity and virtue had to be protected from all manner of potentially corrupting influences.

Notions of purity and authenticity are critical to ideological constructions of sport, and the impression that sport is under threat from external forces underpins efforts to preserve its 'true nature'. From elite-level administrative decisions and international advertising campaigns through to grassroots junior clubs and educational programmes, sport is celebrated uncritically as a benign and positive influence, though one in dire need of protection from a range of disruptive forces. The Olympic movement's 'Celebrate Humanity' campaign, for example, encourages people all over the world to recognise the Olympic Games as 'a reflection of our noblest human qualities', and was designed to engage 'our deepest emotions' to remind us 'that the Olympic Games embody the ideals to which we all aspire' (IOC 2005). The Australian Sports Commission defines 'The Essence of Australian Sport' to 'provide a statement on what sport in Australia "stands for"'. This 'essence' is underpinned by the key principles of 'Fairness, Respect, Responsibility and Safety', and concludes that it is 'vital the integrity of sport is maintained' (ASC 2007). Similarly, the World Anti-Doping Agency's 'Spirit of Sport' campaign highlights six core values of sport, namely 'respect, dedication, character, excellence, solidarity, and courage' (WADA 2005), whilst a host of policies from sports and anti-doping agencies internationally concur that securing the 'integrity' of sport is the most critical challenge they face (see ASADA 2006; ISC 2006; NADA 2006; UK Sport 2006; USOT 2006). Whilst these philosophical precepts are foregrounded, references to competitiveness and the pursuit of success and records, which are fundamental to elite sport, are noticeably absent. Although embedded in the Olympic motto of *Citius, Altius, Fortius*, these traits appear to diverge from the patrician qualities of sport.

Although seemingly incompatible, quantitative and qualitative values coexist in sport and form the centre of the modern sporting paradox. In an effort to come to terms with this conflict, Verner Møller (2003) has noted the discord between the 'essence' and the 'spirit' of sport. The 'essence' of sport includes sport's inner driving force, such as striving for greater performances, the will to victory, its inherent comparative nature and the desire to measure and record performance. Eugen König (1995: 253) similarly argues that sport demands competitors to 'push on until the limits of human performance capacity are reached'. This is the practical reality of sport, and deviates from what Møller (2003) defines as the 'spirit' of sport. The spirit encompasses those external ideals that have been imposed on physical recreations. The notion that sport can build character, engender sportsmanship or teach fair play as well as transfer these ideals to 'real life' lies at the heart of this 'spirit' (Reid 1998). The discord between the realities of elite achievement sport and the ideals of traditional physical recreations, or between the 'essence' and 'spirit', is evident in concerns about the increasing technologisation of sport.

As sport is supposed to promote ideal human characteristics as well as restore the body, the scientific-based incursion of technology into the sports realm seems to undermine these basic principles. Rather than being a naturalistic activity that allows for freedom of movement and the bodily expression of physical potential, sport becomes a highly disciplined, scientised endeavour that emphasises performance and outcomes rather than any kind of organic virtues. Thus, as Lois Bryson (1990: 143) argues, 'drugs represent an infringement of the aristocratic code' for they symbolise 'a triumph of rationality or instrumental reasoning', and expose anxieties about the meaning of sport. As a consequence of exercise science's search for techniques and supplements to improve performance, the 'spirit' of sport seems to be gradually ebbing away. The insatiable search to secure an 'edge' over competitors and the supplementation and augmentation of the body's own capacity has meant that, for many, sport has now become little more than a contest between scientific and pharmacological systems and

20   *The nature of sport*

their indiscriminate application of technology to the exercising body (Garnier 2007; Verroken 2003; 2001; Tuxill and Wigmore 1991; Voy 1991). Entrenched in such wistful reflection is a longing for that time when sport truly represented individual human performances, yet it is difficult to determine when this 'golden age' might have been, given that in the early twentieth century, some were already lamenting the rise of exercise science and the waning 'spirit' of sport. In 1933, Otto Riesser noted that 'sportive competitions are often more a matter of doping than of training' (cited in Hoberman 1992: 131), which mirrors sentiments expressed nearly seventy-five years later in WADA Medical Director Alain Garnier's (2007: 18) open letter to 'those promoting the medical supervision of doping'. In it, Garnier (2007: 18) suggests that condoning doping in any form 'would mean that prizes and medals would no longer be awarded to athletes but to pharmaceutical companies and research teams'. His letter appeared in response to a growing number of academics, sports physicians and others who have begun to question the ethical basis upon which doping in sport is banned, suggesting instead that permission to use performance enhancing substances under supervision would create a more level playing field, such that sport would become 'less of a genetic lottery' (Savulescu *et al.* 2004: 667). Technological intervention into the functioning of the human body to create a fairer athletic system seems abhorrent to those firmly set against the use of enhancement technologies, yet what it does is reject nature as omnipotent, instead suggesting that humans have the 'capacity to improve ourselves on the basis of reason of judgement' (Savulescu *et al.* 2004: 667). Nevertheless, nature, and its preservation, remains a forceful concept within debates about sport and performance technologies.

The nature of nature

This discord between measurable outcomes and an intangible philosophy, which underpins fears about performance enhancement, rests largely on the nature of sport, both in terms of sport's *intrinsic* nature as well as in its relationship *with* nature. Sport is predicated on an alleged organic, or 'natural', origin as well as on human mastery over nature (Bale 1994). It is imaged as an activity located in green environments, as, from grassy fields to pristine waterways, bodies run, jump, swim and move through nature. Fresh oxygen powers through their lungs as athletes craft and push their bodies to, and beyond, their limits. Golfers stroll along tree-lined fairways, mountain-bikers career down rocky paths, surfers tame the ocean's fury and skiers conquer mountains. Many other sports that are no longer staged within the 'unspoiled' environment have been moved to enclosed spaces that are built, named and decorated to resemble the landscapes in which the activities were once held (Bale 1994). Furthermore, a plethora of extreme sports, including snowboarding and rock-climbing, exemplify human mastery over both the elements and the body, which further cements the image of modern sporting practices as those through which participants escape the urban to commune with, and test the body against, nature, whilst seeking solace and physical restoration. As such, sport is juxtaposed against the rigid world of labour, representing freedom of physical expression and the opportunity to test the limits of the body's physical capacity.

It is no coincidence that images of nature, tamed or wild, are central to the rhetoric of modern sport. Concerns about environmental degradation and its elevation to one of the arms of 'Olympism' reinforce the primacy of nature in contemporary sporting practices. Locating sport within a discourse of nature is a consequence of the Romanticism of the late eighteenth and early nineteenth centuries, which, in response to growing industrialisation and its concomitant urbanisation, sought to engage with and celebrate the natural realm. Nature was positively regarded as wild and untamed, untouched by human activity, and was thus contrasted against the rationality of industrial culture (Adam 1998). By juxtaposing nature and urban scapes, wilderness and natural areas became a refuge from the industrial city, whereas, much like today, the countryside symbolised a return to healthy, organic values. As such, nature was relegated to the 'margins of modern industrial society' (Macnaghten and Urry 1998: 13), and, uncontaminated, it offered the potential for liberation from the manipulated, exploited and rationalised industrial landscape.

Recreational activities that were performed in natural settings similarly acquired a rejuvenatory purpose and were encouraged as antidotes to urban life. In continental Europe, gymnastic systems, such as the German *Turnen* movement, were founded in the early nineteenth century to allow boys and men to 'return to nature' through freedom of movement and expression, at a time of political consolidation (Eichberg 1998). Groups of young men would tramp through forests, perform gymnastics in open pastures and learn to appreciate the countryside as part of their national culture. Across Europe, naturists similarly celebrated nature and the naked body's recreation within it as part of a 'nostalgia for bygone eras when people's attachment to the land and/or their attitudes to the body could fulfil the new cravings for self-actualization and spiritual plenitude' (Bell and Holliday 2000: 129–30). Despite images of carefree individuals, clothed or otherwise, frolicking in wilderness areas, modern sport emerged in Europe as a corollary of industrial capitalism in the late nineteenth century, and thus more closely resembled these modernising forces.

Throughout the century of industrial revolution, the changing nature of production required the large-scale movement of labour from rural to urban areas. The new industrial working classes were temporally and spatially precluded from engaging in traditional recreational activities, and they found refuge in the pubs and taverns of the city (Holt 1989). Furthermore, the alienation caused by the new work practices had emerged by the mid-nineteenth century as a cause for concern for many political and social theorists. They feared the interplay between humans and technology and

22 The nature of sport

the alienation and loss of humanity that would result from factory life and the incorporation of the body by production: labour was becoming part machine, part human and the cyborg worker resulted (Stern 1998; Haraway 1991). Concerns about the immorality of pub sports, which largely revolved around gambling and alcohol, coupled with fears about the potential for disease and disorder, prompted reformers to encourage sport as a means of creating a healthier and more genteel working class (Holt 1989).

The dehumanising aspects of the industrial age were to be counter-balanced by the provision of leisure and recreational activities, which were thought to offer an escape from the efficient tyrannies of these new labour forms. Whilst the 'body at play' has long been recognised to be a 'counterweight' to the 'labouring body', the confirmation of its role, particularly in the urban environment, was secured partly in response to the crises in health and hygiene in the rapidly expanding cities. In industrialising settler societies, untamed wilderness areas represented avenues of escape from the 'swollen' cities, opportunities to retreat to and recreate in a natural landscape (Dunlap 1999). The body was similarly rejuvenated and refreshed through sport, which came to symbolise the antithesis of the confined, dirty and unwholesome world of work and became synonymous with good health and clean living. These relationships have only intensified throughout the twentieth century. The role of healthy play away from the belching smokestacks of industrial life reveals a perception of the emancipatory potential of the countryside, and early, organised physical activities focused as much on restoring health as on pleasurable recreation (Aron 1999). The wealthy middle classes would take to the fresh air in the mountains or to the waters of medicinal springs to seek refuge or recovery from illness and other urban threats, as 'Nature, many believed, could be enlisted in the cure and prevention of disease' (Aron 1999: 18). In these spas and resorts, natural symbols adorned the interior design, yet, significantly, all manner of machinery was used in the treatment of various ills (de la Peña 2003). In addition, the emerging recognition of the physiological benefits that ensue from participation in vigorous physical activity meant that men, and eventually women, were gradually encouraged to take up some form of exercise. Since then, modern sport and physical activity have been associated with, and thought to be a precursor to, health and well-being, a naturalistic escape from the confines of the urban environment, offering a release and freedom of movement in limitless space.

Nineteenth-century sporting ideologues, such as Baron Pierre de Coubertin, founder of the modern Olympic movement, were committed to the potential for sport and other rational recreations to rectify what they regarded as a host of social ills that resulted from industrialisation and urbanisation (Holt 1989). The population explosion in urban areas and its attendant social maladies such as disease, discontent and proximity to the middle classes meant that a range of educational and legislative reforms were necessary for the preservation of Victorian standards of morality, health and hygiene (Baldwin 1999; Conrad 1994; Wohl 1983). In this context, sporting practices, the development of parks, and later the sporting spectacle, were crucial, for not only could they distract the masses from their daily plight, they could also be imbued with a higher moral purpose that would educate and reform the working classes of the day (Bednarek 2005; Crawford 1984; Whorton 1982). The amateur philosophy that underpinned, in particular, middle-class sport imposed dictums on how sport should be played; not just the rules and style, but the philosophy of play was prescribed (Allison 2001). Sport, it was reasoned, should be played with a particular spirit and thereby aim towards some higher moral imperative.

It is no coincidence that sport was used to instil moral virtues into its participants, given its conceptualisation as a natural activity. Understanding nature as a site of morality had re-emerged during the Romantic era in response to the Enlightenment's rationalisation of nature. Rather than praising reason and logic, the Romantics conceived nature as possessing intrinsic value and beauty that could instruct and inspire humankind. Nature became the standard against which the corrupting influences of industrialising societies could be measured and served as a moral 'touchstone' or 'arbiter' that offered a means of assessing behaviour and determining acceptable cultural traits (Lock 1997). A 'return to nature' was celebrated in Romantic art, poetry and literature, where untamed and wild scapes were thought to offer redemption and salvation from the intruding technological world (Adam 1998). Nature was thereby conceptually dissociated from culture, relocated on the fringes of the industrial city and regarded as an emancipatory force (Macnaghten and Urry 1998).

The Romantic idea of nature in many ways remains current. It is idealised as a sublime space that offers liberation and salvation and is envisaged as an authentic site that has not been 'intentionally altered' by human interference (Michael 2005: 55). In this way, nature is defined as that which is without human influence, an external, immutable and above all pure concept that operates as a 'source of social norms' (Smith 1996: 41). Contemporary debates about biotechnology, genetic engineering and performance technologies remind us that nature is still conceived as largely independent of human influence, and attempts to manipulate it through cloning, doping or genetic engineering are considered deeply disturbing. The Enlightenment might have made it permissible to scientifically expose the natural world, but the Romantics warned of the consequences of tinkering with nature.

If humans are not supposed to interfere with nature, then in a sense they are positioned *outside of nature*, and as such, are able to conceive of and appreciate nature as an external reality. Nature thus becomes something that is other than, and different from, the corporeal experience, which essentially allows humans to understand, consume and ultimately manipulate nature. Nevertheless, bodies are also seen as *of nature*, immutable entities that suggest a sense of purity and timelessness, which have meanings beyond culture. This dual understanding of humans as both of and

24 The nature of sport

beyond nature means the body is viewed as simultaneously nature and progress, an authentic site as well as an artificial one; one that is and one that can be made. The tensions arising between the immutability of the natural realm and the engineered corpus are evident in athletic bodies, at once natural and created, both of and beyond nature.

A critical element in this view of nature and its implications for bodies is the sense of purity or authenticity, the idea that nature represents some kind of true or real state juxtaposed against the inauthentic modern world. Ecologists, according to Kate Soper (1996: 22), 'tend to evoke "nature" as an independent domain of intrinsic value, truth or authenticity'. Conceiving nature as authentic implies it is fixed, a static entity posited against the vitality of human progress. This narrow conception, however, negates nature's own internal dynamic, ever-changing landscapes where plants seed, grow and die, animals create habitats, reproduce and move on (Adam 1998). There is in fact very little about nature that is immutable or timeless, and a reductionist conception of nature as fixed negates the vibrant and interdependent relationship it has with human society. This is critical because nature does not exist without reference to human or technological culture, and, as such, must be understood as essentially relational. Critically, as Soper (1996: 25) argues:

> Untamed nature begins to figure as a positive and redemptive power only at the point where human mastery over its forces is extensive enough to be experienced as itself a source of danger and alienation. It is only a culture which has begun to register the negative consequences of its industrial achievements that will be inclined to return to the wilderness, or to aestheticise its terrors as a form of foreboding against further advances against its territory.

Nature is thus only knowable when posited against that which is not, or may threaten, nature, and in fact, only ever requires delineation when confronted with something that appears unnatural. As such, nature can never be independent or authentic, but instead must be regarded as a social construct that offers a mirror through which we can come to understand human culture.

Meanings about nature are mediated through a complex interplay between the environment, culture, politics and ideology, and the construction of nature as, for example, a redemptive force, as a site for respite from an urban world, as a source for life-sustaining materials, or as an aesthetic locale, is neither intrinsic nor essential but rather is a reaction to contemporary sociopolitical concerns. In short, 'nature' is the organic response to our material reality (Lovell 1998). Of course, as Macnaghten and Urry (1998: 30) suggest, nature cannot serve as a 'simple or unmediated' moral touchstone if it is understood as socially constructed. It can only operate as a source of moral guidance if it is conceived as having its own intrinsic values independent of the human realm. Similarly, if we accept that, like nature, sport is a social construct, then it is clear that the physical acts of hitting a ball, running a specified distance or throwing an implement cannot possess values that are independent of culture. Although the physical acts in sport do not embody an inherent morality and are unlikely to offer ethical instruction, sport itself, nevertheless, remains imbued with a range of philosophies that are firmly embedded within a discourse of nature.

The nature of sport

Appreciating the social constructedness of nature and the ways in which it serves as a moral barometer is particularly useful when examining conceptions of nature in sport. Nature appears throughout sporting discourses in reference to the unaltered, 'natural' body, in descriptions of 'untainted' performances and in the names of arenas in which sport is conducted. Madison Square Garden, Wrigley Field and Lang Park all suggest a rural, natural setting for the various events that are held there. Although it does not represent the experience of most people, who are confined to the artificial sporting scapes of pools, gymnasia and stadia, the image of sport as a green, healthy return to nature and a simultaneous escape from the oppressive urban world prevails. Sporting arenas gesture towards their natural counterparts, becoming essentially a kind of stylised retreat from urban life. These scapes are thus not quite as untamed as 'real' nature, though they are often constructed to resemble natural locations and, as in the examples above, may be referred to as parks or gardens. Nature is thus simulated within various sportscapes, though often it is only the superficial veneer that need resemble their organic counterparts. If its verdant skin is peeled away, a golf course, despite its parkland appearance, is not a pristine, natural environment, but rather a carefully terraformed scape that conceals a crisscrossing network of pipes and drainage systems. An extensive use of chemicals, pesticides and dyes in conjunction with the daily manicuring of the greens are each required to keep the course looking as 'natural' as possible. A mountain-biker's path is carved out of the hillside so that athletes can battle 'nature', whilst kayakers compete in thoroughly artificial courses that are outfitted with 'natural' obstacles to overcome. The skier's run is supported by a complex system of lifts and, on occasion, artificial snow, and the equipment used to golf, bike, surf or ski are all rigorously and scientifically researched, developed and tested before they reach the marketplace. Even those activities that seem to exemplify human mastery over the nature and its elements reveal an intricate interplay between the environment, culture and technology, where as much of nature as possible is removed from the event.

Sporting arenas can really only ever mimic nature because the 'geographical "sameness" of sports space' is critical (Bale 1994: 63). Untouched environments are typically too variable and unpredictable for elite-level

26   *The nature of sport*

sport, where the space must be as disciplined and regulated as the bodies that perform there. Without standardised arenas, performances are not easily compared, for the result may be influenced by external factors that essentially detract from the athlete's ability to showcase their 'true' ability. Nature, then, must be perfected to create a fair setting that allows for the pure expression of biological potential. In this respect, 'fair' performances are thought to be unadorned, unaided and uninfluenced and are embedded in the idea of the 'level playing field'. This notion insists that a true measure of a performance can only occur if all obstacles external to the competing body are removed from the field of competition. It is a delightful concept because it embodies the relationship between sport, performance, the body and landscape, and suggests that the internal motivation, or essence, of sport is essentially to compare the physical capacities of participating bodies. Neither the playing field, nor any other external force, should influence the outcome, so that the recorded performance is a pure reflection of the athletic capacity of the competitors, or as James Keating suggests (1964: 33) the 'objective and accurate determination of superior performance'. In order to ensure such an accurate determination, bodies are often removed from nature and the physical spaces in which sport is played are standardised so that no competitor has an environmental advantage over another. Such modifications are supported by decades of rule changes that ensure the athletic competition is a 'true test of respective abilities' (Keating 1964: 34). Tracks are levelled, pools lose their wash, clothing becomes lighter so that the victory of the athlete is purely a function of their unrestricted physical efficiency. Even sports that require the unpredictability of nature for their conduct, such as surfing or yachting, are contained as far as possible to ensure that competitors have similar, if not equal, environmental circumstances to contend, thus ensuring that it is an athlete's actions, rather than inequitable conditions, that determines the outcome. Modifications, however, are not just made to those physical conditions that might impinge upon the athletic performance. Environmental factors that might boost a performance, such as a tailwind, are also mitigated, so that the outcome represents the distilled essence of sport: the pure physical performance, unimpeded by the unpredictable 'natural' environment. Nature is, thus, deliberately removed from the performance for 'pure nature has too much variation in it' (cited in Bale 1994: 42). The athlete performs beyond nature.

Just as nature is posited as a kind of authentic landscape, as a site of moral as well as physical redemption and as a static, knowable entity, the natural body is similarly regarded as immutable and sporting prowess innate. As such, it is not only the sporting arena that must be 'fair'; the sporting body too must appear to be 'natural' and similarly unaided in its pursuit of excellence. Athletic achievements are regarded as an expression of an inherent gift or talent, a natural ability that is developed through hard work and training, yet such 'natural' bodies and performances are only recognised when juxtaposed against those that have been augmented through technological intervention. Of course, within elite sport, there is no such thing as 'untamed nature' as participants have each been transformed by a range of technological and disciplinary practices. Rather than embodying freedom and expression, athletes are poked and prodded, tested and tamed, and measured and modified with the latest scientific gadgetry. Sports scientists observe, predict and improve the body and its performances, creating highly efficient, trained specimens in the process. If we regard the elite athletic form as a kind of industrial achievement, perhaps even as an industrial scape, then the modified body itself may become a 'source of danger and alienation' (Soper 1996: 25), as we recognise the 'negative consequences' of technological innovation and its impact on the human body. Enhanced and natural bodies are thus contrasted, with the unnatural Other posing as an explicit reminder of what the Self should not become.

Assumptions about the naturalness of both the body and the sportscape reinforce the idea that nature is fixed, that either one is only ever manipulated by human intervention, which is itself presumed to be necessarily detrimental. Yet, Soper (1996) suggests that there is really no such thing as 'untouched' nature: every landscape is in the form it is in today because of either direct or indirect human interference. Although the body seems to be a natural biological entity, its very form and function is a product of human intervention, and this is clearly observable within elite sporting practices. Fears about the 'unnatural' intrusion of technology rely on the assumption that the body is fundamentally untouched, and yet, every ability, capacity and achievement is the result of external influence. As Soper (1996: 24) states: 'If nature is too glibly conceptualised as that which is entirely free of human "contamination", then in the absence of anything much on the planet which might be said to be strictly "natural" in this sense of the term, the injunction to "preserve" it begins to look vacuous and self-deprecating'. By applying Soper's (1996: 24) argument to sport, it is clear that trying to preserve the 'naturalness' of such an overtly social activity by removing contaminating and corrupting influences, including illicit technologies, is equally vacuous, for it is clear that sport is not, and cannot ever be, 'entirely free from human "contamination"'.

The absence of a truly 'natural' sport has implications for those philosophies that derive from Romantic conceptions of nature, including the presumption of an inherent moral dimension upon which the idea of 'fair play' is based. The notion of fairness underpins contemporary sport and typically represents the main casualty of the doping culture (Schneider and Butcher 2000; Gardner 1989), and though there have been many attempts, this concept has no systematic definition within sport, varying from adherence to the rules through to complex philosophical explanations (Sheridan 2003). In essence, however, a 'fair' competition appears to be one in which each athlete competes under standardised conditions with a fair and equal chance to prevail (Gusfield 2000; Schneider and Butcher 1993/4). Doping, it is thought, allows the tainted athlete to generate an 'unfair' advantage that

28   *The nature of sport*

leads to an 'inevitable victory' (Reid 1998). Yet, given that sport is far from a 'natural' activity and that athletes are 'artificially produced' (Black and Pape 1997), there has been increasing discussion about the validity of prohibiting performance technologies on the basis that they result in a disruption of fair play. Of primary concern appears to the uncritical assumptions that illicit substances and techniques necessarily disrupt the level playing field and represent both an unfair advantage and an assured victory to those who ingest (Savulescu *et al.* 2004; Tamburrini 2000; Gardner 1989).

It is, in part, the assumption that doping equates to automatic success and that, by implication, other physical and environmental factors are irrelevant once an athlete ingests illicit pharmaceuticals that has prompted many to question the moral foundations upon which doping is banned and to suggest that 'fairness' may not be threatened by such performance technologies. These critiques instead argue that enhancement, in all its forms, may instead '*reduce* inequality, injustice, and unfairness' by ensuring that everyone receives 'a fair go' (Savulescu 2006: 321) and that widespread and legal access to performance enhancing technologies would reduce any 'competitive advantage' that one athlete has over another (Black and Pape 1997). Indeed, Black and Pape (1997) suggest specifically that bans on performance enhancing drugs are, in actual fact, responsible for creating unfair sporting competitions, given the sports community's inability to ensure that all athletes are untainted, whilst Christian Munthe (2000) similarly argues that even the incorporation of genetic technologies may enhance rather than detract from the nature of sport. Despite the emergence of such arguments, the hegemonic construction of sport as inherently natural and fair prevails, and the systematic detection of illicit substances continues.

Conclusion

Although it is clear that scientific advances have created athletic feats unimaginable even a decade ago, the increasing reliance on technology has caused considerable disquiet amongst those who believe that an athlete's performance should reflect their biological capacity, unimpeded or unassisted by external factors. For many, this is the defining quality of sport where a natural propensity or talent, carefully nurtured, forms the basis for performance. By contrast, enhancement technologies represent little more than a disruption to, and an unnatural augmentation of, the athlete's body. Compromising nature, it is argued, negates the very purpose of sport by removing 'fair' competition and assuring victory to the chemically enhanced. Much of this argument is founded on the conception of sport as a natural activity that is embedded within a human sense of play and relies on promulgating a philosophy of sport that locates it firmly within nature. Sport, it is reasoned, offers humankind an escape from the world of labour and a recreational site that returns the dispirited soul to the natural realm. The working body, it was feared, was being disciplined and contained by the requirements of labour, whereas sport was thought to offer a kind of release from industrial tyranny. Played in open pastures or other natural spaces, sport seemed far removed from the debilitating urban landscape, yet increasingly, the spaces in which sport was conducted were regulated and controlled to create standardised arenas where performances could be accurately measured. Yet, nature remains a powerful force within contemporary constructions of sport, obscuring the structural and functional parallels between sport and industrial capitalism.

Yet, far from being a site that disengaged people from the threats of urban life and the limits of the time clock, sport functioned as an institution that disciplined its participants into the structures of the capitalist enterprise. Nature was, in many respects, removed in favour of a more thoroughly regulated enterprise that sought to evaluate, compare and record the biological capacity of competitors through the negation of external hindrances and influences. 'Nature' became stylised in venues that were engineered to mitigate the unpredictability of the environment and to ensure that performances were pure measures of the athlete's ability. Nevertheless, the primacy of nature in sport is evident, providing a seemingly objective reason for rejecting intrusions that are deemed to be 'unnatural'. Various technologies, for example, are thought to disrupt the integrity of sport and threaten the authenticity of not only the bodies that compete, but the very meaning of the performances themselves. Such constructions rely on a static representation of nature and the sporting body, but neither sport nor nature is immutable. As each embodies and reflects the culture in which they are produced, their meanings shift and slide according to changes in ideological and cultural positions.

Whilst nature plays a critical role in contemporary constructions of sport, the very nature of nature is often neglected in discussions about sport's inherent qualities. Rather than being timeless and immutable, nature is dynamic and, like sport, is the product of the culture and era in which it is located. Nature, most significantly, is a variable that is only knowable in the presence of that which is not nature. It is something of a mirror through which human and material culture can be measured, and for this reason, it is difficult to base a philosophical foundation of sport on such a slippery concept.

Although there are a variety of arguments for and against the application of performance technologies, what they essentially reveal is that the nature of sport is elusive and highly contested. Whilst the Victorian ideals of sport as noble and character building still function as a powerful tool within contemporary sport to maintain and legitimate the activity as set apart from the rest of society, embedded in Romantic conceptions of nature as a salvation from the threats of the industrialising world, the reality of the twenty-first century, results-oriented and commercially driven sports industry is significantly different. Nevertheless, the presumed 'spirit' of sport remains a focal point around which objections to performance technologies, specifically

30   The nature of sport

doping, coalesce. Embedded within the nature of sport are, of course, specific concerns about the integrity of the natural body and its potential disruption through performance technologies. The construction of the athletic body as unproblematically natural and the concerns surrounding the unnatural transgression of bodily borders is discussed in the following chapter, which initially examines the origins of the natural body and its conceptual transformation into a mechanised product that nevertheless yearns for a return to nature.

3 The nature of the body

Introduction

In a world where Botox, cosmetic surgery, prosthetic limbs and surgical interventions alter the shape, appearance and function of bodies, it seems incongruous that there should be widespread concern about the technological modification of athletes. Commercial television offers a nightly smorgasbord of pills and potions designed to improve both the efficiency and appearance of our bodies, celebrity culture reminds us that a nip here and a tuck there will sustain a youthful visage, and the fitness and dietary fads since the 1970s and 1980s have made us more body-conscious than perhaps at any other time in history. From Jane Fonda to Dr Atkins, the obsession with appearance over the last couple of decades has made the manipulation of bodily aesthetics de rigueur. At the same time, we expect that all manner of invasive and non-invasive procedures will extend the body's longevity whilst improving its capacity and performance. Pushing the body to its biological extremes to increase the length and quality of life is now routine.

Whilst the body might be acceptably malleable in terms of its appearance and efficiency, manipulating the body at a more intimate level provokes a different reaction. Ongoing debates about genetic engineering and the potential to clone or even replace humans with perfect or perfected versions occur not just in the hallowed halls of academia and theological centres, but increasingly in a range of popular and public fora, indicating that we are not yet quite comfortable with the exercise of human power over the body (Williams and Bendelow 1998). Whilst the potential to cure disease by unlocking the mysteries of the human genome may speak in its favour, the not-so-distant eugenics movements remind us that 'playing God' might again lead to devastating consequences. In addition, the possibility that this knowledge will be used not merely to remedy ill health but to create superhumans capable of extraordinary feats fuels fears of its potential misuse. Thus, it is of little surprise that within international sporting circles, a profound anxiety about the potential of twenty-first century gene therapies to augment athletic performance has emerged (Miah 2004). What these debates have in common is a conceptualisation of the body as the

32 The nature of the body

physical manifestation of humanity in which our very mortality is embedded (Palladino 2003). Interfering with the body at the sub-cellular level is thought to threaten the very essence of what it means to be human.

Apprehension about the changing nature of humanity is not new, and the scientific control, and unfettered intrusion, of technology into the body has caused alarm for centuries. From philosophical and religious treatises through to popular cultural representations, technology has both promised future utopias filled with extraordinarily capable bodies and offered terrifying glimpses at the potential subjugation, or conquest, of humanity. All manner of science fiction texts have pointed to the destruction of humankind as a consequence of the unrestrained proliferation of technology, as evidenced historically in dystopian novels such as George Orwell's *1984* and Mary Shelley's *Frankenstein*, or more recently through film such as the *Terminator* series (Murphie and Potts 2003; Magdalinski and Brooks 2002). Similarly, athletic discourses reveal a considerable level of disquiet about the presence of artificially enhanced bodies, which are thought to portend the imminent dehumanisation of sport (Hoberman 1992). Warnings about systematic hormonal manipulation and the fear of grotesque exemplars laying claim to gold medals and winner's cheques suggest that within sport, the athletic body ideally remains powered by nature and untouched by the contaminating effects of technology (Magdalinski 2001a).

Given its centrality to the sporting performance and the obvious concerns about its purity within this context, it is surprising that the body has only recently emerged within socio-cultural analyses of sport. It has, of course, been the main focus of enquiry for exercise scientists who, for decades, have sought means to understand and improve the body's athletic output (Maguire 2004). Nevertheless, these sports scientific investigations concentrate on the biologically fixed rather than ideologically fluid corpus and, as such, are less concerned with the significance of movement than with its mechanics. In such examinations, bodies are individual, though generalisable, knowable and predictable through experimentation, the results of which can be directly applied for athletic gain. Within the social sciences, however, the sporting body is understood as socially and culturally meaningful, with significance far beyond mere moving limbs. These approaches examine the cultural constructedness of bodies, revealing them to be not merely organic but cultural, their surfaces inscribed with, and reflective of, the ideological positions that underpin the society in which they are found.

Understanding the sporting experience as well as the embodiment of ideology through the practice of sport now inform social and cultural analyses of sport. As such, interpretations of the body can offer insight into the construction of, for example, race, gender, class, sexuality, ability and nationhood. In these narratives, the body is revealed to be both an ideological concept and a corporeal reality upon which cultural, social and political ideologies are mapped. The body is thus textual, communicating ideological positions both along the contours of its surface as well as within its depths (Merleau-Ponty 1962). Critically, the body can no longer be understood merely in organic terms as a purely biological entity and should instead be regarded as 'an open text that is constantly rewritten and reinterpreted' (Armstrong 1996: 10). Even so, the 'natural body' remains a construct that is difficult to dislodge. Recognising the textual dimension of the body has important implications for any discussion of performance technologies. First, it suggests that the 'natural body', which requires protection from corruption and intrusion, simply does not exist, and second, it acknowledges that whilst issues of purity and authenticity may be written onto 'natural', athletic bodies, they are indicative of broader ideological concerns, including gender, nation and identity. In this way, the material body symbolises collective relations, and its margins and edges are policed and defended as valiantly as any national border.

This chapter examines the nature of the body to determine the source of anxiety about the inappropriate intrusion of performance technologies and the potential for disruption that these signify. It analyses the body as natural, mechanical, and, more recently, discursive, identifying it as a site of contestation where ideological positions are inscribed onto and into the flesh. Rather than accepting it as material, organic and isolated, the body is revealed to be constructed, liminal and unsettling, a fluid entity whose meanings shift and slide rather than remaining fixed and predictable. Finally, the body is theorised as a landscape, which suggests that, rather than natural and uncontrolled like true wilderness areas, the athletic body is tamed and regulated like a garden. In this context, the body is reflective of wider societal concerns, as it is conceived in the language of the national landscape, which reveals how scientifically built bodies, including those of athletes, are imagined as natural and authentic, even though they are clearly engineered within a specific technological and cultural frame.

Mechanical bodies

Whilst it is now accepted amongst cultural theorists that the body is socially constructed, to the broader public it seems inconceivable that the body is anything other than a biological and material reality, discrete specimens that are concrete, knowable and, above all, natural (Shilling 1993; Featherstone et al. 1991). Bodies appear to be fixed and self-evident, an image firmly entrenched in post-Enlightenment scientific constructions. Whilst bodies are currently conceptualised as isolated and individual, they have, nevertheless, not always been imagined in this way. The significance and meaning of the body has changed markedly throughout the course of human history and has been variously regarded in religious, political or cultural terms. Most strikingly, for much of Western history, and certainly within the Judeo-Christian tradition, the body has been distrusted as a 'site of unruly passions and appetites', an inconvenient corpus that obstructs the

34   *The nature of the body*

quest for 'truth and knowledge' (Shildrick and Price 1999: 2). The dismissal of the body as insignificant, and indeed, dangerous, was disastrous for early physical recreations, and the Puritan influence was instrumental in restraining and containing the body and its corporeal expression. Fears that personal amusements would tempt men away from more pious undertakings and corrupt their bodies and souls underpinned these religious concerns, and royal proclamations in the sixteenth and seventeenth centuries curbed the conduct of the informal, and often violent, games of the countryside (Malcolmson 1973). Medical interpretations of the body, at this time, were also largely based on religious doctrine rather than 'objective' discovery, and, as ideological and religious positions shifted, the body was gradually opened up to the scientific gaze.

Prior to the Enlightenment, the human body was conceived as a fluid interplay between nature and culture that was produced through both external forces as well as its own internal dynamic. Bodies, therefore, were not thought to exist in isolation, and the physical margins that demarcated within and without were not considered as impermeable as they now seem to be. The baroque body was 'neither ... an autonomous object nor ... a mere instrument', according to Dalia Judovitz's (2001: 67) discussion of philosopher Michel de Montaigne. Montaigne rejected the valorisation of the mind as 'universal' and 'transcendental' and argued the body to be imagined through experience, language, habit and custom, in essence, 'a changing horizon of multiple becomings' (Judovitz 2001: 2). The body was unbounded and unconstrained by its somatic limits, and was thus irreducible to its mere organic components. It was imprinted with cultural traces, 'its definition shift[ing] in regard to its position and demeanour in the world' (Judovitz 2001: 68). As such, the body was explicitly a product of the world in which it was located, rather than knowable simply in and of itself.

Since the Enlightenment, however, the body has been reduced to its biology, with significance only to be found in organs, cells and vessels and their mechanistic interrelationships (Shildrick and Price 1999). As a result, the social and cultural nuances of the body and its changing meanings over time and between cultures, have been obscured by a scientific enquiry that has fixed the body as constant, predictable and enduring. Although scientists during this period represented the body mechanistically, it, nevertheless, retained its organic dimension and, as a result, remained firmly a product of the natural world (de la Peña 2003; Armstrong 1996). The body's relationship within and between nature and culture was redefined based on emerging anatomical and physiological theories as well as the gradual manifestation of a technical and mechanical discourse that reconceptualised nature in mathematical terms (Judovitz 2001). Whilst the body/ mind dualism predated this era, the strict separation of the two was effected by a mechanistic interpretation of the body that reflected a changing industrial landscape in which the relationship between the human body and labour had been dramatically altered (de la Peña 2003; Benthien 2002; Hawkins

2002). Most explicit was René Descartes' theory of the body-as-machine, which exemplified this fundamental shift in the body and marked the consolidation of a strict body/mind dualism that subsequently informed much of Western philosophical thought.

The Cartesian body signalled a radical departure from the fluidity of the baroque body. Inspired by William Harvey's rediscovery of the circulation of blood, Descartes theorised the body as an independent device in which various parts worked together, like cogs in a machine, to house the rational soul. The heart was reasoned to be like a pump, food was like 'fuel' and other organs were similarly imbued with mechanical properties and functions (de la Peña 2003). The relationship between the body and nature/culture played little role in the body-as-machine as Montaigne's transitive body was fixed, its limits carefully determined. The material body, at least, was visible, and its mysteries could be discerned through purposeful dissection and analysis. According to Judovitz (2001: 68), Descartes' conceptualisation of the body reflected a technological position that signified the 'objectification and instrumentalization of the body through its reduction to a ... machine' and occurred at the same time that changing manufacturing processes radically modified an individual's relationship to their own labour (Ashworth 2002). This paradoxical 'organic' machine was conceived in the new language and terminology of industrial capitalism, which had a significant influence on corporeal representations (de la Peña 2003; Hawkins 2002). Bodies, like equipment, could 'break down' or be serviced or 'repaired' (Shilling 1993: 37), and each part or system could be individually manipulated, improved or, on occasion, replaced. This metaphor persists, particularly with the invention of diagnostic systems to weed out inefficient segments and replace them with prosthetics and other artificial replicas that work more efficiently than the organism itself (Williams and Bendelow 1998; Foster 1997). Yet, likening bodies to machines meant that they were similarly imagined to have a fixed capacity that could not be extended. Bodies could, therefore, only ever be made more efficient within the confines of their limits. As such, the body-as-machine metaphor served to explain the body and its systems and to suggest measures to improve its efficiency; however, it did not indicate how the body could be enhanced beyond its presumed threshold (de la Peña 2003).

The conception of the body as a fixed machine has fundamentally influenced modern constructions of the athletic body. Within the sports scientific realm, the body is understood in biological terms, and performance improvements are effected through the careful application of rigorous scientific principles. Through its various incarnations over the past century, the athletic body has essentially become a piece of equipment, designed and built to elicit greater performances through improved output. There is something quite impersonal about this kind of body. Each action, each ingestion, each input is coordinated to achieve specific outcomes, and, like a machine, the athlete is reduced to parts and systems that can be specified,

36 *The nature of the body*

isolated, transformed, honed and finely tuned to produce a more rational and efficient body (Shilling 2005; 1993; Brohm 1978). To this end, each part of the overall machine is investigated, mapped and modified, as sports scientists are made responsible for fine-tuning increasingly smaller bits of the body. As such, Chris Shilling (1993: 5) makes the compelling suggestion that the body can be read as an ongoing project in which bodies 'become malleable entities which can be shaped and honed with the vigilance and hard work of their owners'. Indeed, it is this kind of 'protestant bodily work ethic' that is respected in sport, as athletic bodies, and, more specifically, the performances they deliver, are valued only if they are the consequence of vigilance and hard work; in short, if they are earned. To this end, bodies require taming, programming and monitoring to be 'shaped and honed' into a fit and proper athletic specimen ready to test itself against similarly prepared competitors. A 'quick fix' or shortcut is not only unacceptable, but antithetical to the basic tenets of sport, suggesting a disregard for the physical sacrifice that is thought to be the essence of athletic training.

Although the sporting body might be understood as scientifically malleable, it, nevertheless, remains an organic specimen that, although it may be finely tuned, must not be contaminated. The authenticity of performance depends on the pure body, for any real or suspected corruption of the athlete means the outcome may no longer be 'genuine' (Bose 2005). Whilst this concept appears critical to contemporary constructions of sport, determining what is 'natural' about the athletic body is, nevertheless, a difficult task. It is, to a certain degree, predicated on the relationship between sport and nature identified in the previous chapter, which argued that modern sport derived, in part, from Romantic conceptions of nature and landscape as an escape from the strictures of the industrialising world. The conception of nature as pure and untainted was incorporated into the ideology of sport and has had an enduring influence on constructions of the sporting body. Athletic performance, therefore, is understood to be an authentic expression of natural capacity, whilst technological modification threatens to render it unnatural and inappropriately enhanced. As such, performance technologies are assessed, in part, on their potential to reinforce or disrupt the natural body, and for this reason, determining the nature of the 'natural' body is critical.

Natural bodies

Much of the public concern about the prevalence of performance technologies in sport derives from fears that particular techniques or substances threaten the purity of athletic bodies and damage the integrity of competition. Just as sport is regarded as a natural endeavour, sporting bodies are similarly assumed to be 'natural', uncontested entities that reflect institutional 'values'. The athletic body symbolises health and well-being and is considered the logical consequence of hard work, or, in other words, a body stretched to, and perhaps beyond, its own physical limits without intrusive external augmentation. Such conceptions of the athletic body are fixed within a discourse of nature that underpins modern sport and supports the rejection of technologies that jeopardise the integrity of the athlete. So pervasive are images of nature within sport that some have argued the body is becoming increasingly 'dehumanised' through advances in exercise science (Hoberman 1992), and, furthermore, that the presence of 'nature' is being eroded in favour of contests based on competing technologies. In particular, the marked increase in drug use in elite sport is thought to represent, more than any other, this process of dehumanisation, which is deemed not merely a transgression against the 'natural' body, but against sport itself. To suggest that bodies are being dehumanised, or indeed, superhumanised (Miah 2006), through the intrusion of drugs, technology or other techniques is to argue that without intervention bodies are essentially unspoiled. Yet, the 'natural' body remains remarkably elusive within a sporting culture that relies on all manner of intervention to extract record-breaking performances.

Although theorists have written convincingly about the social constructedness of the body, the concept of the body as 'natural' retains primacy in the public consciousness. To many, the body is undeniably biological, rooted in the natural world and a product of organic processes (Turner 1996). It is a fixed reality that finds its meaning within its fleshy depths, a conception that is supported by bio-medical discourses that reduce the body to little more than an independent collection of organs and bones. Furthermore, naturalistic approaches locate a range of social, political and economic attributes firmly within the body, suggesting that culturally generated qualities emerge from, and are controlled by, the corpus (Shilling 2005; 1993; Turner 1996). Feminist scholars have identified how medical science, in particular, has contributed to the construction of femininity as an inherent, biological fact, whilst race, sexuality, sanity and class, to name but a few, were similarly thought to result from a defective or substandard body (Terry and Urla 1995; Vertinsky 1990). Whilst regarding the body as exclusively biological may seem compelling, it nevertheless neglects the ways in which the body is discursively constructed.

Whilst the natural body may be fanciful, it is nevertheless a potent image within the context of sport, confirmed by a range of textual and discursive devices that present it as inevitable. Advertisements, news and current affairs programmes, sporting federations and governmental policies as well as athletes and coaches themselves each reaffirm the existence of, and preference for, the natural sporting body. Popular representations of sport evoke images of bodies powering through the natural landscape as sweat pours from their brows, suggesting that the desire, energy and capacity to perform come from within rather than from without. Anti-doping programmes similarly reinforce the authority of the natural body, utilising images that warn of the monstrous consequences of illicit enhancement. Through their study of such campaigns, Davis and Delano (1992: 4) confirm

38 *The nature of the body*

that 'media texts assume, reinforce, and help to naturalize the notion that the human body is or can be purely natural' unless, of course, it is specifically 'disrupted by artificial substances'. In these images, female bodies are digitally altered so their genitalia resemble male organs, or are adorned with hairy chests and faces (Skins 2006), which both visually confirm the 'unnatural' state of these doped women and suggest that bodies that do not conform to normative gendered expectations are themselves evidence of illicit treatments.

Nevertheless, 'natural' bodies are the stuff of sporting mythology, presented and represented to remind us of the horrors of technology and their potential to disrupt the otherwise uncontaminated. In this sense, the natural body insists that it is an entity unto itself, which, though it may be located in culture, remains steadfastly isolated from it. Its sovereignty is protected by visible edges that both demarcate its limits and create a locus of contestation. Although imagined as stable, these borders are unreliable, exposing the vulnerable body to invasion and corruption. Discourses of health and hygiene confirm that the body is susceptible to contagion that enters from the outside, whilst fluids that leach from within confirm its permeability and leakiness (Shildrick 1996). The body is, thus, constantly at risk, and fears about its disruption derive from the threat of an unnatural or unauthorised transgression of its borders.

Binary bodies

Like nature, what constitutes a 'natural body' is only apparent in the presence of an 'unnatural' one, revealing that it is an essentially relational concept that only exists when juxtaposed against an Other (Murphie and Potts 2003). As such, the unnatural body represents an ideological counterpoint to the natural body, and, whilst it symbolises a potential threat to the latter's integrity, the impurity of such marginalised bodies is critical to establish the natural body's own identity. Crucially, without an Other hovering at its margins, there would be no need to establish and police the borders of the natural body, no need to protect it against potential contamination and no need to define it negatively in terms of what it is clearly not. The body would simply be, and it would require no further explanation because there would be nothing to remind it of what it is not or, more ominously, what it might become. In the face of technology, however, the natural body commands recognition; it requires its borders to be carefully defined, as its very identity relies on establishing and confirming its limits. Consequently, the natural body is positioned within a simple, hierarchical binary that privileges nature over not-nature, such that the natural/pure/authentic body is confronted directly with its unnatural/impure/inauthentic counterpart.

Binaries are not, of course, restricted to the body and underpin the construction of broader personal and social identities. Accordingly, the twin concepts of 'us' and 'them' are embodied in national discourses that similarly define the Self in relation to the Other, as well as within the competitive structure of contemporary sport where nation states, through their individual representatives, submit themselves to be measured and, most importantly, compared against one another. Whether personal, social or national, identities, then, rest largely on the construction and maintenance of binaries, even as the border between the two is assaulted by liminalities. For the purposes of this study, a Lacanian model of identity formation can inform a discussion of sport and its commitment to the natural body by illustrating the psychosocial processes through which the Self is distinguished from the Other and by identifying how these are evident within an institution, where various binary relationships are established and re-established to ensure its integrity. Within such a framework, the anxiety that is generated as a consequence of the development of independent social identities is mirrored in the disquiet provoked by performance technologies and the potential disruption to the natural body that these represent.

In analysing the psychological processes through which children determine a sense of Self, Jacques Lacan (1977) distinguishes between several stages of identity formation, including the initial 'mirror stage'. Simply put, the mirror stage is that developmental moment when an infant comes to recognise itself in a 'mirror', a significant milestone, as it represents the point at which the child is 'first able to imagine itself as a coherent and self-governing whole' (Sarup 1992: 66). Specifically, the mirror allows the child to recognise her/his own limits, and, as Elizabeth Grosz (1989: 21) notes, 'internalis[e] as its own image an externalised representation of itself, a view of itself from the outside'. At this point, the child learns to accept as its identity an external, yet artificial, image of itself as a discrete Other, separate, for the first time, from its mother (Sarup 1992: 66). The child enjoys its reflected image, indeed the promise, of itself as unified and stable, yet this is not the 'real' subject. Although the reflection seems complete, the body is, after all, visibly detached from other bodies, it does not correspond with what the child feels. As it experiences alienation and is 'split between what it feels (fragmentation, the body-in-bits-and-pieces) and what it sees (the image of itself as a *gestalt*, as a visual whole)' (Grosz 1989: 22), the search for identity becomes a quest to find the illusory 'whole' mirror image.

The mirror stage assists the child in distinguishing itself 'spatially', allowing it to imagine its identity as separate from other bodies and objects (Grosz 1989: 21). By sensing its 'discrete separation', the child begins to recognise and, indeed, desire boundaries between it/Self and Others (Sarup 1992: 66). These become critical for maintaining the child's newly discovered sense of independence and, consequently, the preservation of the discrete Self through the maintenance of these borders becomes a priority. By keeping 'Others' outside of those psychosocial boundaries, an artificial sense of cohesion and 'purity' is maintained: that which is 'not-pure' is

40 *The nature of the body*

identified as that which is, and must remain, outside the Self. Meanings about 'us' are thus generated through 'our' relationship with 'them'. According to Lacan, the Self, the 'I am', is clearly 'that which I am not' (Moi 1985: 99), suggesting not only that identity is negatively defined, but that it is characterised by a lack, an unsettling recognition that the Self is fundamentally split between what it senses in its body and what it sees in its reflection. The individual is thus compelled to sate that lack and endlessly seek wholeness. Of course, the mirror is but a metaphor and, for the subject, symbolises ideological frames and cultural mechanisms. Individuals, then, seek their sense of Self through multiple 'cultural mirrors' that reflect back a range of subject positions and identities, each of which further reinforces a sense of alienation.

Although Lacan's theories explicitly refer to the formation of the subject, the search for identity through the juxtaposition of Self and Other is useful for this discussion, and not simply because sport lends itself well to simple binary constructions. Athletes certainly use the Other as a direct and indirect measure of themselves; however, institutions and other groups may similarly recognise their respective identities within the 'mirror's' reflection. The ideological identity of sport, for example, is predicated, in part, on nature and humanity, which is expressed through its earnest desire to protect and nurture the natural body in the face of pressing technologisation. Nevertheless, the pressures of the modern sporting industry mean that these ideologies are constantly threatened by an overarching emphasis on winning at the expense of more intrinsic motives, financial incentives and illicit performance enhancement. In other words, the internal conflict between the essence and spirit of sport, on one level, represents a fundamental split within sport's identity, and this lack sustains the search for sport's imagined wholeness, that mythical golden era when amateurs reigned without the insidious threat of professionalism, commercialism and doping. This split is, in many ways, reduced to a natural/unnatural or nature/artifice dialectic, so that the natural body comes to symbolise the true, uncorrupted nature of sport, whilst the latter represents that which 'I am not' and would never wish to be. The search for the pure body is, thus, the search for the soul of sport, its true meaning and identity; however, in a Lacanian sense, these represent the illusory and unattainable imago.

Abject bodies

It is clear that the dialectical relationship between Self and Other underpins the quest for a pure, natural body within the context of sport, yet despite increasing legislation, the 'problem' of illicit enhancement seems to be worsening. As noted above, part of the reason lies in the fact that the construction of distinct 'us' and 'them' categories may obscure the dependent relationship that exists between the two (Cranny-Francis 1995), for simply recognising arbitrary boundaries between pure and impure does little to explain, for example, why drug-use and drug users cannot be contained. Despite such an unambiguous objective, it would appear, from the discussion above, that the 'Other' can never fully be expelled for it is the 'Other' that gives the 'Self' definition. Yet, it is not merely the presence of a discrete Other that is critical, but rather it is the fluid nature of the boundary that purports to segregate them that is most instructive. To this end, theories of abjection offer a useful heuristic for considering the mutually sustaining and interwoven relationship between Self and Other.

Julia Kristeva's (1982) work in *Powers of Horror: An Essay on Abjection* draws on the work of anthropologist Mary Douglas, who locates the relationship between Self and Other within a cultural concept of the body as either 'pure' (Self) or 'defiled' (Other). Although 'pure' and 'defiled' are positioned antagonistically, they are not absolutely independent. Not only are the boundaries between the two porous, fluid and, thus, open to disruption, but the 'defiled' and the 'pure' are both necessarily part of the same body. Despite being intimately linked, 'pure' and 'defiled' are, nevertheless, characterised by the search for independence from one another. In terms of the body, for instance, purity can only be attained through the removal of impurities, including bodily wastes, such as vomit, urine or faeces, which are excreted. According to Kristeva (1982), these fluids represent the abject and must be continually expelled from the body as part of its pursuit of purity. Yet, as the abject both comes from within, and is generated by, the body, it can never be completely discharged; the cycle of production and excretion is continuous. The abject is thus a recurring contaminative threat to what would otherwise be the pure or natural body, so that the search for Self therefore becomes a never-ending quest for the pure, the undefiled or Lacan's illusory whole body. Yet, as Grosz (1989: 73) points out, 'the abject attests to the impossibility of clear borders' and disturbs boundaries between Self and Other to threaten the 'apparently settled unity of the subject with disruption and possible dissolution' (Grosz 1989: 71). Consequently, the abject has a dual nature within the body: though excreted, it remains essential to the normal functioning of the body. Thus, as Grosz (1989: 71) contends, 'what is excluded can never be fully obliterated but hovers at the borders of our existence. ... It is impossible to exclude these psychically and socially threatening elements with any finality', confirming that purity can never be attained.

Although the abject is typically applied to the individual body, it can also provide a framework for understanding broader cultural or social bodies. Whereas individually, the defiled relates to bodily waste, within a society, the social abject are groups that are 'represented as a threat to core values' (Sibley 1995: 41). Across history and cultures, various groups have been condemned as a social threat, including criminals, the insane, people of colour, illegal immigrants, those with disabilities, disease or a different religion or politics, women and the poor. These various 'Others' are compelled to occupy the margins/fringes of society, yet remain embedded

42   *The nature of the body*

within definitions of Self. David Sibley (1995) recognises the variety of measures that are employed to protect the pure 'us' from being contaminated by the defiled 'them', including legislation that formally identifies 'impure' groups or movements and seeks to reform and/or purify them. The most common technique, however, is the erection of physical or psychosocial boundaries designed to spatially and/or socially exclude the Other by groups who 'consider themselves to be normal and mainstream' (Sibley 1995: xv). This process is clearly intended to preserve the Self, for without evidence of the not-Self, that which the boundary excludes, there is no Self, there is no Other.

Various groups within sport have been abjectified. Professionals, women, homosexuals, and people of colour, for example, have, at different times, been represented as a threat to the 'core values' of sport and various rules and regulations have been introduced to preclude their entry into the athletic arena. More recently, 'steroid-fuelled' or doped athletes have come to occupy this position, and comprehensive strategies have been introduced to excrete drugs users from the sporting body, just as waste is eliminated from the corpus (Fairchild 1989). The integrity of sport is thus dependent on the strict policing of its margins in order to sustain this process of purification, and sporting bodies regularly flush their systems of all that threatens to disturb. In addition, there are processes in place to capture the body's composition, to record a snapshot that is safely stored until technology progresses even further. Specifically, bodily fluids are taken, tested and then frozen, to be reanalysed at that future time when detection technologies are expected to have improved, meaning that the outcome of a particular event will remain unconfirmed, in flux, until all possible examinations have been exhausted. This is a somewhat curious position to be in for an institution that is so quantitatively driven, yet, at the same time, it confirms the desire for absolute certainty and confidence that an outcome is a measure only of physical capacity.

Recording the body's state at any given athletic moment is realised by freezing blood or urine samples and storing them for future analysis. This recent practice illustrates how the transient and defiling abject is actually and symbolically seized for self-defining and celebratory purposes. Abjected bodily fluids are gleefully appropriated as a means of eliding ambiguity and fortifying binary oppositions, whilst the process of collecting these waste products moves the abject out of a dependent relationship with the body. That the samples are frozen is particularly significant, as the act of freezing fixes the abject, capturing and then warehousing that which is normally quickly flushed away. Thus, the frozen samples are a metaphorical attempt to reestablish immutable boundaries between the Self and the Other, as freezing these body products removes their fluidity and prevents them from crossing back across the porous boundary from whence they came. As such, the abject is stabilised and can no longer disrupt established binaries.

Critically, freezing samples can only ever be a temporary gesture, because in order for them to serve their purpose, they must be unfrozen and returned to their liquid state. Yet, it is the very fluidity of the abject that makes it so unsettling. In its original form, not only is the abject free to traverse corporeal borders, it also reminds us of the abject's existing relationship with the body and, thus, its capacity to defile. These samples will, therefore, always be transgressive and will never lose the potential to disrupt fair/cheating, pure/defiled, nature/artifice and Self/Other binaries. Furthermore, as the abject is never entirely eliminated, it is essentially unable to determine Self without reference to the Other.

Drug-users will never be completely expelled from this body, because they represent the logical consequence of an institution that encourages aspirations for records, victories and medals by embodying *Citius, Altius, Fortius* within its very structure. Those who seek technological enhancement and alternatives are inevitably produced by such a system, which itself inevitably relies on such athletes for its success. Like all bodies, sport yearns for, though never attains, purity, thus, calls to 'excise the cancer of sports drug use' from an otherwise healthy sporting body is (Magdalinski, 2000a), therefore, merely a futile attempt to eliminate the abject completely, just as the subject repeatedly tries to expel impure or defiling bodily fluids. Yet, the abject lingers on the margins of the body, revealing an unsettling, liminal space between inside and out, which contests the certainty of borders and exposes binary categories to be more elastic than fixed.

Liminal bodies

Whilst the natural body seems to be a discrete and inevitable category, the border demarcating natural from unnatural is not, in fact, fixed, for binary opposites, once established, do not remain uncontested. They exist in a constant state of flux as boundaries shift to include or exclude, repairing their fractures and eliminating instability. This is clearly apparent within sport where the natural/artifice binary has altered over time according to ideological changes and variations in accepted training practices. Whilst illicit technologies now represent the antithesis of all that sport is supposed to represent, it must be remembered that these substances are simply the latest in a long line of potential 'contaminants', as, across the decades, various perils and moral panics, each located on the margins of what is 'natural', have threatened to disrupt and 'pollute' sport. During its early stages, the amateur code dictated that a 'natural' athlete, for example, was one who required little, if any, practice; during the Cold War era, 'natural' athletes were those who relied on amateur, self-funded training methods; and in the twenty-first century, 'natural' athletes are those who, though they train professionally and scientifically, do not resort to illicit enhancements to augment their performance. Although the meaning of 'natural' has changed within sport, the hierarchical relationship between 'natural' and 'artificial' has remained constant and is founded, for the most part, on the construction of a binary relationship between Self and Other.

44 The nature of the body

In many respects, the 'us' and 'them' binary is omnipresent in sport. Athletes who belong to 'us' and those who belong to 'them' are readily identifiable on the sportsfield; 'we' are represented as heroic and invincible, whilst 'they' are cowardly and ungracious; 'we' are pure of spirit and body, whilst 'they' are immoral and polluted. In essence, 'our' athletes are natural, whilst theirs are plainly not. It is clear that the natural/unnatural binary underpins contemporary constructions of the athletic body in theory, however, in reality, the distinction between appropriate and artificial bodies is harder to sustain. The usual image of 'artificial bodies' is that of the android or robot. Athletes, no matter how artificially enhanced they might be, and even though they may be stereotyped as 'robotic', as communist athletes were in times past, they are still human and so cannot be comfortably categorised as thoroughly 'artificial'. Nevertheless, these bodies are still regarded as materially different from 'us'; 'they' may resemble us but they are decidedly less natural and more synthetic.

Technologically enhanced bodies disturb conventional boundaries between nature and artifice; they are not quite robots, not quite human and yet are both. These athletes are cyborgs, hybrid creatures that seamlessly blend the organic and inorganic and, by their very irreducibility, vitiate the nature of humanity (Haraway 1991). Cyborgs reside within the liminal space that opens up between binary positions, living in the borderland between nature and artifice. This space destabilises and unsettles the boundary that distinguishes 'us' from 'them', confirming the fragility and vulnerability of these essentialist categories and undermining the authority of the entire structure. Accordingly, this space generates anxiety, particularly for those who are 'socialized into believing that the separation of categories is necessary or desirable' (Sibley 1995: 33), and for this reason is regarded as a clear threat to the Symbolic Order. In order to contain this threat, liminal spaces, as soon as they appear, need to be assimilated back into the binary before they can cast anchor and establish an alternative perspective. This process typically requires each category to shift its margins to incorporate the hybrid threat within reconstituted definitions of Self and Other. This is not a hegemonic process, because rather than negotiating an emergent system, the liminal zone is forcibly reabsorbed into the binary to reclaim the border. As such, liminal space is both destabilising and unstable, a potential threat and an inconvenience.

Within the context of sport, 'athletes', such as *Rocky IV*'s boxing automaton Drago, as well as other 'drug-abusing' athletes, exemplify the organic/inorganic and destabilising cyborg. These hybrid bodies slip betwixt and between constructions of nature and artifice, human and robot, and body and technology. They are considered neither entirely human because of their chemically/technologically/artificially enhanced physiques, nor robots, for they still have the fleshy form of humans. They are decidedly liminal, resist being confined to either category, and are confounding, for they shift and slide between the organic and inorganic to jeopardise the sporting body. For this reason, they must be assimilated into the binary; however, whilst it is critical that liminal space is dissolved, it is inconceivable that technologised bodies can be accepted into the category of 'us'. Yet, by their very nature, they are also not 'them', the category that, in this construction, is reserved for the truly artificial robot or android. To accommodate, the latter is revised to provide for the previous anomaly of chemically altered humans, suggesting that binaries are never fixed and are necessarily fluid and responsive. As soon as borders between the modified categories 'clean us' and 'drug-tainted them' are reestablished, they are, however, again challenged by the appearance of new liminal zones. For example, if 'our', presumably clean, athletes are caught with banned substances in their bodies, they too transgress the boundary that separates 'us' from 'them' and create a new, threatening liminal space. In addition, those athletes who have been suspected of, but have not been caught, taking performance enhancing drugs similarly contest the binary. Though they reside in the same unsettling zone, these groups are, nevertheless, treated differently. The transgressions of 'our' athletes are typically framed as 'innocent' mistakes, ensuring that despite their tainted bodies, they remain firmly part of 'us'. If their drug-taking is, for example, rationalised as a therapeutic measure designed to restore their health, then they may be 'forgiven' and recategorised as 'innocent', if, temporarily, not 'clean' (Magdalinski 2001b). By contrast, 'other' athletes, regardless of whether there is evidence against them, are, often with little prompting, immediately suspected of systematic drug use, which confirms that they represent incontrovertible exponents of the drug-taking 'them'. Crucially, the reincorporation of 'our' athletes back into the sporting body is not secure, and athletes who take drugs to enhance performance can be expelled from the Self and forcibly resituated within the category of 'drug cheat'. The public is certainly not uncritical, and the reincorporation of too many drug-taking athletes, even those cast as 'our' innocent heroes, risks the complete dismantling of these binaries, which sport can ill afford.

Surveilled bodies

In order to maintain the integrity of the nature/artifice binary, athletic bodies are surveilled by sporting organisations, international federations, governments and the public. Their bodies become, in a sense, a kind of public property, where all interested parties have a right to know what they ingest, how they are trained, or their respective hormone levels. After an event, athletes are whisked away before they even have a chance to catch their breath to provide bodily fluids for analysis, or they may be selected for random, out-of-competition tests. To facilitate the latter, their movements and travels are closely monitored, as athletes must notify anti-doping authorities of their whereabouts at all times. After prisoners, athletes are perhaps the most highly surveilled social group, meaning that they, too, can

46   *The nature of the body*

never be quite sure when Big Brother is watching. The systematic organisation of in- and out-of-competition testing, suspensions or expulsions and the more recent threat of criminal prosecution combine with subtle and discursive strategies to create a docile athletic body that is compelled to 'toe the company line' (Morgan 2006: 178).

The carefully monitored athletic body reflects wider issues of power and control within society, as effectively theorised by French philosopher Michel Foucault (1977). Foucault (1977) was concerned with the means by which social authority and power could be maintained, and focused largely on disciplinary practices that created easily, and self-, managed citizens. These 'docile bodies' were produced by networks of institutions and techniques that relied on panoptic surveillance strategies to guarantee compliance with desirable behavioural norms. Drawing on Jeremy Bentham's eighteenth-century design, Foucault (1977) argues that the regulatory power of the panopticon, a model prison that was constructed to observe inmates who themselves were unaware if, and when, they were being watched, is sufficient to ensure obedience and, thus, social order. Rather than exercising power through direct enforcement, the panopticon alleges that the mere threat of being observed can be enough to provoke self-scrutiny and behavioural regulation.

Although it was conceived specifically to control the incarcerated, panoptic strategies are evident within other institutions and social contexts. Whilst the growing network of CCTV cameras provides a direct, though unsophisticated, example of surveillance, other, more subtle, strategies utilise panopticism to regulate and enforce not only behavioural but bodily norms. Schools and factories, Foucault (1977) contends, function like prisons to subordinate and control the body, teaching individuals to respect authority, obey instruction and respond to bells. Yet, it is not only formal institutions where surveillance strategies are evident. Margaret Carlile Duncan (1994: 49) utilises panoptic principles to identify how women's fitness magazines 'invite a continual self conscious body monitoring' from its readership. In this case, the threat of scrutiny from others prompts women to internalise their gaze to evaluate their bodies against, and modify them to, established feminine norms. Similarly, the mirrored walls of gyms and fitness centres not only 'invite' but force visitors to dissect their own bodies, and those of others, as each segment is carefully, thoughtfully and deliberately honed (Frew and McGillivray 2005; Sassatelli 1999).

David Kirk (1994) identifies specifically how sport and physical education programmes have been complicit in the disciplining of, particularly young, bodies. The regulation of time and space as well as the reduction of the body to a series of moving parts mirrored industrial labour practices, as did the repetitive drills that characterised early physical education models. Contemporary theorists, furthermore, note that power, surveillance and discipline remain a constituent part of sport and physical educative practices (Webb *et al.* 2004; Kirk 1994). Since the 1950s, however, surveillance within sport has concentrated on the cleanliness and, thus, naturalness of athletic bodies as increasingly sophisticated systems are advanced to monitor, test and, potentially, expel those bodies that do not conform to untainted ideals.

The formal regulation of athletic purity began in the 1960s with the formation of the International Olympic Committee's (IOC) Medical Commission, which was initially asked to examine the extent of doping within sport and was only later entrusted with the broader mission of protecting athletes' health. Whilst the Commission quickly prohibited a range of performance enhancing substances, the lack of rigorous analysis meant that at the 1968 Mexico Olympics, the first Games after it was established, the only significant testing for which it was responsible was the chromosomal test that was carried out on female athletes to confirm their sex (Todd 1992). That the Medical Commission was responsible for both the drug and sex testing of athletes is, on one level, not particularly astonishing, as health practices are firmly entrenched within broader disciplinary techniques that establish and reinforce bodily norms. Despite the Medical Commission's purview, until the 1990s, individual nations and sporting federations were largely responsible for their own anti-doping policies. Yet, after the 1998 Tour de France scandal, in which athletes and teams were disqualified following the discovery of large amounts of recombinant erythropoietin (rEPO) in a team van, the IOC organised the World Conference on Doping in Sport, held in 1999 in Lausanne, which recommended the creation of an international umbrella organisation to coordinate and monitor a global anti-doping strategy. In response, the World Anti-Doping Agency (WADA) was founded in 2000 to 'harmonise' anti-doping policies, though the zeal with which this organisation has pursued its mission has created something of a global 'police force' charged with arresting athletes for 'crimes against humanity', prompting many to question the degree to which individual and civil rights are being infringed (Morgan 2006; Houlihan 2004; Magdalinski and Warren 2004).

Whilst the WADA initiatives are extensive and pervasive, they are, nevertheless, rather like the CCTV of the sports world. They are an obvious and direct method of surveillance that, whilst effective, is not as alarming as the more insidious methods that compel athletes to comply with the 'natural body' norm. Whilst international federations and other statutory bodies establish and uphold regulations, laws and invasive testing, the media and public, at a more practical and immediate level, also become expert at recognising illicit enhancement by examining athletes' physical dimensions. Images in the sporting press confirm that chemically or unnaturally enhanced bodies exceed accepted physical norms, which means the body itself becomes a marker of guilt or innocence (Magdalinski 2001a; 2001b). Women, for example, with 'masculine' characteristics and men who are hypermuscular each appear to provide visual evidence of their culpability. Their 'unnatural' appearance invites careful scrutiny to confirm that these

48   *The nature of the body*

bodies cannot possibly be 'normal' and, by consequence, must be unnaturally altered. Spectators are also ably assisted by the complicity of other athletes, who helpfully and eagerly point out physical anomalies in their competitors, reinforcing that enhancement is visible on the body's surface.

At the 2000 Sydney Olympic Games, the differential treatment of American shot putter C. J. Hunter and Romanian gymnast Andreea Raducan reveal how inappropriate enhancement is recognised through a visual analysis of the body. Hunter had returned positive tests for nandralone, whilst Raducan, an 'elfin gymnast', had been stripped of a gold medal following a positive test for the pseudoephedrine she had taken to ward off a cold. Although she was included in *The Australian* newspaper's 'Olympic Hall of Shame', Raducan, unlike Hunter, was treated as an 'innocent victim' by the media, and, as her situation represented 'rough justice', was publicly absolved of guilt (Harris 2000a, 2000b; Stewart 2000). The media constructed Raducan 'in stark contrast' to Hunter, because it was 'impossible to lump sixteen-year-old Raducan into the same drug-cheating category as ... C.J. Hunter and hammer throwers Vadim Devyatovsky from Belarus and Mihaela Melinte from Romania, all of whom tested positive recently to steroids, two of them in extraordinarily large quantities' (Harris 2000b: 19). Strength athlete Hunter was thus demonised as representative of the bulked-up, steroid-abusing drug cheat, similar to the 'three Bulgarian weightlifters ... who had shamed their sport and their country' (Harris 2000b). Whilst IOC vice-president Jacques Rogge admitted Raducan's case was a 'very painful' decision and IOC Medical Commission chair Prince Alexandre de Merode acknowledged that such young athletes are often required to follow orders of athletic officials and coaches, Hunter's explanation for his positive test was summarily dismissed by these same representatives as 'impossible' (Forbes 2000).

What is significant in the Raducan and Hunter examples is that the sex, size and, potentially, race of the athlete played a considerable role in determining their relative guilt. Large, powerful bodies, the public has learned, are representative of illicit drug taking, whilst petite feminine bodies are innocent victims, reliant on a masculine Other for guidance and nurturing. The head of Australian Gymnastics, Jane Allen, even 'doubted whether steroids or other banned drugs even helped female gymnasts, given their small size and youth' (Harris 2000b: 19), confirming that, at least in the public mind, small, feminine bodies can not be confused with oversized doped ones. It appears that by simply gazing at the external contours of athletic bodies, a kind of athletic phrenology perhaps, the guilt or innocence of athletes can be ascertained, and the public has thoroughly accepted that a series of bodily measures, including physical appeal, offer clues as to an athlete's guilt or innocence.

The examination of bodily surfaces to determine illicit performance enhancement is an important point that is discussed in later chapters; however, what is critical from a theoretical perspective is the suggestion that bodies do not necessarily have to *be* strictly natural, but that they must, at the very least, *resemble* nature, or rather, an idealised vision of what nature is. This is a critical distinction, revealing a tension between actual and imagined nature. José van Dijck (2001) suggests that although there is a cultural preference for 'natural' rather than human-made or artificial items, confirming Barilan and Weintraub's (2001) notion of 'technophobia', the production of artificial replicas of natural products has altered our vision of what 'nature' really is. She suggests that the ubiquitous plastic flowers and fruit that epitomised 1950s consumer culture has been replaced with a marked preference for the 'real' thing, yet we are so used to the perfect artificial versions that we now accept nothing less than perfection from natural products. The rosy blush on an apple, the flawless red tomato or the perfectly formed rose are now expected, so that each organic item must correspond to the image presented by their plastic, and culturally recognisable, replicas. Van Dijck (2001: 99) submits the example of the tulip, genetically modified to produce standard sizes, colours and shapes, which essentially reduces variation from the culturally established norm of how a tulip should look, to argue that although we now want the 'real' thing, we need it to reflect a kind of 'perfected nature', because we are no longer content with 'nature's own imperfect products'.

Like the tulip, the body too has 'become an intricate object, an amalgam of organic material, cultural norms, and technological tooling' (van Dijck 2001: 99), as it is subjected to intimate modifications to conform to cultural standards and imagined ideals. This is particularly evident within elite sport, where, despite appeals towards nature, bodies and performances are deliberately crafted and engineered. Just like the sportscapes that are denuded of environmental variability, athletes too are purpose built to conform to van Dijck's (2001) 'perfected nature'. In this way, athletes, and the spaces in which they compete, are analogous, such that examining corporeal topography can provide an intriguing insight into the significance of nature in the discursive construction of both body and landscape.

Landscaped bodies

The landscape has played an important role in the conception of modern sport as a naturalistic activity. The provision of a spatial counterpoint to the crammed conditions of industrial life and the rejuvenatory potential of green spaces revealed natural landscapes and recreation within them to be the perfect antidote to the ills of the modernising world. Yet, as sport was gradually formalised and the comparison of bodies became a more serious national enterprise, the environmental vagaries of these natural spaces that impinged on performances made it difficult to assess the actual physical capacity of athletes. Dedicated spaces were engineered to ensure that the landscape would not inadvertently influence outcomes so that a result was an accurate reflection of the pure human performance. It is within these modified

50 *The nature of the body*

sportscapes, where nature and culture collide, that athletic bodies perform and are viewed, scrutinised and ultimately judged, and it is no coincidence that the ambiguity of the sporting landscape and the tensions within the nature/ artifice binary are reflected in, and inscribed upon, athletes' bodies. Yet, these bodies are confounded by an institution that admires both architectural spectacle and environmental symbolism, yet expects nothing less than purity from its athletes. Like the sporting landscapes themselves, athletic bodies are at once artificial and organic, their seemingly natural topography belying their systematic manufacture. Despite this paradoxical reality, 'pure' human, rather than technologically induced, performances, are expected. Just as the environment is moulded to become as neutral as possible in the sporting performance, so too must the body appear to be uninfluenced by externalities, becoming a 'sculpt[ed] landscape' in its own right (Bale 1994: 52).

In conceiving the athletic body as a kind of landscape, it is clear that geographical concerns are played out, in part, on the surface of the body, where anxieties about nature and artifice, and the boundaries between them, are realised. Owing to their deliberate manufacture, athletes cannot represent unbounded and untouched nature and, as technological artefacts, are produced by external, rather than intrinsic, forces. Like landscapes, they are 'highly artificial constructions' that are 'created for particular types of use' (Aitchison *et al.* 2000: 77). The athletic body resembles the mastered nature of the sportsfield, where nature is regulated to ensure consistency and efficiency and, for that reason, corresponds more closely to manicured gardens than to undomesticated areas. Gardens represent a spatial and ideological interface between nature and culture (Crozier 1999), and are typically understood to be 'natural' landscapes that have been adjusted by technologies into a rational form that can be managed and replicated. As an interface, gardens are necessarily liminal spaces, not quite wild, but despite technological and rational intervention, neither completely predictable nor controlled. Nature might be domesticated in the garden, but it can never be completely ordered. At the same time, gardens are bounded, tamed spaces, demarcating culture and ownership, and preventing the threatening encroachment of the untamed wilderness (Beilin 1999).

If sporting bodies are read as gardens, then they too must be liminal; they are not representative of sublime wilderness, but nor are they machines, fully of the technical realm. They reside in the hazy space between the two, just like the unstructured English garden that was popularised in the eighteenth century. The change in preference from formal, geometric gardens to the more popular 'English' style, which were constructed to approximate natural wilderness, suggests that the obvious presence of human intervention in these 'natural' spaces has been gradually concealed in favour of rambling parks that appeared to blend seamlessly into the surrounding countryside (Roberts 2004). The English garden, thus, offers a wonderful metaphor for the athletic body. As a garden, the space is clearly constructed. It is designed, planted and maintained under the careful eye of the gardener. Yet, the English garden does not appear to be one; there are no walls that establish the limits of either the garden or the countryside, the planning is hidden beneath an apparent random array of plantings, and its deliberate construction is obscured to project an image of nature, or, rather, the gardener's vision of how nature looks, such that the garden could be mistaken for part of its non-garden surrounds.

The athletic body is also tamed from a kind of 'wilderness' state. A cadre of support personnel produces a competitive body from raw material, in essence 'construct[ing] a "natural" landscape' (Roberts 2004: 264). These bodies operate as both nature and artifice, blurring the boundaries between them, which is a problematic position, for the very existence of these nature/artifice bodies exposes tensions between the external spirit and the intrinsic essence of sport. These liminal bodies reveal sport to be not of nature but decidedly cultural, constructed and technological. The engineering of the body is, nevertheless, obscured, for the body's dimensions and proportions are designed to conform to accepted bodily norms, yet few recognise the irony in admiring the architecture of a sports stadium whilst, at the same time, overlooking the same built quality in the athlete. According to the former, the sportscape is appreciated as a technological site that has reduced or removed nature, such as in the notion of a 'fast' pool. In terms of the latter, the body is more respected the more 'natural' it appears to be. As such, it is clear that acknowledging athletes to be engineered threatens the authenticity of the natural body, and of sport more generally, by revealing these bodies to be synthetic scapes that are effected by extreme and constant technological intervention, surveillance and manipulation. To expose athletes, in this sense, would be to acknowledge the seamless, interdependent relationship between sport, the body and technology, and to render arguments against technological enhancement unsustainable.

Whilst allegations of the inappropriate use of performance technologies expose the rational design, structure and production of athletic bodies, as gardens, athletic bodies are certainly rational and efficient, not unruly as nature can be (Shildrick 1996: 2). Conceiving the athlete as a form of tamed wilderness, a rationalised garden that is surreptitiously controlled, is apparent when nature, in the form of unnatural/untamed bodies, intrudes on its territory. Just as gardens are threatened by the unwelcome intrusion of nature, the unexpected appearance of non-athletic bodies in the sporting arena is similarly confounding. Eddie the Eagle and Eric Moussambani are but two examples of the introduction of essentially untamed, and untrained, bodies into elite sport, and whilst their exploits may garner international attention or prompt viewers to regard them as evidence of the 'true spirit' of sport, they, nevertheless, remain a laughable curiosity rather than a serious contender, confirming that nature seems 'deeply disruptive' when 'set against culture' (Shildrick 1996: 2). Until their appearance, the gardened athlete resembled nature, yet its artifice was exposed by the presence of a truly irrational, 'natural' body.

Conclusion

The natural body is both conspicuously present in, and noticeably absent from, sport. On the one hand, administrators and officials declare their desire to preserve the sanctity of the natural athlete, yet, on the other, the application of external devices, methods and substances to improve physical performance counters that the elite athlete is far from, and likely has never been, an exemplar of inherent talent and ability. Nevertheless, concern that the integrity of sport is under threat from the technological corruption of body underpins strategies designed to both assert and preserve the 'natural' body; however, determining what precisely this is may prove difficult. The 'natural' body is a notoriously fluid concept that changes according to fluctuating social, cultural and scientific ideologies. A 'natural' competitor from the nineteenth century, for example, would not recognise that today's scientifically prepared, nutritionally supplemented and mechanically trained athletes embody 'nature'. A further complication is that both 'nature' and the 'natural body' are necessarily relational concepts, as each only establishes its identity when juxtaposed against the other. As such, the natural body is embedded within a meaningful binary relationship that posits it against an artificial, technologically enhanced version. Whilst the construction of simply binaries is compelling and may offer some insight into the nature/artifice binary, it is, nevertheless, important to thoroughly interrogate the margins of the boundary between these two concepts, for it is here that potential disruption resides and reveals significantly more about the relationship.

A simple 'us' and 'them', or Self and Other, binary offers a limited insight into the way that sporting bodies, as representatives of broader social interests, are set against each other in combat. Spectators can identify with one side or the other, and cultural stereotypes may be applied to each team to bolster one's own sense of belonging. Using this binary to explain the discontent with performance enhancement, however, is to neglect the detailed and complex ways the categories natural/Self and unnatural/Other intersect and interact. Importantly, Self and Other are not exclusive concepts, and, as Lacan suggests, one essentially serves as a mirror for the other, revealing a disparity between Self and the Others confronted within the Symbolic Order. Kristeva, on the other hand, reminds us that Self and Other, or the 'pure' and 'defiled', exist not independently but are very much part of the one body, institution or society. In a never-ending search for purity, bodies expel contaminating waste, just as institutions eject those who do not abide by its rules, and societies incarcerate those who disrupt social order. Yet, the boundary between Self and Other is not merely a transition point across which fluids are transported, but is a location in itself, a liminal space that, by its very presence, has the potential to dissolve the binary couplet. This is a destabilising zone and to prevent their dissolution, binary opposites shift their margins in concert to incorporate

The nature of the body   53

those who may otherwise fall outside their territory. Critically, liminal spaces betray these boundaries to be neither solid nor porous, but amorphous or even foggy.

Each of these theories makes a significant contribution to an analysis of the relationship between natural and unnatural bodies; however, it is at the corporeal level that these theories are embedded in specific and identifiable actions. The surveillance of athletes to determine their relative purity concretises the Self/Other and nature/artifice binaries, as the material invasion of the body to collect, and later test and freeze, body fluids establishes the impure Other as a very real and tangible threat. At the same time, the panoptic monitoring of athletes' physiques by sporting institutions, the media and the general public reveal that it is not only the body's depths that divulge secrets, but that its very surfaces can be scrutinised for evidence of illicit enhancement. Bodies that exceed normative dimensions are considered to be visible and incontrovertible evidence of inappropriate augmentation, whilst those who conform to the shape and size of the ideal are appreciated for resembling 'natural' bodies. Having already established that 'natural' bodies do not exist, it is perhaps more accurate to suggest that those bodies that most closely conform to our conception of the natural corpus represent an ideal and 'perfected' nature, which is, nevertheless and ironically, engineered by complex scientific and technological practices.

It is significant that the primary focus in debates about performance technologies concentrates on the body and its interaction with technology, yet we do not condemn 'body technologies' or fear the effects of 'body enhancing substances'. Indeed, the notion of 'performance' is curiously absent from discourses on sport and enhancement and is typically only gestured to as a mere consequence of doping. Yet, the very purpose of enhancing the body, either legally or illicitly, is to push the body beyond its previous achievements and to create superior performances that challenge personal bests and formal records. As such, it is critical that this analysis contends specifically with performance as a social and cultural phenomenon. Accordingly, the following chapter theorises the nature of performance to identify its significance to analyses of technology, the body and enhancement.

4 The nature of performance

Introduction

As each Olympic Games approaches, the quest to find additional tests to detect the presence of a new wave of illicit drugs intensifies. Calls for tighter controls are answered in rigorous scientific protocols, and extended lists of dubious substances are circulated widely to ensure that no athlete remains unaware of the penalties for their deliberate or inadvertent ingestion. The public discusses with some expertise the notion of performance enhancing substances, and the media raises immediate questions about athletes who 'burst' onto the scene only moments prior to an opening ceremony. New world records, personal bests and outstanding accomplishments are scrutinised to ensure their authenticity, and victorious athletes are unable to avoid the mandatory testing of their bodily fluids. It is clear that within sport an athlete's performance is a serious matter, requiring independent verification and validation to ensure its integrity.

Whilst performance enhancement has become cause for concern in the world of sport, determining what the 'enhancement' of a 'performance' means is a little more complex. Part of the problem is definitional. Precisely what constitutes 'performance enhancement' and how it can be recognised has confounded sports administrators, coaches, athletes and lay spectators, and many definitions have become so obtuse as to render them useless. Fundamental to early efforts to define performance enhancement, or 'doping', was the notion of intent and character. Traditionally, if an athlete engaged in illicit practices for the specific purpose of gaining an 'unfair' advantage over their competitors, then this constituted deliberate performance enhancement. Sir Arthur Porritt, the first chair of the IOC Medical Commission, which oversaw early testing procedures, acknowledged the difficulties in trying to establish what doping was and insisted that the 'definition lies not in the words but in the integrity of character', adding that 'everyone who takes part in competitive sport or who administers it knows exactly what it means' (cited in Mottram 2003: 26). Of course, measuring intangible motivations such as intent, integrity or even character is hopelessly fraught generally, let alone within the narrow confines of performance sport. Nevertheless, anti-doping codes around the world still refer to integrity as a core issue (ASADA 2006; UK Sport 2006; USOT 2006), though in WADA's *World Anti-Doping Code* (2003) doping is defined essentially as the violation of one or more of the eight anti-doping rules, though substances and methods are analysed for their potential to violate the 'spirit of sport' (Miah 2006).

Formal definitions aside, if we look carefully at what performance enhancement means, at its most basic, any action, method, substance or intervention that improves an athlete's performance is rightfully 'performance enhancing'. Yet, few in the sports world today would agree that running around a track, swimming lengths of a pool or manipulating one's diet should be banned as an unnatural interference. These are recognised as normal and expected training routines, not 'performance enhancement' *per se*. In fact, the idea of 'performance enhancement' has become so stigmatised over the past several decades that athletes themselves valiantly search for alternative ways to describe improvements in their sporting capacity. When testing Adidas's new full-length swimsuit prior to its introduction in 2000, for example, Australia's Ian Thorpe reported at a press conference that the suit did not 'enhance' but rather 'optimised' his performance (Channel 10 2000). Clearly, it was imagined that the radical design would offer the swimmer an advantage over his competitors, yet Thorpe's careful choice of words reveals the dishonour attached to 'enhancing' one's performance, even though, essentially, that was the purpose of his chosen attire as well as the rationale behind his gruelling training schedule.

Defining 'performance enhancement' and establishing its relationship to various technologies is thus critical to understanding the concerns that surround this concept in modern sport, and deconstructing it is the initial step towards developing a more nuanced understanding of the nature/artifice binary. But whilst we might ponder the subtle semantic variations in a range of definitions, there remains an important oversight. Although determining what constitutes 'clean' or 'unenhanced' might be critical to sports administrators, the media and the public, on a theoretical level, there has been a tendency to focus solely on 'enhancement' without ever considering the concept of 'performance'. This is especially puzzling, as understanding 'performance' in the context of sport is critical to determining how and why it must be protected from unauthorised improvements. As such, the very nature of performance within sport requires scrutiny before performance enhancement can be addressed. For this reason, this chapter initially examines the concept of performance within a broader cultural context, drawing upon the rich literature of performance and theatre studies and applying these theoretical approaches to the particular circumstance of sport. It notes the similarities and, most notably, the discord between theatrical and athletic performances, as the former is essentially deceptive whilst the latter is embedded in a discourse of authenticity that suggests the athletic performance is a true reflection of not only the capacity, but also

56 The nature of performance

the motivation of a competitor. Finally, the enhancement of performance is traced historically to determine why scientific intrusion into the body is only sometimes regarded as terrifyingly inappropriate.

Understanding performance

Although we admire athletes for their feats on the track or in the pool, the concept of performance has traditionally been embedded in the creative arts. These range from musical and theatrical presentations through to performance art and dance, and are typically organised productions staged primarily for the entertainment of the viewing public. Performances are temporally and spatially defined, conducted in a confined space with a clear beginning and end, and are generally scripted. Nevertheless, performance is not limited to aesthetic experiences and describes other accomplishments, either individually or collectively, publicly or privately, such as those in the bedroom or at work. In the case of the latter, performance has become embedded in industrial notions of efficiency, productivity and output. The performance of a computer network, economic system or employee suggests less an emphasis on creativity and more a concern with measurable outcomes and an assessment of the way in which assigned tasks are conducted (McKenzie 2001). Indeed, 'performance management' strategies in the workplace suggest that labour can be identified, regulated and improved. It is this dual, almost contradictory, notion of performance as simultaneously aesthetic/creative and measurable/recordable that reflects its role in sport.

Given the multiple ways in which 'performance' is applied, finding a singular definition that effectively serves an analysis of sport is difficult. This is compounded by the fact that performance studies, the overarching discipline that has emerged in the last couple of decades from theatre studies, both raids and informs academic disciplines such as history, sociology, anthropology and cultural studies. As a result, performance is a contested term that resists definitional closure (Carlson 2004), and is understood variously as the creative delivery of written texts, social drama (Turner 1988), or ritual action (Schechner 1988). More recently, theorists have extended the term to encapsulate a broad range of social interactions, trying to understand how culture is enacted through performative acts, and how meanings are embodied in these social and ritual performances (Carlson 2004; Butler 1990). Performance now is used to describe everything from artistic installations and memorial services to political activism and fashion (Auslander 2004). Given the diverse ways in which this concept is utilised, it is evident that performance is not merely theatre or theatrical in nature, and its dissociation from a literal stage has freed theoretical approaches from the 'constraints of architectural location', allowing us to recognise that 'all of culture is in some ways performative' (Dolan 1993: 431).

At its simplest, performance is human action and behaviour, a bodily experience or a demonstration of acquired skills (Carlson 2004; Schechner

2002). Actors stand on the stage, delivering a pre-prepared, organised and directed dialogue, dancers move according to choreographed steps, and clowns juggle balls and somersault through the circus. Performances are acts, but it would be erroneous to categorise every action as 'performance'. What distinguishes performances from other acts is a self-awareness on behalf of the performer. The actor knows that s/he is on stage and is conscious that his/her actions are scripted, premeditated and delimited. For this reason, performance is regarded as a 'created event' (Szerszynski *et al.* 2003), one that exists outside of 'everyday life' (Hymes 1975; Bauman 1989; Goffman 1956), something that is knowingly 'put on'. Yet, as James Peacock (1990: 208) indicates, this is not to say that performance is more important than the mundane happenings in life, but to recognise that it is 'a deliberate effort to represent, to say something about something'.

Peacock's (1990) assertion reminds us that performances are essentially communicative, embodying a range of ideological positions that offer a view of the world. By extension, this suggests that there must be someone to whom the message is directed. Whether it is a paying audience, a group of strangers or work colleagues, performances require the presence of observers. These observers may be an external group, a company of actors might perform in front of no-one but themselves, or an individual could self-reflexively be their own audience (Palmer and Jankowiak 1996). Erving Goffman (1956: 22) foregrounded the significance of the audience when he noted that performance is 'all the activity of an individual which occurs during a period marked by his continuous presence before a particular set of observers and which has some influence on the observers'. As it influences and can be influenced by an audience, performance is perhaps more accurately described as a 'relationship' between actor and observer (Schieffelin 2005; Robinson 2004). Edward Schieffelin's (2005: 82) notion that all performance is 'contingent' is particularly compelling, as it reveals that the performance act, as a 'social event', is 'co-created' between the performer and the audience, where meaning is generated through the presence of, and interaction between, both parties. This suggests that the audience must be aware that the actions presented in front of them are by design so that they may recognise them as a performance. Whilst the self-consciousness of the actor is certainly important, as noted above, Goffman argues that 'performance' occurs at the site of the audience, confirming that the audience must also perceive the events as staged.

Nevertheless, the audience's role is not merely to observe actions unfolding in front of them, but to assess these performances against some 'standard achievement' (Carlson 2004: 4). Marvin Carlson (2004: 5), drawing on Richard Bauman, suggests that 'all performance involves a consciousness of doubleness, according to which the actual execution of an action is placed in mental comparison with a potential, an ideal or a remembered original model of that action', implying that performances are ultimately scrutinised by audiences, who judge their respective success or failure. Performances

58   The nature of performance

are thus measured against previous 'great' events, or imagined or ideal versions, which is, as Carlson (2004: 4) reminds, 'not the responsibility of the performer but of the observer'. Nevertheless, the very act of scrutiny suggests that the audience appreciates that what occurs on stage is not 'real', and that it is the approximation of realness that is noted and appreciated.

Reducing performance to a mere binary between the 'real' and the 'performed' (Crane 2001: 169) or between 'authentic' and 'inauthentic' provokes tension and negates the multiple readings that any one performance may generate. Furthermore, performance has had a troubled relationship with the notion of 'real', offering on the one hand an actual, live event, whilst, on the other, self-conscious that it is an enacted version of 'real life'. The consciousness that they are 'on stage' means that performers are aware that their actions are necessarily 'put on' and not reflective of their actual life. That the audience is aware that the moment is staged means they too recognise the event as disconnected from the performer's own lived experience. Both actors and observers thus realise that the performance is produced, that it represents an illusory or theatrical version of life and that it is little more than a series of scripted acts, which each confirm that what they are seeing is not 'real'. A reenactment of a Civil War event can never be the actual Civil War and will only ever be a 'representation of a prior reality' (Crane 2001: 169). A play does not reveal the actual lives of actors, and the popularity of 'reality' television, such as *Big Brother*, demonstrates that even 'real life' is staged. The authenticity of these latter performances is questioned by a public who are increasingly sensitive to the fact that editors impose narrative structure on random events and construct archetypal 'characters' out of 'real' people (Hill 2005). Whether the Civil War reenactment or *Big Brother* are regarded as authentic and thus legitimate, or inauthentic and therefore inferior, reveals a binary that juxtaposes 'living' and 'acting', where the former is presumed to be 'honest' and the latter 'deceptive' (Magnat 2002: 147).

Although the theatricality of performance has been dismissed as evidence of its inauthenticity, there is nevertheless something quite real about performance. A Civil War reenactment is, itself, a tangible event, a moment in time that is actually occurring. This means that as an event the performance is authentic; it exists and is real, even though its subject matter might gesture to past events or reenact the lived experience of others. This is partly because performance is necessarily an embodied act. As noted above, performance, at its simplest, is human action, framed as distinct from other social practices (Taylor 2003). It is thus clear that performance must be 'an activity of bodies' (Wallis and Shepherd 2004: 191). It is active and dynamic, implying the presence of a body that 'does'. The fact that performance is embodied also reveals that it is temporally unstable, having only a transitory existence. They are momentary, fleeting, and ephemeral, occurring only in the present in a 'state of appearing and vanishing' (Franko and Richards 2000: 1). They resist capture for as soon as they happen, even *as* they are happening, they are over, never to be experienced again (Berlin 2006; Franko and Richards 2000). Actors never perform the same way twice; a politician does not deliver a speech in precisely the same way; and an athlete cannot score the same goal.

It is the sense of immediacy, of being in the present, and of 'liveness', that is a defining characteristic of performance (Auslander 1999; Kirshenblatt-Gimblett 1998; Phelan 1993). The liveness of the performance suggests a sense of authenticity that is seemingly lost when looking at dramatic or musical performances on television or via the internet (Sherlock 2004). 'Liveness' is particularly critical when examining sport, for more than many other activities, sport is temporal, having significance in the moment it occurs. Nevertheless, with the increasing sophistication of sports media, 'live' performances are not necessarily viewed in person, but can be watched via satellite across the world. 'Liveness' is thus no longer strictly about spatial proximity, but about temporal consistency. Knowing that we are watching as events are actually unfolding can still make sport a compelling experience. But for many, an event that is broadcast after its conclusion loses its appeal. The fact that the outcome has already been established means there is no longer a sense of unpredictability, which reduces its value and often renders the experience unsatisfying. The authenticity of sport derives, in part, from the relishing the unknown, pondering the outcome and appreciating the performance in the moment, which means that sports performances are valued not for being a staged deception but for being unpredictably, and satisfyingly, 'real'.

Understanding sports performance

As noted in the introduction, performance lies at the heart of sport. Delivering a performance is the task of athletes; improving performance is the purview of coaches; appreciating performance is the role of audiences; and enhancing performance is seemingly the task of a range of technological interventions. 'Performance' is used in a variety of ways, and refers, for example, to an athlete's actual output, a coach's ability to influence an athlete, and to an entire category of sport. A glance through a number of sports science texts confirms that 'improving' or 'positively impacting' or 'affecting' performance is the aim of most training programmes (Wilmore and Costill 2004; Hoffman 2002; Hill 2001), yet significantly, in each of these texts, the meaning of performance is assumed to be the physical motions and actions that constitute the sporting act. Hargreaves and Hawley (2003: 1–2) note that a 'successful sports performance of any sport depends on the skilful and coordinated activation of an athlete's skeletal muscles to produce power to overcome resistance (or drag) due to air, surface friction (water, snow or asphalt) or an opponent'. Yet, a sports 'performance' is more complex, incorporating broader social and cultural values that are obscured by essentialised definitions. Determining what is

60 / *The nature of performance*

meant by 'performance' is challenging, as sports performances embody almost contradictory elements. On the one hand, athletic performances incorporate the creative, aesthetic and emotive elements of traditional theatre or artistic performances. Audiences gaze upon the well-formed body, admire feats of strength or endurance and marvel at the athlete's ability to overcome the usual constraints of the human anatomy. There is a range of aesthetic pleasures to be had through both watching and playing sport, and the relationship between art and sport is one that is explored critically (Hughson *et al.* 2005; Rinehart 1998; Arnold 1990). Yet, on the other hand, sporting performances are measurable and recordable. Results are documented; records are kept for comparison with future and past events; and performances are quantified, sometimes to thousandths of a second, to ensure the best is recognised and appropriately rewarded (Guttmann 1978).

Given that sport has these ostensibly contradictory dimensions, the discussion of performance above offers a valuable starting point for understanding its significance to sport. It allows us to appreciate sports performance as more than simply moving a body from point A to point B and provokes a reading that contextualises it within broader social and cultural performances. Furthermore, it is important to note that the embodied act itself is performative. Not only is athletic performance a physical action, but the meanings communicated through and derived from it are significant. Drawing upon other aspects of performance studies, we can determine the role and significance of the audience as 'co-creator' and scrutiniser of the athletic performance. Finally, the notion of authenticity is critical for any discussion of sport, and is especially pertinent when discussing performance technologies.

It may seem unusual to mine the rich theories of theatre and performance studies to discuss sport, particularly as the two are often regarded as antithetical: one is creative, the other physical; one is seemingly real, whilst the other, self-consciously 'fake' (Fotheringham 1992). Nevertheless, sport has theatrical dimensions, both in terms of its structure and execution. Playing sport is a conscious act on the part of the athlete, and the action is staged for the entertainment, and in front of, an interested audience. The event is out of the ordinary, a display of practised skill and a temporally bounded experience. Above all, like theatre, sport is a deliberately 'created event', which is 'marked out from the everyday' (Szerszynski *et al.* 2003: 3). There have been a number of studies that have examined the relationship between sport and theatre, highlighting the dramatic, or melodramatic, aspects of athletic performances or analysing the common juxtaposition 'sport versus the arts' (Fotheringham 1992). Whilst the two might not sit easily alongside one another, the overt theatricality of sport is nevertheless nowhere more evident than in professional wrestling. Although some have disputed whether professional wrestling should even be considered a sport, it is nonetheless a physical performance that has been variously described as a dramaturgical spectacle, a 'masculine melodrama' (Jenkins 1997) or 'a theatrical entertainment that is not theatre' (Mazer 1998). Regardless of its status as 'sport', it is a useful example of the interplay between theatre and sport, even whilst it may, according to Sharon Mazer (1998), deliberately parody both genres. But other 'real' sports also embody a sense of the theatrical. Normand Berlin (2006) describes boxing as a form of theatre without words, an unscripted drama in which participants construct their own narrative through their actions and their bodies. He contends that boxing is 'theater stripped down to its essentials, a serious conflict in a small space, witnessed by spectators who get caught up in the action' (Berlin 2006: 24). Sport and theatre, for Berlin (2006), are one and the same.

There are, nevertheless, several ways in which sport and theatre differ. In contrast to Berlin (2006), Bob Rinehart (1998) argues that narrative is not inherent in sport, but rather is imposed after the fact to make linear sense of a series of physical acts. Commentators, journalists and spectators each discern meanings from sporting events, and the 'story' of the game, its social and cultural context, and the significance of the outcome is rarely consistent between these parties. For this reason, sport more closely resembles popular cultural forms such as reality television where storylines are determined after the event in order to offer continuities, cause and effect and a basic structure to a multitude of otherwise disconnected moments (Hill 2005). Theatre, on the other hand, brings an established narrative to life, enacting words on a page, offering a sense of certainty about the destination the players will reach. Even with a carefully conceived plan or strategy, sport, at least in its ideal form, remains inherently unpredictable.

Unpredictability derives from the assumption that each participant is similarly skilled and is doing their utmost to perform at their best as well as from the belief that the sports field offers an equal chance for each participant to win (Eitzen 2006; Gusfield 2000; Tuxill and Wigmore 1991). Furthermore, those physical performance activities that have, as an essential component of their being, predetermined outcomes or scripted actions, such as professional wrestling or even ballet, are regarded as less authentic than 'real sport', and whilst participants may need to be in excellent shape, they are not thought to be 'real' athletes. Such performances lack the competitive element that, in part, distinguishes sport from other recreations. The outcome, even when suspected, predicted or hoped for, is never assured until the final whistle blows (Gusfield 2000; Fotheringham 1992). In cases where sports events have been fixed by players, judges or both, there is considerable dismay and even a sense of betrayal experienced by the audience. Spectators come to watch a 'genuine', competitive event where athletes share the goal of trying to win. To then discover that the outcome was predetermined diminishes the value of the event, and it is relegated to mere theatre and the acting out of a script. The significance of the 1919 Black Sox scandal in the American psyche today, for example, reveals the lingering national impact that such scripted outcomes in sport can have (Nathan 2003).

62   The nature of performance

The fact that the audience's assumptions about the 'realness' of the event is relevant, suggests that, as in theatrical or other artistic presentations, the meaning and significance of sport is constituted through the relationship between performer and audience (Schieffelin 2005). In this instance, the audience need not be an external group of fans, but might consist of coaches, other participants, the referee or any other person associated with the staging of the event. The media too operates as a powerful observer, providing immediate and subsequent commentary on the event, the athletes and their performance. Some observers have a specific investment in the performance, such as coaches or other competitors, whilst others may only draw symbolic value from the outcome. But it is not simply a matter of having an audience present to confirm a performance. Unlike traditional theatre, the competitive nature of sport *requires* the presence of something resembling an 'objective' other to verify the performance. Whilst a group of actors might act only for and in front of themselves, simultaneously performer and audience, and even be impressed by their efforts, a world record broken by a sprinter on her own or in front of her coach has little meaning in the context of sport. Without confirmation from another, non-participatory and 'objective' party, the new record simply does not exist. Similarly, a beautifully executed and aesthetically pleasing movement in sport may be appreciated by the performer themselves, but is only meaningful, in terms of a competition, if observed.

Not only is an audience required to assure the competitive aspect of the performance, they are also partly responsible for qualitatively or quantitatively assessing those performances. In the latter, the audience determines the relative merit of the sporting performance that unfolds before them by comparing them to standard or invented measures (records), past athletic feats (by 'the greats') and ideal performances (a perfect ten). Their role is to establish success or failure, for as Rinehart (1998: 5) confirms, performance in sport is not restricted merely to the athlete; the audience '"knows" better what makes a good performance'. Of course, if the audience knows a good performance, then, conversely, they are also acutely aware of what makes a poor one. Cheating in its various guises, unexpected interruptions, not abiding by the rules or their 'spirit', significantly differing abilities and inaccurate refereeing are some of the factors that will alter an audience's perception of an outcome. An athlete, for example, who does not try to win weakens not just the value of their own performance, but that of the others in the field. A competitor who is allowed to win, for example, knows that their victory is hollow, not a true test of their abilities nor a reflection of their actual capacity to triumph over their peers. A convincing sporting event thus requires both competitors and audience to be assured of the legitimacy of the outcome, suggesting that there is an 'assumed contract' between the two (Tuxill and Wigmore 1991: 121). This confirms that Schieffelin's (2006) contention that performances are co-created between audiences and performers holds in athletic as well as artistic contexts. If a

The nature of performance   63

sports performance is understood to be co-created between the audience and the performer, then the audience has a direct and essential stake in determining the authenticity of the performance, and, furthermore, 'purity' of the event.

Authenticity has been discussed in a number of ways in sports studies, from the notion of self-actualisation and the development of an 'authentic self' (Feezell 2004), through to research on sporting subcultures, where participants posit their authentic, non-commodified sport against commercialised, mediated versions (Wheaton and Beal 2003). Nevertheless, when it comes to discussing performance technologies, the concept of authenticity is conceptualised as a sense of 'purity' or 'realness'. Realness in sport emerges from the performance itself, which differs markedly from the way that this term is applied to theatrical performances. The temporal and spatial delineation of a theatrical performance contributes to the perception that it is set aside from real life, and its self-conscious execution of a predetermined script confirms for the audience that they are not encountering 'real life'. Theatre is 'put on', staged, created and is thus, on one level, an inauthentic event (Taylor 2003). In this context, authenticity is found by comparing the enacted performance with the written script, such that an authentic performance is one that accurately reproduces the meaning or intent of the text (Kidnie 2006). As such, a performance can never really be independent from the script and is 'measured in relation to the text in degrees of *in*fidelity and *in*authenticity' (Kidnie 2006: 104).

If performance is regarded, at the level of theatre, as something 'not real', then it might follow that athletic performances are similarly thought to be 'not real'. Yet, this is not the case. Although sporting performances are understood to be outside of the everyday, they are not perceived to be inauthentic as a staged play might (Gusfield 2000; Tuxill and Wigmore 1991). Rather than being a pretend or inferior version of the 'real' thing, sporting performances are understood as 'real' in their own right. They may also be held in 'intentional spaces' (cited in Carlson 2004: 37), but they are an actual feat, conducted in real time, in front of a real audience, with real and direct outcomes. Whilst a play might be a real moment in and of itself, it is, nevertheless, representing another moment, either actual or imagined. Sport seems to be neither referential nor imitative. It is neither directly orchestrated to present an alternative reality nor to enact a script, but is considered expressive of the athlete's, team's or other stakeholder's motivations to succeed. Unlike theatre, there is no original text that athletes are directed to enact, and as such their performances are neither contingent on accurately portraying an author's intent nor based on a script that offers direction and guidance on how the performance should occur. Authenticity is, thus, embodied within the performance itself, and the body operates as the text against which the performance is assessed. If an athlete performs to what is thought to be the best of their ability, then their efforts are considered to be real, and if the performance is a genuine reflection of the athlete's physical

64   *The nature of performance*

capacity, they receive the accolades and prizes. In theatre and film, on the other hand, the director and producer as well as other non-performing staff may, in addition to actors, receive honours for their contribution to the final performance. Yet, for coaches, there are no Oscars.

Although we judge athletic performances to be authentic or not, authenticity is neither a fixed or static concept nor an objective measure. Rather, it is socially constructed, suggesting that its boundaries are flexible and malleable (MacCannell 1999). For this reason, what we agree to be authentic at any one time reveals more about the observer and their ideological proclivities than any intrinsic value of the observed. Furthermore, Janelle Wilson (2005: 58) suggests that notions of authenticity are bound up in nostalgic recollections of the past and that seeking authenticity is essentially a search for an 'idyllic past ... something unattainable'. It is a way of drawing upon idealised versions of the past to critique the present. If authenticity is another of those slippery concepts, then its application to sport is equally unstable. Authenticity does not, therefore, reside objectively in the sporting event, nor in the athletic body itself, but is imposed on performances as a result of a complex interplay of ideologies, so that an authentic performance for Victorian gentleman amateurs differs significantly from Olympic competitors in the twenty-first century.

In terms of contemporary sport, authentic performances are those where both the performer and the audience are assured that no extraneous factors have deliberately or inadvertently impacted the outcome. It is an accurate expression or measure of an athlete's actual physical capacity, a record of what the performer's body can genuinely do when, unaided, it is pushed to its absolute limit. Such 'real' performances are those that are untainted by external factors, such as a predetermined script, illicit substances or training techniques, or third-party involvement. Authentic sporting performances are thus thought to be those that truly pit 'man' against the odds without ancillary technologies or devices. Hank Aaron's home run record seems 'more authentic' than Barry Bonds' success, given the latter's access to technologically advanced equipment, more games per season as well as his well documented use of illicit pharmaceuticals (Fainaru-Wada and Williams 2006).

Measuring the pure performance of the human body lies at the heart of sport, whilst technological enhancements threaten that purity by introducing confounding variables that detract from an assessment of the athlete's physical ability. If sport is a demonstration of human capacity, then, in the presence of external or internal technologies, an individual's performance can never be understood as a genuine reflection of their own physicality. An observer cannot be sure whether the split second difference at the end of a sprint was owing to the individual's superior physical ability or whether the competitor's high-tech, ultra-light cycle, or fastskin swimsuit or drug regimen proved the decisive factor. Of the two, internal technologies cause the most disquiet within the context of sport, primarily as they are integrated into the body, invisible to scrutiny and, unless detected, unaccounted for in the final outcome. On the other hand, external technologies are more easily reconciled with dominant notions of sport and performance. We rationalise that the presence of technology in the velodrome is a requirement for the sport of cycling, and that whilst a cyclist with an advanced piece of machinery certainly benefits, s/he nevertheless must still produce the requisite performance to win. The bike might remove friction or ensure a smoother ride; however, each athlete has the ability to access such technology and the performance is a measure of what each competitor can do with this equipment. Furthermore, the advances in bike technology are, in part, designed so that what ultimately is measured is the athlete's pure performance without hindrance, such that the bike is merely the means to the end and neither detracts from nor adds to the performance.

Whilst technologies are regarded with some suspicion in sport, what is regarded as a 'technology' shifts between sports and across time, adjusting to suit the search for greater performances and renewed records as well as developments in equipment and training. If we accept that technologies are essentially a 'tool that helps extend our capabilities' (Kolcio 2005: 107), then essentially all aspects of an athlete's preparation are a technological intervention that alters the athlete's final performance. But whilst training might be a technology designed to improve the final performance of athletes, it is not considered to be illegitimate, because, as Shilling (2005: 113) points out, the effort that goes into training is compatible with late capitalist ideologies that revere success based on hard work and a commitment to a 'productive lifestyle'. Performances that represent the outcome of the productive disciplining of the body, through hard work and training, are regarded as authentic, whilst illicit chemical substances, for example, are rejected as an artificial and passive enhancement of performance. Such illegitimate means to augment performance are perceived to be a 'chemical shortcut' (Reid 1998) or a 'quick fix' (Slattery 1998) to circumvent the honest toil that is required to train the body for competition.

Enhancing sports performance

Although sport and technology have had a troubled past, their relationship is now undisputed and, in many respects, celebrated by an industry that welcomes the application of new technologies in the pursuit of outstanding performances. The development of improved equipment, new surfaces or faster pools is seen as directly responsible for substantial advances in performances, making the spectacle of sport even more valuable, attracting larger audiences and generating greater revenues. Yet some of the most significant improvements to sport have been in the area of the science of human performance. Not only have researchers focused on upgrading equipment or facilities, but, for most of the twentieth century, there has also been a growing interest in the capabilities of the human body. Scientists have searched for new training methods and substances that will

66 The nature of performance

extend the body's capacity and boost its physical output. As a result, the highly technologised body has emerged in a global sports arena where technical training equipment, testing, filming, digitising and the physical and biochemical manipulation of the body have become commonplace. Whilst some of these advances have been categorised as legitimate athletic endeavour, those substances and techniques that seek to go beyond the body's 'natural' capabilities and aesthetically pleasing dimensions have largely been rejected as unethical or unhealthy.

Although questions of morality and health are applied to technological innovations in sport, whether or not a new substance or technique is permitted rests to a large extent on its propensity to 'enhance' an athlete's performance. Yet, without a consistent definition of enhancement, this assessment remains largely arbitrary. On the one hand, enhancement implies a sense of 'going beyond' the normal or 'adding to' the body's existent capacity. That the body's functioning is extended past some kind of natural limit suggests that enhancement is a relative concept that is dependent upon normative frames (Juengst 1998). It is thus only meaningful in the presence 'normal' bodies with 'normal' functioning, with the augmented body serving as the lens through which the natural can be recognised. For this reason, enhancement must be understood to be socially and culturally dependent, and as it lacks a 'substantive transcultural meaning itself', it cannot be usefully employed universally (Savulescu 2006: 322). This is particularly pertinent within the context of sport. Not only are various enhancements arbitrarily defined, their use across cultures and historical periods suggests that, like the 'natural' athletic body, performance enhancement is an elastic concept.

Whilst improving performances seems to be a logical and desirable outcome of rigorous training regimes, significantly, the strict 'enhancement' of physical capabilities has not always been the objective of sports scientists, coaches and athletes. Soon after the emergence of modern sport at the peak of industrialisation in the mid-to-late nineteenth century, doctors and scientists only gradually turned to the exercising body as a new area of study, yet their interest did not initially centre on extending the physical capacity of athletes. The amateur ethos that dominated sport at the time, coupled with a Victorian urge to measure and record all aspects of living things, produced a scientific area of enquiry that focused on establishing the limits of the human organism (Massengale and Swanson 1997; Berryman and Park 1992; Hoberman 1992). Humans were believed to have fixed capacities, like machines, that could only be improved in terms of efficiency. Drills and training techniques were more concerned with refining what the body already had rather than trying to increase its performance potential and were not strictly concerned with 'systematically increas[ing] physical power, speed, endurance, and agility' (Beamish and Ritchie 2005: 415–16). Preparing for athletic contests required little more than healthy living and the repetitive practice of technique to ensure efficiency of movement, as coaches had no conception of exploiting physical potential.

The discipline of sports science was still some years away, when, by the end of the nineteenth century, a conflict emerged between 'two opposed theories of human potential: an older doctrine of natural limits and the new doctrine of expanding biological limits' (Hoberman 1992: 9). Scientists started to recognise the body's capacity to adapt effectively to external stressors, revealing that rather than being fixed, the body could be extended beyond what was considered its normal functioning, such that 'bodies were given by God but perfected by man' (de la Peña 2003: 24). Whilst many of these early studies used athletes as subjects, there was no systematic or specific application of their research results to enhancing sports performances. Beamish and Ritchie (2005: 414) suggest that this was owing to a noticeable lag between the generation of theoretical models and their application in sport, and it was not until after the Second World War that there was a significant 'paradigm shift' in the 'ontology of human performance'. To a large degree, this shift was prompted by the changing import of sport internationally, which encouraged state and institutional investment in exercise science and elite sport. Enhancing an athlete's capacity became a scientific pursuit in its own right, and the advances made by, in particular, the Soviets gradually filtered through to the West, spawning a kind of athletic Cold War as performances became closely and, with the increased media coverage of international sport, publicly aligned with the nation.

Since the Second World War, the sports industry has boomed, and science has assumed a central role in the quest for athletic success. Subdisciplinary areas have contributed to the mapping of the exercising body in order to elicit greater physical outputs from athletes that can be translated into improved international and internal prestige for nations. The development of new testing techniques, equipment and biochemical analyses, as well as growing commitments from international federations and governments to invest in sports science research, have combined to challenge the 'frontiers of human performance' and produce athletic feats unheard and unthought of even just a decade ago (ASC 2008). With the large amounts of money injected into elite sport and exercise science, it is clear that, in essence, enhancing performances is central to all forms of sport. Athletes eagerly submit their bodies to technologies that seek to chart, forecast and, most importantly, improve their abilities, perfecting their bodies on what is essentially a factory production line. Much like the Taylorist model of specialised production, each element of this finely tuned organic machine is refined to enhance its capacity and output. All manner of techniques and procedures have been utilised, including hypnosis, to break records and obliterate performance landmarks established by previous competitors. Yet, these advances have not always been readily embraced, particularly when scientists shifted their focus onto what were considered essentially unnatural or synthetic substances or techniques to boost athletic performance (Park 1992). It is in this context that 'performance enhancement' acquired the negative connotation that still persists.

68 *The nature of performance*

Today, 'performance enhancement' popularly refers almost exclusively to illicit substances and practices, evoking a sense of dishonesty of even criminality. It is thought to be deliberately deceptive and is held to be largely responsible for the dissolution of traditional sporting values. Yet, athletes and coaches have always experimented, to a greater and lesser degree, with a range of methods, techniques, supplements, diets, and concoctions of drugs and other agents to prepare the body for competition (Yesalis and Bahrke 2002), and so it is futile to try to establish the moment when sport was 'free' from such maligned practices. In the late nineteenth century, for instance, athletes ingested amphetamines, caffeine and other drugs to 'pep' them up prior to and during a race; in the mid-twentieth century testosterone, the newly discovered 'fountain of youth', was applied to athletic bodies with noticeable effect (Hoberman 2005); more recently, designer drugs are customised to assist athletes to dope effectively with little chance of detection; and finally the spectre of gene doping casts a menacing shadow over the future of sport (Miah 2006; 2004; Sweeney 2004).

Despite the intermittent use of pharmacological substances by athletes, it was only in the post-war era that performance enhancing drugs began to be used more systematically by athletes. By the mid-1950s, the Soviets' use of testosterone to bulk up their weightlifters had become something of an open secret, and after returning from the 1954 World Weightlifting Championships, US team doctor, John Zeigler, along with several other weightlifters, began experimenting on themselves. Their concerns about the androgenising effects of testosterone were mitigated with the release of Dianabol in 1958, a synthetic 'anabolic steroid' that was created for therapeutic use but was used by strength athletes who craved the additional mass testosterone supplied (Todd 1992). Whilst steroids were enormously popular, they did not benefit all athletes, and those in, for example, endurance events sought other products to augment their performances and by the 1970s and 1980s the pharmaceutical industry responded with synthetic hormones, including erythropoietin, human growth hormone and a host of other supplements and substances that found their way into a growing black market industry. Since then, untraceable designer drugs as well as the potential for gene doping have emerged as further threats to the nature of athletic performance.

By the mid-1960s, doping had become so widespread that sports federations were forced to take action to protect the health of athletes, if not the very spirit of sport itself. Whilst anti-doping laws had been enacted in both France and Belgium in 1965, it was only in 1967 that the IOC formed its Medical Commission to examine what they felt was a growing problem in international sport. The commission developed a working definition of doping, namely 'the use of substances or techniques in any form or quantity alien or unnatural to the body with the exclusive aim of obtaining an artificial or unfair increase of performance in competition', and initially banned a number of substances under these guidelines (Todd 1992: 322). Significantly, steroids, likely the most widely used substance at the time, was not included on the banned list until 1975, confirming that efforts to stem the use of performance enhancers critically rely on the ability to police their use. Testing procedures designed to detect the presence of banned substances in bodily fluids have notoriously lagged behind pharmacological innovation, prompting many observers to lament the 'cat and mouse' game that is required to remain in control (Mottram 2003). Interestingly, some argue that testing practices are specifically 'hamstrung by significant limitations in technology' (Yesalis *et al.* 2001), whilst others recognise that 'powerful technologies' are needed to 'combat drug abusing athletes' (Birchard 2000: 1008). It is certainly ironic to suggest that within the 'natural' realm of sport, increasingly sophisticated technologies are required to ensure that athletic performance remains untarnished, whilst at the same time, performances are legitimately enhanced by technologies that seemingly do not corrupt.

Conclusion

Within our contemporary visual and media savvy society, performances are all around us. From television and cinemas to the theatre and sporting arenas, we are exposed to displays of physical, creative and intellectual skill. In each of these fields, audiences admire the prowess and discipline that it takes to produce such performances. For many, artistic and athletic presentations epitomise the human spirit and its will to master even the most complex of routines. To discover, however, that a ballerina takes amphetamines or that an athlete bulks up on steroids is thought to diminish their achievements because technology 'threatens to replace the embodied human endeavour' (Kolcio 2005: 107). Yet, the relationship between technology and performance is not fixed and to understand the concerns that surround illicit enhancement within sport, defining performance is crucial.

A careful examination of sports scientific disciplines reveals that 'performance' is a critical area of enquiry. From sports psychology and nutrition through to biomechanics and motor learning, scientists and coaches try to solicit the greatest output from the raw material of individual bodies. Within the socio-cultural study of sport, performance too is significant. In these studies, for instance, the dominant and/or contested meanings of sports performances are analysed with reference to the social, political and economic contexts within which they are staged. In essence, performance appears to be an uncontested concept within sport, referring explicitly to the successful conduct of specific motor skills. But given the theoretical approaches to understanding performance within theatre studies, it is important to problematise and critically evaluate athletic performance, and such an analysis is especially pertinent to a discussion of performance enhancement. As such, determining what is meant by 'performance' is as crucial as defining 'enhancement'.

Performances are essentially communicative, are spatially and temporally defined, and are typically a self-conscious act on behalf of the performer staged in front of interested observers. Athletic performances share these broad characteristics; however, whilst theatrical performances are necessarily 'put on', 'staged' and 'apart from everyday life', those that occur in sporting arenas are characterised by a sense of authenticity that is embodied within the physical act itself. Sport may also be put on, staged and apart from everyday life; however, its validity hinges on the audience's conviction that what they are observing is real: a real athlete competing to the best of her/his ability under real conditions against real competitors who are similarly motivated to prevail. Actors, audiences realise, are not living out their own personal hopes, dreams and desires on stage, whereas the athlete's performance is believed to be the product of their personal motivation, genetic capacity and training. In other words, performances in sport seem to be 'authentic'.

The narrative of integrity that underpins sports performances is fragile and easily ruptured by enhancement technologies that are thought to fundamentally alter the nature of the performance. Rather than reflecting a 'real' athlete, performance technologies are confounding, if not duplicitous, obscuring the body's capacity and thereby creating an insincere performance that is more staged than authentic. But it is not only the performance that is threatened; these technologies have the potential to corrupt the health of athletes. The following chapter examines health as a social and cultural phenomenon, locating it within broader ideological constructions, and suggests that protecting the 'health' of athletes and protecting the spirit of sport are closely linked within a discourse of morality that is rooted in nature and promulgated through social institutions and practices.

5 The nature of health

Introduction

Athletes who power down a track, carve their way through the snow or lift three times their own body weight generate powerful images that clearly establish the relationship between the body, movement and health. Engaged in wholesome physical activity, these well-crafted, fit and taut specimens appear to be the epitome of health, as their sculpted bodies represent well-being, progress and control. Inactive bodies, on the other hand, seem slothful and selfish, as children are dislodged from their computers and nudged outside into fresh air to engage in energetic play. The enfeebling of the world's youth is thought, in large part, to result from a declining level of physical activity and a preference for more sedentary entertainments. For this reason, fitness and health movements have, since the nineteenth century, reminded citizens that it is their social obligation and personal responsibility to fashion a healthy body, free from disease and other contaminants. Physical education has been central to such health promotional activities, and it is fair to say that by the twenty-first century, sport, exercise, fitness and health have become so thoroughly integrated, and their relationship so completely naturalised, it is now difficult to conceive of sport as anything other than an antidote to a range of social and physical ills.

Yet, organised sport, particularly at the elite level, is anything but healthy. Athletes risk their bodies each time they step out onto the field to play or train. In sports such as boxing, it is expected that the competitor will sustain some form of injury, given that the purpose of the sport is to physically incapacitate one's opponent, whilst it is not uncommon to see bodies stretchered from the field in heavy contact sports such as rugby union, rugby league or, despite the extensive protective padding, American football. Playing whilst in pain is largely normalised, and 'no pain, no gain' is an athletic mantra that seems unlikely to disappear from the sporting parlance as young athletes are taught not to question the authority of coaches and trainers, even when their own physical well-being may be jeopardised through intense regimens (Howe 2004). Heat illnesses, exhaustion, chronic pain, mechanical injuries and in extreme cases, malnutrition and death, can

72 *The nature of health*

result from the extreme physical and psychological demands placed on sportsmen and women. Furthermore, numerous studies confirm that the early onset of some diseases and potentially premature death await former elite athletes who have dedicated their lives to the pursuit of 'healthy' sport (Waddington *et al.* 2006). Even junior and recreational sports are notoriously dangerous, with millions of children presenting at emergency rooms around the world each year with sprains and other more serious injuries that may have long-term consequences (Adirim and Cheng 2003). Given its risky nature, it may even be more appropriate to suggest that sport is not particularly healthy, and that the strain placed on, and the injuries sustained by, athletes' bodies require the relationship between sport and health to be fundamentally reconceived.

Nevertheless, health and sport remain closely aligned such that sports medicine and other industries have developed to ensure an athlete's body remains in good working order and, if damaged, is quickly restored to its competitive best. Professional and national teams each have a growing number of medical support staff whose primary purpose is to ensure that their 'patients' remain in peak competitive condition, ready and able to perform. In addition, sporting federations authorise rule changes and permit the use of safety equipment to further protect athletes, suggesting that health, despite the inherent risks in sport, remains highly prized. Indeed, it would seem that anything that jeopardises an athlete's well-being is quickly contained to ensure that, as far as possible, sport remains a wholesome endeavour, and it is for this reason that the proscription of illicit performance enhancing substances and methods seems justified.

Doping practices have, since the 1960s, been outlawed, in part, to protect athletes' health. Long lists of side effects are presented as evidence of the irreparable harm that is wreaked upon an abuser's body, offering a useful justification for the prohibition, and eventual eradication, of specific substances and methods from sport (Mottram 2003). Furthermore, international anti-doping policies reinforce the sanctity of physical well-being. The Australian Sports Anti-Doping Authority, for example, suggests doping to be 'the use of a substance or method, potentially dangerous to athletes' health, and/or capable of enhancing their performance' (ASADA 2006), whilst the Tough on Drugs policy reveals that doping 'carries serious health risks for individuals' (DISR 1999). The German *Nationale Anti-Doping Agentur* refers to the increased 'health risks' facing athletes who dope (NADA 2006); the Canadian Policy Against Doping in Sport is similarly committed to 'protect[ing] the health of individuals'; and the US Anti-Doping Agency seeks to 'ensu[re] the health of athletes' (USOT 2006). Throughout the world, sporting federations and governmental agencies confirm that alongside their concern for the 'integrity' of sport, they are particularly troubled by the potential impact of banned substances on an athlete's health. That questions of morality and health are given equal billing in the 'war on drugs in sport' suggests that this issue is framed by a medico-moral discourse that regards drugs as not merely a threat to individual health but to the broader institution of sport and, potentially, other collective identities as well.

Despite global accord, prohibiting doping because it may damage athletes' health is not sustained when examined more critically, particularly as the sweeping assumption that all substances taken into the body to promote performance are necessarily harmful is simply not supported by rigorous scientific analysis (Dawson 2001; Black and Pape 1997). Yet, this chapter does not seek to examine individual performance technologies to assess their health implications, but is instead more concerned with establishing how the nature of health offers a further insight into how such substances and methods generate discord in the sports and broader communities. It draws on a growing critical theory that recognises health not to be merely the 'absence of disease', but a socially, politically and economically crafted concept that reveals more about accepted cultural boundaries in society than it does about infections that risk individual biological borders. Furthermore, health is not simply a physical concern, but a moral issue, and bodily well-being is equated not merely with desirable character, but, more broadly, with social order. Within the context of sport, then, the health and physical purity of athletic bodies can be read as a marker of national worth, so that anti-doping strategies need to be interrogated as part of a discourse of societal well-being and stability. Yet, before examining its relationship with sport or the effect that performance technologies and doping practices may have, it is critical to understand the meaning and significance of 'health'.

Understanding health

Health is a multifaceted term that is variously used to describe an individual's physical disposition, the state of a nation or economy or the relative success of a business. It suggests a sense of well-being that is worked for, achieved and protected by both individual commitment and community support. Yet, health is more than simply a physical state and is increasingly linked to other desirable attributes, such as happiness and, more significantly, attractiveness. As health and beauty are conflated, all manner of 'health' promoting programmes are devised, which do little more than produce aesthetically appealing, rather than fit, specimens (Bordo 1993). Indeed, 'fit' is currently used to describe beauty or physical appeal rather than cardiovascular or athletic capacity, suggesting that, in this context, it is largely immaterial what a body is capable of doing as long as it looks proficient. Indeed, we specifically value bodies for 'looking well' or for being 'the picture of health' (Jutel 2005). Despite these conflicting values, 'health' has become the fashionable project of the latter part of the twentieth and early twenty-first century as Western cultures are saturated with advice on how to gain, and even excel, in being healthy. Governments commit millions

74   *The nature of health*

to promote health, and billions more on recovering it, at the same time that thousands of recommendations, suggestions and tips, many of them conflicting on an almost daily basis, flood the public domain. The latest medical developments in the pursuit of perfect health are featured on the evening news, whilst, during commercial breaks, a plethora of pills and potions promise to deliver requisite levels of health to consumers. It is clear that, for individuals, health is a personal concern, one towards which we are each responsible, and rewarded, for working (Crawford 2006).

Although it seems to be a self-evident concept, ascertaining what 'health' means and, for the purposes of this chapter, how it is risked through performance technologies, is not as straightforward as it may first appear. For instance, health is probably best understood as a relational rather than independent concept because defining health positively, in terms of what it is, in and of itself, is difficult. Essentially, what constitutes a healthy body is only apparent the moment that the body falls ill or is incapacitated. As health is essentially temporal, it is typically measured at those moments when symptoms seem to suggest that the body may be compromised, which means that 'health' itself is never really established. It is, therefore, only meaningful when the body is confronted with a disease or other contagion that threatens to disrupt it, which means that health can curiously be regarded as 'the absence of non-health' (Callahan 1973: 85). Like most social identities, then, health is most often defined negatively, in terms of what it is not, rather than what it is, which is clearly apparent when it is characterised simply in relation to expected physical competencies (Boorse 1977). Such medical models frame health essentially as the absence of illnesses, injuries or disabilities, suggesting that the ideal healthy state is achieved by the removal or mitigation of disruptions and the restoration of the body to 'normal functioning' (Allmark 2005; Lorber and Moore 2002). Simply put, without illness, there is health. Although it presents a compelling, and relatively simple model, further definitional problems emerge. 'Normal functioning', 'illness' and 'disease', rather than being self-evident, each require further delineation. Like health, disease and illness are not easily defined independently of the body and, therefore, exist uncomfortably in isolation as their meaning is determined primarily through their relationship with the corpus.

'Normal' functioning is particularly difficult to establish, as humans vary significantly in the ways their bodies operate. As such, 'normal' functioning is most effectively represented as a range or a series of statistical averages, rather than some kind of fixed constant that is universally applied. Yet, defining ill-health as deviations from a statistical norm, proves inadequate, particularly, as Peter Allmark (2005) notes, some deviations, such as extraordinary intelligence, are regarded as desirable rather than disease, whilst certain 'normal' functions, including hair loss or an aging libido, are treated as 'illnesses' that require intervention and remedy. Furthermore, symptoms that are perceived to be 'disease' or 'illness' may not, in fact, be negative

The nature of health 75

disruptions at all, but rather the body's usual, and welcome, adaptation to a changed set of circumstances. Given that statistical ranges seem inadequate, it might be more appropriate to recognise that individual bodies define their 'own norms and parameters within the context of its basic design' (Lewis 2001). In other words, 'normal functioning' for an individual body is that specific physiological state to which it feels 'compelled' to return after having been affected by illness or disease. Yet, as Christopher Boorse (1977) contends, such a model is also inadequate because many of the body's functions are not intended to be homeostatic. Instead of returning the body to a state of equilibrium, what locomotion or perception, and we can include strength and aerobic training for example, are designed to do is upset stasis and challenge the body to respond and adapt.

Nevertheless, the medical model predominates in Western societies, though other, more 'holistic' approaches try to incorporate broader mental, social and spiritual dimensions into their definitions of health, whilst 'wellness' frameworks aim for 'better than normal' states, particularly in Western nations where there is an expectation of not merely sufficient but 'excellent' health (Larson 1991: 2). In essence, there is no widely agreed definition of health, and even the World Health Organisation (WHO), which adopted an holistic approach, offers a summation which is largely inadequate (Callahan 1973). The WHO states that health is 'a state of complete physical, mental and social well-being and not merely the absence of disease or infirmity' (WHO 2007). In retreating from a purely medical model, the WHO presumes health to be a transcultural, transhistorical phenomenon, yet it is clearly rooted in a post-war era that regards 'happiness' and peace as critical elements of world health, even at the risk of medicalising these concepts (Callahan 1973). It is clear, however, that most models of health remain largely focused on individuals and their personal well-being, revealing that in popular and professional discourses, health is firmly rooted in the body. Yet, the WHO definition implicitly recognises that cultural factors are as important in defining health as the absence of biological contagions.

Critical theorists, by contrast, contend that health is a socially, culturally, politically and economically specific phenomenon that has no fixed meaning and cannot be located specifically in the individual (Crawford 2006; 1984; Lupton 2003; Robertson 2001; Larson 1991). Instead, 'particular discourses on health emerge at particular historical moments and gain widespread acceptance primarily because they are more or less congruent with the prevailing social, political and economic order within which they are produced, maintained and reproduced' (Robertson 2001: 294–95). James Larson (1991: 1), for example, has identified significant changes in the United States where health has shifted from mere 'survival' through to the achievement of 'happiness' and 'well-being', which corresponds to a growing affluence and its influence on what constitutes the ideal lifestyle. Yet, individual and public health has not always been such a critical concern, and it was a set of rapidly changing social circumstances, and a concomitant

76   *The nature of health*

secularisation of society, that created the conditions whereby the body's physical state acquired personal and political significance.

The origins of contemporary notions of health can be traced to the Enlightenment where a growing focus on secular and earthly priorities prompted a concern with both protecting and improving physical health (Crawford 2006). Whilst it initially remained an individual issue, with the rise of industrialisation and the construction of foetid urban environments, the promotion and protection of health became firmly entrenched within broader social and political frameworks. The Victorians feared that the squalid and cramped living conditions that resulted from unregulated and rampant urbanisation would breed filth and disease, and their aversion to the unfettered spread of contagion was reflected in social movements and government policies that tried to ensure access to hygiene practices was widely available (Baldwin 1999; Wohl 1983). Whilst some reformers were certainly concerned about the physical state of the labouring classes, for the most part the urgent need to sanitise them revealed something of a disdain for the urban poor as well as a fear that their lifestyles would contaminate society's more refined. Disease and filth were, thus, firmly linked to the working classes, and health reformers agitated, on behalf of these groups, for the provision of public bath houses, sanitation and sewerage, fresh and nutritious food and access to clean water (Hardy 2001). At the same time, the Victorian middle classes were defined, in part, by the maintenance of increasingly healthy and hygienic lifestyles, or, in other words, a 'cult of cleanliness' (Wohl 1983: 76). They eagerly embraced new health innovations, hygienic measures and even sought rejuvenation beyond the city walls in spas, seaside resorts and mountain retreats. The growing transport networks provided easy access to locations where one could take to the waters or otherwise engage with the restorative power of nature, dusting off the filth of the industrial cities and those who were confined to them (Macnaghten and Urry 2000; Aron 1999).

Whilst these spas were spaces where the body could be refreshed and renewed, health was more than a personal concern, but was, in conjunction with a 'pure environment', the very foundation upon which social progress could prosper. Individual health was thought to be indicative of social health, so by improving the physical well-being of citizens, national strength and vitality were also advanced. This was particularly pressing in the early twentieth century where, despite declining mortality rates, there was grave concern that the British race was degenerating as a result of the ill effects of industrialisation and urbanisation, and Britons themselves were becoming enfeebled compared with their colonial counterparts (Hardy 2001). Furthermore, for the Victorian middle classes, 'there could be no moral, religious, or intellectual improvement without physical improvement' and early health reformers found themselves on something of a 'crusade' to better living and physical conditions (Wohl 1983: 6–7). In urban centres, filth and disease were closely associated with other social disorders that threatened the fabric of industrial society, and, therefore, health became, first and foremost, a moral concern (Brandt and Rozin 1997) as 'immorality was rooted in physical impurity', and 'the abolition of evil' could only occur through the 'abolition of dirt and disease' (Wohl 1983: 7).

Nineteenth-century reformers, like John Harvey Kellogg and Sylvester Graham in the United States, became health evangelists, combining physical and moral health within integrated programmes that promised bodily and spiritual salvation (Whorton 1982). These philosophies were not dissimilar to the Muscular Christianity of the public schoolyard and university quad, in which physical fitness and moral rectitude were regarded as two sides of the one coin. *Mens sana in corpore sano* was understood literally, as the pure soul was secured, in part, by rigorous corporeal management. Health and hygiene were, thus, anchored within a Protestant discourse that associated physical and moral well-being with self-control, denial and the strict control of bodily temptations and appetites (Turner 2003). Graham, for example, preached that overeating was as sinful as masturbation and promoted austere bodily regimens to ensure that the moral character remained unimpeachable. Indeed, the body did not simply house, but also reflected, the soul, such that the healthy exterior was thought to attest to the individual's 'internal goodness' (Jutel 2005: 120).

Despite medical advances and a more sophisticated approach to its promotion, health remains closely associated with appropriate appearance and appropriate behaviour, the former often providing evidence for the latter. Allmark (2005: 2) thus suggests that health is less a set of facts but rather 'a judgement on the facts', whilst Robert Crawford adds that health has essentially become a 'key word' that says something about the 'goodness' of individuals and society (Crawford 1994). The discourses of weight loss, for example, praise dieters for 'resisting' and admonish them for 'succumbing' to the delights of a 'sinful' chocolate dessert. These same dieters internalise such values by proclaiming that they are 'being good' when they decline the offer of a sugary treat, or declare themselves to be 'bad' should they fail to display the requisite self control and moral fortitude to resist temptation (Bordo 1993). In other words, dieting is popularly framed as a 'virtual battle between good and evil' (Conrad 1994: 388), reinforced by television programmes such as *The Biggest Loser* or *Fat Chance*, which not only make losing weight competitive but which frame the victors as those who display the greatest level of self-control. 'Falling off the wagon', whether with drugs, alcohol or food, suggests a fundamental weakness of character and a lack of appropriate control, which is popularly thought to be visible in the shape and state of the body. For this reason, Crawford (1984: 76) states explicitly that 'health is a moral discourse, an opportunity to reaffirm shared values of culture; a way to express what it means to be a moral person', confirming that health represents much more than mere physical condition.

Understanding health as part of a shared cultural discourse recognises how it is employed as an 'identity strategy and dividing practice', where the

78　*The nature of health*

healthy Self is juxtaposed against, and protected from, the diseased Other (Crawford 2006: 414). Disease and the diseased body each represent a tangible threat to social stability by reminding the Self that health is fragile and easily disrupted, but it also suggests that with sufficient will these threats can be contained or even eradicated, both personally and collectively. The protection of individual health during the nineteenth century was, for example, not merely the avenue towards personal redemption but a social duty, and the Victorian association of individual hygiene and national vigour is replicated in contemporary debates about obesity, smoking and other 'epidemics' that threaten a society's well-being. Reforming social behaviour thus remains firmly part of modern health promotion, and this is evident within the context of modern sport, where performance technologies, like diseases, are thought to represent a material risk to both an athlete's health and the broader institution of sport. The prohibition of performance enhancing substances and methods for reasons of health is, thus, embedded in a specific social agenda where health and morality are not discrete but rather are essentially integrated to ensure that sport and other social identities remain unblemished.

Sport and health

To consider sport to be anything other than a fundamentally healthy endeavour is difficult in a society that so closely equates physical well-being with an active lifestyle. We are reminded on almost a daily basis that working out will lead to improvements in cardiovascular health, decrease the risk of lifestyle diseases and contribute to an overall feeling of wellness. Strategies to combat numerous public health concerns rely heavily on the promotion of physical activity through organised sport, whilst, at the same time, physical education programmes, once in decline, are being revived to ensure the health of the young. Elderly citizens are not immune to interventions and are encouraged to exercise to improve their quality of life by stabilising their bodies and preventing injury. Governments of all descriptions explicitly state that health, both national and individual, is the critical foundation upon which their sports policies are based, and the relationship between sport and nature further confirms physical activity as essentially restorative. As a result the sport–health nexus has been constructed as a thoroughly natural and self-evident phenomenon (Waddington 2000).

Given the close association between the two, it would seem that those who participate in physical activities are assured of a healthy body and a bright future. Accordingly, athletes, more than any other population, are thought to exemplify good health and clean living, which means that when they engage in risky activities, such as binge drinking or smoking, they are subject to particular condemnation for jeopardising their physical health and, as role models, for setting a poor example. It is, however, ironic that sport is uncomfortable being associated with unhealthy behaviours. Numerous studies attest to the deleterious effect that sport can have on an elite athlete's body, and even casual participants are exposed to potential physical problems as a result of their exercise regimen (Waddington *et al.* 2006). Indeed, given the number of injuries in junior, casual and elite sport, it could be argued that sport represents a very real public health issue, as well as a significant economic cost, in and of itself (Finch and Owen 2001). Rather than representing an activity dedicated to, or motivated by, improving health, it could easily be argued that sport is not a particularly healthy enterprise and might even justifiably be described as a 'violent and hazardous workplace' (Young 1993: 373). Nevertheless, those who perform in these risk-laden environments are expensive commodities, and accordingly, professional team owners, national governments and sporting organisations are typically concerned with safeguarding their investments.

The professional and elite sports industries have burgeoned since the 1950s, and athletes are required to play longer and harder than ever before. Cricket and rugby, once scheduled only during summer and winter respectively, are now essentially year-long sports, as their earning potential in international competitions has increased; baseball has lengthened from 140 games at the beginning of the twentieth century to the current 162 game season; and swimmers, who traditionally focused primarily on the Olympics every four years, now have a series of national and international championships, short course, grand prix and other events peppered throughout the intervening years. As a result, greater physical demands are made of athletes' bodies, which require increasingly specialist care to ensure they remain fit, healthy and ready to perform. Rule changes, improved training programmes and techniques, and the inclusion of safety equipment have each contributed to protecting athletes from injury and illness, but it is perhaps the rise in sports medicine that has made the most significant impact on the health and well-being of competitors.

The ubiquitous presence of doctors within professional and national sporting teams would seem to suggest that athletes' health must be a critical concern. Yet, the aims of medicine and the aims of sport are not always in concert, particularly when physicians are employed by teams rather than engaged by players. In this sense, the employment contract between the sports doctor and their employer may influence the type of care that is offered to athletes, whose bodies, beyond the confines of the game, may ultimately be regarded as expendable (Waddington 2000). For athletes, symptoms of ill-health are framed within a performance context, such that a player may be offered painkillers for a persistent headache for the short-term goal of returning to the pitch, rather than a scan that may reveal a more substantial condition. Furthermore, medical staff may be entreated to 'patch up' injuries for a timely return to the game or to recommend a course of treatment that is influenced by the needs of the team rather than the best interests of the player. For example, an athlete who suffers from cartilage damage to the knee might be advised by the team doctor to have

80   *The nature of health*

the offending tissue removed rather than repaired. The former would require only a brief disruption to the season, though, given the joint is hyper-mobile, this treatment could lead to arthritis later in life, whilst the latter would require six or more months, essentially an entire season, of recovery and rehabilitation after which the knee would likely be fully restored to its prior strength. This is not to suggest, of course, that sports physicians specifically or deliberately operate unethically, but to acknowledge that the athlete's best 'health' interests may not necessarily be the primary or sole concern of their doctor (Dunn *et al.* 2007; Mathias 2004).

Sports organisations regularly amend or update rules or permit the use of new technologies to ensure the safety of participants (Miah 2006). Helmets, padding, boxes, shinguards, mouthguards, eye protection, knee pads, wrist guards and chest protectors are among a seemingly endless list of devices that can be strapped to the body to shield almost every inch from the dangers of rigorous physical activity. Rule changes, such as the 2006 decision in Little League baseball to implement an age-based pitch, rather than innings, count or the implementation of a 'no head checking' in ice hockey, are each designed to protect competitors from serious injury. Nevertheless, invoking changes to promote health and reduce injury is often slow and inconsistently applied across sports, such as in the case of netball.

Developed in the early twentieth century as a version of basketball that was appropriately modified for young ladies, netball today suffers from a high rate of knee and ankle injuries at all levels of the game. These are, in part, a consequence of the 'no stepping' rule, which differentiates netball from basketball and which was initially designed to encourage a slower, more modest playing style. The pace of the game would now be unrecognisable to those early adherents, and to stop abruptly in the midst of a sprint down the court places extraordinary stresses on the players' lower limbs, causing injuries from twists and sprains through to ruptured ligaments and patella dislocation (McGrath and Ozanne-Smith 1998).

Netball is, of course, not a lone exemplar, and at the elite level there are numerous examples of how sport can be 'unhealthy', particularly for junior athletes. Young female gymnasts can develop symptoms of osteoporosis as a result of amenorrhoea; junior baseball pitchers risk the integrity of their growth plates through overtraining; bowlers in cricket can suffer long-term spinal damage as a result of a poor or 'mixed' action; football players are prone to injure almost every part of their bodies; whilst discus throwers may require knee reconstructions in their teenage years (Caine *et al.* 2006; Adirim and Cheng 2003; Sabatini 2001). To many, then, it seems contra-dictory to prohibit performance enhancing substances simply to safeguard athletes' health, when other risky or dangerous practices are not similarly outlawed, and in fact may even be encouraged (Kayser *et al.* 2005; Savulescu *et al.* 2004; Schneider and Butcher 2000; Tamburrini 2000).

To rationalise the prohibition of various substances and methods for reasons of health appears to be rather more complex in light of the various risks to which athletes are routinely exposed in high-level performance sport, and the issue is further confounded by several key assumptions about the impact of illicit performance enhancement on health, which underpin anti-doping strategies. There is popular consensus that substances that appear on the prohibited list must be harmful simply because they are included, whilst those that do not appear are consequently presumed to be harmless. Yet this argument is fallacious, particularly when many proscribed drugs, such as Ventolin, are freely available to members of the public, and many permitted drugs, left unregulated, may cause significant harm. By denying athletes these substances, sporting officials may harm them further, and might even imply that the health of an athlete is more important than that of a non-athlete. Furthermore, many banned substances have a therapeutic application and can be safely ingested without the horrendous, and typically overstated, consequences predicted by those who control sport (Street *et al.* 1996). Indeed, this appears to be accepted by the WADA, for athletes can apply for a Therapeutic Use Exemption (TUE) to utilise substances or methods on the prohibited list in the event of a documented medical condition (WADA 2007).

This is not to suggest, of course, that all drugs are harmless, though without solid empirical evidence, the effects of extreme drug abuse, where athletes ingest extraordinarily high doses, have only been anecdotally recorded (Dawson 2001; Black and Pape 1997). Given that many of these substances can be administered therapeutically, there is little evidence to suggest that the use of ergogenic aids under close medical supervision is equally risky (Kayser *et al.* 2005). Rather than cleansing sport, prohibition has driven the doping culture underground, and the inclusion of many performance enhancing drugs in controlled substances legislation has prompted athletes to resort to equine and bovine drugs with little or no professional advice as to their dosage or administration. Moreover, in a bid to avoid detection, athletes may ingest more harmful substances than necessary, such that their health is further jeopardised. To assume that those substances and methods that do not appear on the banned list are necessarily risk-free is also problematic, given the dearth of research into the long-term effects of permitted supplementation such as creatine (Tokish *et al.* 2004).

Other inconsistencies suggest that health *per se* may not be the overarching concern when determining the legitimacy of performance technologies. Additional, non-medical considerations may contribute to the assessment of potential enhancements, which could explain the differential treatment of substances and methods that provoke the same physiological outcomes in the body. For instance, blood doping, where an athlete's blood is drawn and later returned to the body, and the injection of rEPO are each banned as 'unnatural' or 'artificial' enhancements. Yet, altitude training and hypoxic chambers, which simulate the density of oxygen at altitude, are currently accepted as legitimate preparatory measures, though the latter has been at

82   *The nature of health*

the centre of recent controversy, such that WADA considered its inclusion on the 2007 prohibited list (Levine 2006; Miah 2006; Kutt 2005; Savulescu *et al.* 2004). In essence, each of these treatments is designed to increase the level of haematocrit in the bloodstream, which enhances the body's capacity to transport oxygen to the working muscles, thereby improving an athlete's endurance capacity. Each shares the same health risks, as the increased cellular density increases the blood's viscosity, which prompts the heart to work harder to circulate blood. Coupled with dehydration, this can heighten the risk of stroke, myocardial infarction and pulmonary embolism, and deaths have been recorded (Tokish *et al.* 2004).

Although there are clearly risks associated with an increase in haematocrit, not all of these technologies are prohibited, and there is no useful physiological reason why this might be the case. Yet, if the discussion is removed from the medical sphere and regarded as a cultural or social construct, it becomes clear that the 'natural' body and the protection of its integrity is a critical issue. These technologies are divided carefully into 'natural' and 'artificial' enhancements based largely on the manner in which they interact with, and their potential effects are transferred to, the body. In this example, the re-injection of blood and rEPO are essentially mechanical actions, whereby a substance penetrates the body's outermost layers to gain entry. Transgressing the body's boundaries in this way is considered materially different from training in real or simulated altitude environments, which, rather than introducing a foreign agent, encourages the body to increase its production of endogenous EPO. This outcome is considered more 'natural' as it relies on the body's adaptive capacity, rather than the 'unnatural' approach of injecting rEPO or blood, which provokes a specific and certain outcome by 'bypass[ing] all the body's natural feedback control mechanisms and overwhelm[ing] the normal adaptive responses' (Levine 2006: 298). By contrast, Benjamin Levine (2006: 298), in defence of this new technology, likens altitude training and hypoxic chambers to 'a component of training' whereby bodily responses to the intervention are 'quite variable and unpredictable', depending on a host of other physical and environmental factors. The 'naturalness' of such physiological responses, according to Levine (2006), is what distinguishes these techniques from one another and justifies the prohibition of artificial substances, like rEPO, and methods, such as blood doping.

It is clear then that health is not always the determining factor in the prohibition of particular performance technologies. Rather, cultural conceptions of the body as pure, natural and discrete are significant. Yet, according to Kristeva (1982), the desire to preserve an untainted body is negated by the fact that the body is never, and will never be, isolated from other individuals or the world. The body is always open, always porous and thus always exposed to potential adulteration, and the intake of sustenance and the excretion of waste across its borders, whilst necessary, are a constant reminder of the body's incompleteness. These transgressions expose

The nature of health   83

'points of contact' where contamination may be introduced (Turner 2003: 3). Furthermore, Kristeva (1982), drawing on Mary Douglas, suggests that particular revulsion is reserved for the body's waste products, those substances, such as faeces, urine, semen or blood, that leach from the body and open the inner self to the outer world. These fluids are abhorrent because they disturb bodily and social harmony by disrupting the carefully maintained boundaries that distinguish bodies and demarcate the inside from the out. The thought of re-ingesting these substances provokes universal disgust (Curtis 2001), an emotion that is also vigorously directed towards athletes who 'unnaturally' augment their bodies with hormones or other human or animal by-products.

Injecting blood, synthetic or natural testosterone or human growth hormone, once harvested from cadavers, evokes an intense response that is not evident even when athletes engage in other performance enhancing practices (Magdalinski 2000a). For as David Fairchild (1989: 77) succinctly argues: 'The deliberate reinsertion into the body, through ingestion or injection, of substances that have traversed the body's boundaries is both an abrogation of the fundamental inner/outer distinction that determines our clean selves and a culturally revolting practice', and he cites blood doping and anabolic steroids as instances where the return of bodily fluids, or their simulants, generates revulsion. Similarly, rEPO is rejected as 'unnatural' and undesirable, though it presents a particularly curious case, as endogenous EPO, produced by the body, and rEPO share an identical amino acid structure and are, therefore, effectively indistinguishable. Triggering the body to produce the former is not, however, as objectionable as introducing genetically constructed substances, for it is a 'natural' physiological response to changed conditions, whereas injections must artificially transgress the body's border, by penetrating the skin, in order to take effect. It is clear, then, that rather than protecting the health of an athlete, it is their purity, and hence authenticity, that is most valued. For this reason, doping sanctions are severest for those who deliberately permit substances to cross their borders, or even just utilise 'unnatural' methods of delivery that invade the body.

The 'unnatural' use of 'natural' substances was, in part, responsible for the removal of Australian cyclist Jobie Dajka from the 2004 Olympic team. Following allegations made by former teammate Mark French, Dajka and four other cyclists were accused of self-injecting vitamins without medical consent. Dajka denied the claims; however, DNA evidence secured from vials and syringes provided irrefutable evidence of his involvement, and, for bringing cycling into disrepute, he was expelled from the Olympic team (Kelly and Aiken 2004). Admissions of involvement from several of the other cyclists prompted a rapid response from both the Australian Institute of Sport and the Australian Olympic Committee, which each developed policies to ban athletes from self-injecting any substances with the exception of insulin and adrenaline for medical conditions (Anderson 2004;

84　*The nature of health*

Editorial 2004). Whilst others, including team doctor Peter Barnes, found no significant difference between the injection or oral administration of legal substances, the Anderson Inquiry, established in June 2004 to investigate the doping culture in cycling, found that the Australian Sports Commission and the Australian Institute of Sport were acutely aware that the public perception of self-injection was that it is 'a sinister and unacceptable practice' (Anderson 2004: 22). Dajka remarked, following his unsuccessful appeal for reinstatement, that he was 'probably the first to be ejected from an Olympics for taking a vitamin' (BBC 2004), and the fact that he is popularly remembered for a doping infringement is tinged with more than a little irony. What it does suggest is that the unnatural penetration of athletic bodies, even with legal substances and regardless of its health promoting potential, represents an unacceptable transgression of the body's boundaries akin to the use of illicit substances.

Restoration, medication or enhancement?

Although exposing the body to the corruptive forces of external contaminants is reviled in sport, there are instances when athletes are sanctioned in their use of foreign agents, and even substances derived from the body's own fluids may be celebrated as a welcome, and necessary, remedy. When athletes are ill, injured or are suffering from diseases, their physicians prescribe pharmaceuticals or recommend techniques that are intended to return their bodies to a healthy state. These 'medications' thus restore the body to 'normal' and work within the limits by which a body is socially, culturally and biologically imagined, and are mirrored against 'performance enhancers', which, as the appellation suggests, stretch the human body past a 'normal' stage to the level of the hyper-normal. Although performance enhancers are banned, on occasion these need to be therapeutically administered to athletes, revealing that they too have legitimate medicinal applications. Therefore, a substance that enters the body for therapeutic reasons is deemed appropriate, whereas if the same product enters the body for less than pure motives, it is rejected as unlawful contamination. 'Restoration' and 'enhancement' are thus materially different within the context of sport, and it is only the intention behind using the substance that seems to distinguish them.

Medications and performance enhancers are treated disparately by sports officials committed to keeping sport 'clean', yet substances that are prohibited for athletes also have non-athletic therapeutic applications. Human growth hormone, for example, is used to treat patients with growth hormone deficiencies, chronic renal failure or HIV-related cachexia (Tritos and Mantzoros 1998); anabolic steroids can be administered to those suffering from, amongst other conditions, age-related sarcopenia (Evans 2004); whilst rEPO is prescribed for those diagnosed with anaemia (Fisher 2003). Yet, despite the fact that these drugs each have medical functions, it is their application to what are presumed to be otherwise 'healthy' bodies that is considered problematic. Medications, it seems, are only acceptable to repair a body rather than improve upon it, yet the distinction between restoration and enhancement is not easily established as each concept fundamentally rests on the presumed existence of bodily norms (Parens 1998). Biomedical models accept, for the most part, that health is a kind of statistical standard, which provides medicine with the specific mission of restoring an incapacitated body to physiological equilibrium. Trying to improve the body beyond the accepted norm, however, is to 'enhance' the body and to utilise 'interventions designed to improve human form or functioning beyond what is necessary to sustain or restore good health' (Juengst 1998). Yet, as Julian Savulescu (2006: 325) points out, 'the mutually exclusive distinction between treatments and enhancements is a false one', because 'treatments are enhancements', and, as such, others have reframed the debate in terms of 'health-related enhancements' and 'non-health-related enhancements' (Walters and Palmer 1997: 110). In other words, all interventions into the body are designed to better it from its current position, however well or ill it might be. It is, essentially, the degree to which the body is improved, as well as the motivation for doing so, that is under interrogation.

Medical ethics debates are inconclusive about the appropriateness of treatments that try to extend the body beyond its usual limits, and within sport, strict regulations ensure that any intervention is confined to the restoration of health rather than the enhancement of capabilities. Nevertheless, there are many examples of treatments that are used by elite competitors to improve the bodies that nature allotted. For example, dozens of professional athletes, including, most notably, Tiger Woods, have used LASIK eye surgery to improve their eyesight to a 'better than normal' level of 20/10 or 20/15, yet for many, this is as indefensible as taking anabolic steroids. There has been, to date, no attempt to have such surgeries outlawed, perhaps as they are represented as 'corrective' procedures designed to restore faulty vision rather than enhance a healthy, well functioning organ. Permitting athletes to submit to such procedures suggests that it is not merely the artificial manipulation of the body that is of concern, but rather the underlying intention that is critical. If one *intends* to enhance performance, then punishment is warranted. Conversely, if an athlete *intends* to correct or restore health, then the motivation for consuming even the same substance is, with permission, acceptable. The Australian Olympic Committee (AOC) in its submission to the 1999 IOC World Conference on Doping in Lausanne, where the WADA was formed, confirmed that intent is critical in determining instances of doping and proposed that 'athletes should be permitted to take prohibited substances for genuine therapeutic reasons'. The AOC insisted that the 'object should be to merely bring the athlete back to the level playing field, not to give him or her an advantage' and further asserted that 'no enhancement of the athlete's *normal* level of performance' should result (emphasis added), suggesting that heath and intent are critical determinants of 'real' cases of doping.

86 *The nature of health*

The 'harmonisation' of anti-doping policies in recent years has invested the WADA with the power to coordinate and monitor international anti-doping efforts as well as establish and maintain, in conjunction with national sports administrations and international federations, an annual list of prohibited substances and methods (Houlihan 2004). As per the AOC's suggestion, WADA has the additional authority to issue TUEs to athletes seeking permission to utilise otherwise banned medications with the intention of restoring their health (WADA 2007). This policy only provides for athletes with a recognised and documented medical condition and is accompanied by a stringent set of guidelines, which state categorically that athletes are restricted to substances or methods that will 'produce no additional enhancement of performance other than that which might be anticipated by a return to a state of normal health following the treatment of a legitimate medical condition' (WADA 2007: 9). To remove any doubt, the guidelines further clarify: 'the return by the athlete to the level of performance possessed before the treated medical condition occurred' (WADA 2007: 10). WADA concedes that 'a certain enhancement of individual performance, due to the efficacy of the treatment, can occur', yet maintains that this improvement 'cannot go beyond the level of performance of the athlete prior to his/her medical condition' (WADA 2007: 10). Not all foreign agents, then, contaminate sport, and substances, even banned ones, that are regarded as 'essential' for health, even if otherwise banned, can been seen as appropriate for ingestion within international sport, though Bordreau and Konzak (1991: 93) erroneously contend that anabolic steroids should be considered independently of other performance enhancers for unlike most prohibited substances, steroids do not 'bring back health'.

Even so, if we accept Savulescu's (2006) argument that all treatments are enhancements, it would seem that an athlete who eases an acute headache with medication shortly before an event, regardless of whether or not the substance is banned, is, in essence, enhancing their performance. Consequently, if taking a headache tablet to restore the body to 'normal' is not considered an 'enhancement', then it seems contradictory that the use of, for example, anabolic steroids is not similarly considered therapeutic, given that these substances are primarily used in the sports community not to enhance performance but to assist recovery. In this sense, steroids perform a similar restorative role, and like headache relief, both provide an accelerated route to 'health'. Of course, these are equated neither by governing bodies nor the public, both of which regard performance enhancing drugs in the same category as illicit drugs such as heroin or cocaine, whilst other pharmaceuticals are constructed as 'medication' designed to 'cure' the body. What this suggests is that there persists a flawed assumption that athletes 'normally' perform in a healthy state, and that disruptions to that 'health' need to be eradicated so that the body can return to its customary state. Establishing what this might be can be difficult as it presumes the existence of a physiological equilibrium that can be restored solely through the therapeutic, as opposed to the non-medical, administration of pharmaceuticals. These assumptions clearly draw upon the biomedical model of health discussed earlier, and as Boorse (1977) cautions, there is no inherent homeostasis to which a body returns following illness, injury or disease. The body functions as a continuum rather than in an either/or, healthy/unhealthy binary. This is particularly significant within the context of elite and professional sport where athletes submit to rigorous training systems to extend their physiological capacity with the expectation of improving their performance. Athletic bodies are, thus, in a constant state of flux as they transform and adapt, and are modified and altered, in response to external stresses and internal processes. Rather than being regarded as evidence of ill-health, greater-than-normal aerobic capacity or muscle strength are typically regarded as a welcome and desirable sign of the body's ability to adapt. As such, it is difficult, even with the WADA guidelines, to determine what the 'normal' health of an athlete is, and how this should and could be measured.

There is, of course, another group of athletes for whom biomedical models of health that presume 'normal' functioning are inadequate. Paralympic competitors each have a recognised impairment or disability that typically prevents them from participating in mainstream sport, yet it would be inappropriate to argue that these elite athletes necessarily suffer from ill health. Nevertheless, their bodies represent a significant deviation from 'normal' bodies, and Western medical and health practices seek to 'repair' these bodies so that they structurally and functionally resemble able bodies (Imrie 2004). Disabled bodies are thus 'treated' with prosthetic technologies, which try to return 'deficient' bodies to more comfortable and familiar state that if not completely 'normal' is somewhat reminiscent of it. These are not regarded as enhancements because they are intended to '*restore* rather than extend people's capacities' (Shilling 2005: 178), though essentially the attachment of lower limbs to a double amputee or the paraplegic's use of a wheelchair creates a 'better than normal' body for an athlete who, without these devices, would have significant mobility problems. Nevertheless, the use of artificial limbs that are built from carbon, embedded with microprocessor technology and designed to replicate the biomechanics of wild cats have prompted questions about the appropriateness of these 'extra-abled' bodies (Longman 2007). In the event that Paralympic performances surpass their Olympic equivalents, disabled athletes are likely to be condemned for 'artificial' enhancements that are not intended to restore health but to extend the body's capacity for the sole pursuit of athletic success.

Protecting national health

Representing the body as fragile and constantly at risk of corruption not only frames anti-doping strategies, but also validates wider cultural constructions of Self and Other upon which national identities are based. In

88   *The nature of health*

these constructions, the pure 'us' is distinguished from impure 'others' by borders that demarcate the physical landscape and psychosocial terrain of the nation, the maintenance of which is designed to sustain a cultural homogeneity that contains the Self and expels the Other (Sibley 1995). Collective efforts to protect the integrity of the nation are replicated in a range of social and civic institutions that remind 'us' of the risks posed by foreign agents, who, not unlike the drugs that pollute an athlete's body, threaten to traverse borders and contaminate 'our' society. In addition, domestic risks have the potential to undermine social harmony, thus national security relies on containing these twin dangers and immunising society from their ill effects.

It is not surprising that narratives of national well-being draw so decisively on discourses of personal health, as individual and social health have long been closely aligned in Western societies. The nineteenth-century equation of personal health and national vigour persists as social and individual progress are inextricably linked in a society that sees the maintenance of personal borders as analogous to the protection of national ones. In many respects, the nation is conceived as a body that, without mindful protection, is subject to injury and disease both from within and without, and the management of personal health and the eradication of contamination mirrors broader social desires to maintain order and expel threats. Bryan Turner (2003: 1) notes that: 'Concepts of social order and disorder are often seen in terms of the balance or imbalance of the body', thus corporeal metaphors are used to describe societal dis/ease, whilst bodily ailments are framed as direct threats to the vitality of the nation. In this way, individual health is contained within a national discourse so that personal borders become a social concern and citizens are expected to take responsibility for their well-being. To this end, bodies are surveilled, monitored and regulated in the interests of the 'greater good', as personal corporeal management is regarded as a cornerstone of social order and stability.

Within the context of sport, athletes are not only inscribed with, but embody national ideologies in an adversarial forum designed to test relative strength and 'precisely delineate our own limitations and shortcomings' (Fairchild 1989: 76). As such, national and other interests are communicated through sport, and the use of cultural stereotypes to reinforce 'drama' and to distinguish between 'us' and 'them' has been well identified by sociologists of sport (Garland and Rowe 1999; Tudor 1992). International athletic success is accepted as evidence of a nation's superior stature, and individual competitors are thereby legitimised as indicators of national worth. In essence, the condition of athletic bodies symbolises the condition of the nation, even though international sporting prowess usually does not correlate with national physical fitness. In this context, protecting the health of athletes and the integrity of their bodies symbolises more than concern about personal well-being. A contaminated athlete suggests a disordered and immoral society, whilst clean bodies signify a pure and virtuous one. It is, therefore, no coincidence that nations keenly pursue 'drug free' sport, embedding a commitment to 'purity' within all levels of government and athletic administration, and, as the United Kingdom's Anti-Doping Policy (UK Sport 2006) confirms, 'the contribution that [drug-free] sport can make to the health ... of the nation' is specifically valued. By contrast, the national 'corporate image' is tarnished when athletes are publicly accused of taking drugs (Kelly and Aiken 2004).

The protection of the national image through the recovery of athletic purity is no more apparent than when 'our' athletes are accused of illicit doping. Rather than immediately expelling these tainted bodies from our midst, sports administrators, the national press and even politicians try to salvage the tarnished athlete by initially expressing their disbelief, horror or outrage, which is later followed by explanations for the 'inaccurate' results and suggestions that some grand conspiracy might just be afoot (Magdalinski 2001a). Typically, the restoration of health is proffered as rationale for the indiscretion, though as health represents both the individual and collective, it is unclear precisely whose health is being recovered.

Conclusion

If protecting the biological health of athletes was a critical concern of sporting bodies and anti-doping authorities, then it would seem that the range of risks that athletes encounter on a regular basis would be dealt with in a more concerted and comprehensive manner. Given George Orwell's equation of sport and war, however, it would appear that bodies are little more than 'cannon fodder' on the sports field and may be largely expendable in the pursuit of national and international prestige. Understanding health, therefore, as a broader social and cultural construct emphasises the multiple ideologies upon which this notion rests, and reveals it to be reflective of issues of national vitality and standing as well as personal morality and collective integrity. Within the context of sport, protecting the 'health' of athletes is equated with protecting national interests, and for this reason, individual boundaries and national borders are synonymous. The expulsion of foreign bodies from the athlete and the recovery of its purity are mirrored in efforts to rid the national body of similar undesirable contamination to preserve social order and stability. In essence, then, anti-doping strategies must be interrogated as part of a medico-moral discourse that is not primarily focused on biological welfare, but which is aligned more closely to issues of 'fairness' and morality than might first be expected.

Despite the fact that 'health' may be a broader social construct, there is nevertheless evidence that doping, as well as other sporting practices, can cause harm to the body. Whilst prohibiting illicit drugs and methods on the basis of health may be unsustainable in theory, and in practice may provoke more damage to athletes' bodies, ensuring the well-being of their charges should be, at least in part, a responsibility of those who benefit directly from their labour. Like any employer, international sporting bodies and national governments have an implied duty of care towards those in their service. Anti-doping strategies are, however, limited and ineffective when it comes to safeguarding physical well-being, and for this reason, Savulescu and his colleagues (2004) suggest that 'health' rather than 'bodily corruption' should be the primary concern. Rather than testing athletes for evidence of illicit substances in their bodies, they should be examined to ensure they are physically prepared for the rigours of sporting training and competition. For example, if, in the case of blood doping, rEPO, altitude training or hypoxic chambers, haematocrit levels in the blood stream above 50 per cent is considered to be the point at which the well-being of an athlete is jeopardised, then all athletes should have their blood tested for haematocrit levels. If they have more than a 50 per cent concentration, then they should be prevented from competing, regardless whether their blood was thickened through 'natural' or 'artificial' means, or was simply a result of genetics.

Safeguarding the health of athletes may lie at the heart of anti-doping policies; however, it is clear that 'health' is an elusive concept, which is inextricably linked to broader moral and national discourses. In essence, these strategies are based on controlling and regulating athletes' bodies to conform to normative standards, which is particularly evident in claims that anabolic steroids corrupt gendered bodies by feminising men and masculinising women. In the following chapter, fears about the monstrous feminine, the apparent consequence of substantial drug abuse, are explored to examine how the enhanced female body unsettles normative, heterosexual expectations. An 'unhealthy', or, more specifically, 'unfeminine', appearance is acknowledged as evidence of the body's essential corruption by illicit substances, whilst an appropriately attractive body, regardless of what chemicals may be swimming therein, is thought to 'look' healthy and so must 'be' healthy. This chapter suggests, then, that the body's own surfaces become visible markers of the guilt or innocence of doping.

6 'Those girls with sideburns'
Enhancing the female body

Introduction

As Le Jingyi climbs from the pool, for perhaps the millionth time, and as the water cascades off her impressive shoulders, slender waist and defined musculature, she reminds us of the terrifying consequences of women's entry into sport. Her presumably soft and feminine features have been replaced by hard muscle, and her womanly proportions are obscured by a masculine physique. No longer strictly female, yet not quite a man either, the image of Jingyi has become the predictable media adjunct to any report on illicit doping in sport, visually confirming that for women to transform their bodies to such a degree, they must systematically consume large quantities of dangerous chemicals. As such, she represents the unsettling outcome of the intrusion of technology into the body, offering a horrifying reminder of what can happen when the nature/artifice binary is disturbed. Thus, Jingyi represents a troubling future, where essentialist categories collapse, where gender fusion and confusion abound and where the nature of femininity is overshadowed by the spectre of the monster.

By re-examining Jingyi's physique each time an allegation of illicit performance enhancement emerges, we are repeatedly compelled to confront the nature of the body and its relationship to technology from the particular perspective of gender. If technology represents an inorganic Other against which the organic Self is defined, then, in this case, Jingyi offers a technologised exemplar that invites, indeed, forces, women to evaluate their own and other bodies. The purpose her body serves is thus not unlike those unrealistic images presented through the bodies of media starlets, celebrities and representatives from the worlds of fashion and entertainment. In both cases, bodies function as explicit reminders of what femininity definitely is, or what it most assuredly is not. Thus, Jingyi, and those with bodies like hers, warn of the gender consequences of tinkering with nature.

What the images of Jingyi reveal is that the female body is particularly scrutinised within the context of sport and is subject to specific sanctions if it transgresses. Of course, the body is the central focus of various discourses of surveillance and their corresponding disciplinary measures. The emergence of medical practices, for example, literally opened the body to scrutiny, which meant, according to Rosa Braidotti (1994: 89), that not only could the functioning of the body be deciphered, but it was 'transform [ed] into a text to be read and interpreted by a knowledgeable medical gaze'. This gaze is not restricted to the medical fraternity, and an increasing emphasis on the visual has meant that 'ways of seeing' have become technologised and integrated into the everyday practices of culture. The media have, of course, refined the gaze to a fine art, not only producing and sanctioning a cultural scopophilia, but circulating and further entrenching normative discourses of gender and the body within society. Through institutions such as these, the female body is reduced to a series of iconic surfaces to be deciphered and judged, and any variation in what is considered the 'appropriate' female form is placed under a cultural microscope. This is particularly evident within sport, where gender binaries reinforce an enduring suspicion of the presence of women within this 'arena of masculinity' (Pronger 1990).

Modern sport has always been firmly linked to a patriarchal project that seeks to establish and maintain strict cultural boundaries that police what is feminine and what is masculine. It is well documented that sport is a gendered institution and since its inception has been utilised as part of the hegemonic reproduction of patriarchal society (McKay 1991; Messner and Sabo 1990; Lenskyj 1986). Numerous researchers have focused on the way that women's entrance into sport is limited through various discourses that render them secondary to men, physically incapable of aggressive physical exertion and as sexualised objects for the male gaze. Studies that focus on the media have identified a variety of marginalising strategies that have restricted women's participation, including the processes of trivialisation and symbolic annihilation (Hargreaves 1994; McKay 1991; Lenskyj 1986). Sport is, thus, rendered a masculinising ritual, embodying characteristics of strength, power, aggression and confidence. By contrast, female bodies are portrayed as weaker, graceful, flexible and attractive. Those who stray from this feminine ideal are regarded as bodily, and perhaps morally, deviant and are often read as poor parodies of their male counterparts. Whilst women are denigrated for their involvement in a range of sports, especially those requiring power, strength and physical contact, their participation is often recuperated through a range of hetero-feminine and heterosexual discourses. Sports magazine covers and calendars that stylise and reduce the female form to a series of desirable and unthreatening surfaces remind the spectators that these women might be athletes, but physically they remain heterosexually desirable and feminine. It is clear, then, that sport, as a 'masculine arena', functions to establish and police the binary oppositions male/female and masculinity/femininity.

Although Michael Burke (1998: 25) suggests that the 'most interesting cases of mythmaking to support dichotomous sex categories occur when females enter sports that have traditionally been gendered male', the situation

'*Those girls with sideburns*' 93

is a little more complex. Attempts to differentiate male from female occur not when women simply play sport, even 'masculine' sport, but specifically when women seek to step outside the traditional feminine form. Unlike in the nineteenth century, or even for much of the twentieth century, women who play sport are no longer regarded with the same level of suspicion or concern, prompting some young women to question whether there even remains a gender divide in sport. Those who 'bulk up', daring to approach or even replicate the masculine athletic physique, are, however, still repudiated as mannish freaks (Cahn 1993). By 'wearing' their bodies in a masculine way (Budd 1997), female athletes, such as tennis player Amelie Mauresmo, provoke reactions that seek to reestablish essentialist gender categories and eliminate the confusion that their appearance augurs. Mauresmo's first grand slam final appearance at the 1999 Australian Open prompted obtuse comments from Lindsay Davenport, who remarked that she thought she was playing against a man, and Martina Hingis, who explicitly declared that the Frenchwoman must be 'half a man' (Hillier and Harrison 2004). *Sports Illustrated* added to the colourful representation of 'muscular Mauresmo' with the following introduction: 'Amelie Mauresmo's thickly muscled shoulders bulge from her dark blue tank-top, and she struts cockily around court like a weightlifter in the gym' (CNN/*Sports Illustrated* 1999). When the tall, muscular Chinese swimmers first came to international attention in the early 1990s, the media constructed their performances as monstrous spectacles and charged them immediately with illicit enhancement. In 2006, Australian swimmers Libby Lenton and Liesel Jones' buffed bodies generated comparisons with former East German and Chinese swimmers, prompting one media commentator to proclaim the duo as 'so feminine' unlike the East Germans and Chinese who had 'real masculine features, like a protruded jaw line' (Williams and Wilson 2006). Clearly, when women exceed the accepted boundaries of the female body and adopt 'masculine' characteristics, femininity is manifestly threatened and is worthy of public comment.

Whilst the institution of sport, constructed as a 'natural' activity, reaffirms sex and gender binaries within the public sphere, technologies have the potential to blur those borders, and performance enhancing agents, in particular, pose particular risks, specifically to female bodies, as they threaten to dissolve carefully juxtaposed gender categories. Yet, 'natural' bodies are believed to be biologically determined rather than culturally ascribed, and the sex categories of 'male' and 'female', in particular, are assumed to be fixed and identifiable through bodily scrutiny (Vertinsky 1990). The use of apparently 'unnatural' substances jeopardises established physical borders that demarcate male from female and exposes the athletic body as a site of anxiety. The disruption of these gendered margins through muscle-building and fat-reducing technologies, for example, allows for not only the masculinising female but also the feminising male. The blurring of biological, particularly visual borders, is seen as a greater threat, than the

94 *'Those girls with sideburns'*

blurring of cultural borders that are understood to be, if not on a continuum, then at least more fluid categories. Male/female, on the other hand, are considered immutable, scientific categories, and are perceived as biologically rather than socially defined. This is not to say that the two are not linked, but it might be possible to accept a code of feminine behaviour that is inconsistent with the hegemonic ideal, but only as long as the body conforms to strict 'natural' sex categories.

This chapter examines a range of cultural responses to women taking performance enhancing substances and contextualises these within wider debates about fears of the monstrous feminine: that is, women who challenge the limits of what signifies 'femaleness'. It interrogates specific cultural responses to female athletes who take, or are accused of taking, performance enhancing drugs, revealing how a fear of 'supra-female' athletic performance disrupts our understanding of both the male/female and nature/artifice binaries and provokes horror at the dissolution of those borders that clearly establish male and female as separate physical and biological categories. At the same time, bodies that conform to normative expectations of 'femaleness' are, despite ingesting chemicals, restored as appropriately female and excused for their 'minor' mistakes. Scrutinising the athletic female body generates a series of narratives that link women, through technology, to the realm of the monstrous, creating an almost hysterical cultural response that condemns the appearance of these potentially transgressive bodies.

Normally speaking

When the gendered body is subjected to public and private scrutiny, the arbitrary concept of 'normal' becomes fixed within a rigid discourse that relies on a continual visual display of socially constructed, and accepted, feminine and masculine qualities and behaviours. Furthermore, the biological differences between male and female bodies are repeatedly asserted to ensure that gender appears to be rooted in the organism and is not merely constructed through culture. Perhaps because Eve came from Adam, the female body has always been more easily conceived relationally, rather than independently. Anatomy textbooks have traditionally utilised the male body to demonstrate the collective inner structure and workings of humans, whilst female bodies typically appear only as a point of contrast, to demonstrate their reproductive deviance from the masculine standard (Vertinsky 1990). As such, female bodies are read against the male form and through the masculine gaze, perceived variously as a 'lack' (Irigaray 1985; Lacan 1977) or as 'men turned outside in' (Laqueur 1987: 2), in essence, a topsy-turvy, somewhat unstable body that remains inferior to the male norm. Perceiving the female body as different from and lesser than has become firmly established within the psychosocial unconscious, through, as Judith Butler (1993) contends, a series of stylised repetition of acts, or performances, that serve to reiterate gender on a personal and daily basis. Because gender is not axiomatic, it must be regularly and forcefully enacted as a constant reminder of what is, and is not, appropriate. Butler (1993) argues that performing what is socially and politically perceived to be 'normal' constructs a 'ritualised production', which is carefully policed to marginalise those who do not conform. The force of prohibition and fear of exclusion contribute, Butler (1993) reasons, to the maintenance of gendered discourses that regard men and women as essentially, and fundamentally, different.

In essence, the repetition of gendered performances creates norms that are enthusiastically embraced by, and embedded within, society, suggesting that rather than universally applicable, these normative categories are culturally, sexually and geographically specific. Yet, this does not mean they are fixed; indeed, gendered norms are clearly responsive to shifts in fluctuating popular and ideological proclivities. Over the past thirty years, there have been significant changes to the ideal feminine physique, revealed by a cursory examination of celebrity culture that suggests female bodies, once soft and round, are now celebrated for their thin, angular appearance. Sports stars similarly remind women that too much floppy flesh is undesirable, and a toned, athletic appearance is a standard that should be desired and aspired to, if not actually replicated. The media contribute by delivering an overwhelming array of images of ideal male and female physiques, inviting scrutiny of their, and our own, bodies. Even the most confident cannot help but be tempted to look critically at their own less than satisfactory examples, at the same time they gaze longingly at the perfect visions walking the red carpet or hurtling down a track. This panoptic strategy is reinforced by increasingly accessible technologies designed to nip, tuck, suck, lift, augment, straighten and smooth a range of 'unsightly' and, thus, undesirable physical attributes. The ability to self-modify is thought to empower women to take control of their bodies and to fashion them into whatever they desire, however, as Foucault (1977) might remind us, these occur within a strict patriarchal paradigm that equates self-determination with physical compliance to established norms and expected behaviours. Whilst these technological modifications are clearly accepted as a necessary part of 'repairing' or 'restoring' the body to an accepted femininity, the use of technologies to take women beyond femininity is rejected. As such, the consumption or use of performance enhancing substances or methods for the specific purpose of altering the female shape is regarded as an infringement against, and even an obliteration of, the very essence of femininity. A female body transgresses the margin that distinguishes male from female by disfiguring the physical attributes that a woman should possess, and is thus regarded as unnatural, abnormal and monstrous for ignoring the nature/ artifice and male/female binaries as well as for potentially impairing its culturally ascribed role of reproduction. As such, alterations to the body are perceived as irrational, unhealthy and grotesque, essentially a pathetic and inferior attempt at embracing the qualities and appearance of maleness.

Visual borders

Although sporting success hinges on an individual's bodily performance, female athletes are confronted by the specific reality that their external surfaces are as important, if not more so, than their athletic ability. For these women, sponsorship deals, publicity, post-sport media careers and a range of other advantages rest largely on their physical attractiveness and sexual desirability (Hargreaves 1994). The media and commercial success of tennis player Anna Kournikova, despite her less than outstanding singles career, attests to the fact that female athletes can gain extraordinary celebrity based on their appearance, whilst more physically capable, though perhaps less visually compelling, athletes are overlooked. In particular, women who compete in strength, power or contact sports are rejected as ugly, butch or manly as their sports demand a level of muscularity that conflicts with popular definitions of feminine appeal (Cahn 1993). Of course, the ideal female form is not fixed and shifts according to changing cultural standards; and over the last three decades, female bodies have become stronger and fitter, accompanied by a growing acceptance of the technologies required to produce them (Pronger 2002; Markula 1995). Nevertheless, there remains a clear demarcation between acceptable levels of muscularity in men and women, whereby women are encouraged to focus on 'toning' rather than growing their muscles to ensure that they do not replicate men but remain identifiably female (Choi 2003; Malson 1998).

When female athletic bodies 'cross' into the realm of masculine shape and size, the masculine/feminine boundary is rapidly fortified to ensure that gendered identities are protected. Her genetic sex, sexuality and possible use of external aids are each interrogated by a public unconvinced that women can 'naturally' become large and muscular. As a result, the mere presence of excessive muscles is sufficient for the authenticity of her body and, by association, her performance to be publicly questioned. The media assumes a particularly aggressive role in the surveillance of female athletes, and following its relentless tutoring, the public too have learned to scrutinise bodily surfaces for signs of technological enhancement. After the insinuation that Lenton and Jones were no longer 'feminine', comments on an Australian newspaper's website reveal how effectively the public internalises these physical codes, applying them on demand when presented with a new specimen to observe: 'Libby is broader across the hips than the Chinese girl, thus the Chinese girl is much broader across the shoulders than Libby. That is where the muscle building steroids have done their work on the Chinese girl, giving her much broader shoulders and narrower hips' and 'There really is no comparison between the two ... Libby looks in proportion' (Williams and Wilson 2006).

The panoptic surveillance of the female body occurs not only from without but from within: by the athletes themselves. Amidst accusations of drug-taking, Australian swimmer Susie O'Neill referred to her Chinese competitors as 'those girls with sideburns' (*Inside Sport* 1999: 13). Furthermore, 'unexpected' successes by Irish swimmer Michelle (Smith) de Bruin and Dutch swimmer Inge de Bruijn were immediately labelled 'suspicious' (Lingard 2000). Despite de Bruijn's markers of femininity, including long, blonde hair, make up and manicured and painted porcelain nails, her strong body and outstanding performances were sufficient to render her 'masculine', 'unnatural' and thus 'suspicious'.

Whilst it is the primary sex characteristics that typically distinguish male from female, other bodily features contribute to the body's gendered identity. The shape, size and overall appearance of the body is coded, whereby largeness, muscularity and hardness signify masculinity, and smallness, softness and fat are deemed feminine (Lindsay 1996). In a society where femininity is correlated with thinness, the presence of an excessive musculature on a female frame violates normative ideals (Malson 1998). Female bodies that are hard and strong perplex as they deny a woman's assumed 'natural' and desired cultural state. As Leslie Heywood (1998: 5) suggests, 'muscular women are a contradiction to, even an attack on, our reality'. Such physiques embody strength and power, presence and solidity, dissolving patriarchal structures by removing the binary relationship between men/strength and women/weakness that underpins political, cultural and gendered power relations (Holmlund 1989).

To reclaim muscle as masculine, women's athletic competitions that require strength and power are labelled 'unfeminine' and the athletes who participate as 'butch' (Cahn 1993). Furthermore, hegemonic femininity has become so entrenched in some sports that it not only influences but is explicitly embedded in the judging criteria. Female gymnasts and figure skaters, for example, are required to demonstrate a level of grace and femininity that is not required of their male counterparts. Elements that emphasise strength and musculature are eschewed in favour of 'dance' routines where the competitors appear to float across the mat or ice with the apparent effortlessness of pixies. In response to concerns that female bodybuilders appeared too 'mannish', the International Federation of Bodybuilders incorporated the undefined and indefinable 'femininity' into their judging criteria. In addition to assessing their musculature, symmetry and density, female competitors were to be assessed on the way they walk to and from their position on stage, obliging the judges to determine 'whether or not she carries herself in a graceful manner' (IFBB 2006: 55). Once the competition begins, the rules firmly state:

> First and foremost, the judge must bear in mind that this is a women's bodybuilding competition, and that the goal is to find an ideal female physique. Therefore, the most important aspect is shape – a muscular yet feminine shape. The other aspects are similar to those described for assessing the male physique, but muscular development must not be carried to such an excess that it resembles the massive muscularity of the male physique.
>
> (IFBB 2006: 55)

98 'Those girls with sideburns'

It is significant that the 'most important aspect' is the 'feminine shape' of the competitor, whilst the converse, a 'masculine shape', is not specified in the judging guidelines for male competitors. What precisely a 'feminine shape' is, however, is not defined by the IFBB, and gestures towards an assumed shared understanding of what a woman's body should look like. The IFBB rules confirm Helen Malson's (1998: 106) contention that 'masculinity can be more easily defined independently of physical appearance than can femininity'. Femininity, she further notes, is correlated with thinness, whereby 'female beauty and (heterosexual) attractiveness' is equated with the thin body (Malson 1998: 106). If women are to remain thin to be feminine, then clearly, as the IFBB suggests, there is an upper limit or 'glass ceiling' of musculature beyond which the body is no longer sufficiently womanly (Dworkin 2001). As a result, some have argued that women's bodybuilding offers the potential for transcendence and the opportunity for competitors to reject hegemonic femininity in order to explore revolutionary or transgressive forms (Heywood 1998), yet female bodybuilders are not immune to the cultural requirements of femininity. These women may toy with the limits of 'femaleness', trying to push beyond them in terms of their size and musculature, yet their own governing body requires them to embrace the cultural mainstream of acceptable femininity, implemented through their costuming, deportment and, more drastically, cosmetic surgery. To obtain the 'ideal female physique' desired by the IFBB, female bodybuilders must retrofit their bodies with the very markers of femininity that have disappeared through their rigorous training regime. These feminine accoutrements are deliberately designed to 'counteract the "masculine" appearance they have worked so hard to create' (Ian 2001: 76). The extreme dieting required to produce a 'ripped' body strips away the very softness that is thought to define a woman, such that 'pockets of softness' must be replaced (Gelder 2005: 389). Femininity is thus externally accessorised through make-up, hair and performance attire, whilst invasive procedures surgically fabricate absent breasts, triggering further anxiety about the naturalness of the female bodybuilder's body. It is thus not surprising that the rise of women's 'fitness' competitions, oft derided by serious physique athletes as little more than beauty pageants, has come at the expense of women's bodybuilding, which has declined rapidly through the 1990s. Male bodybuilders thereby retain their monopoly on muscle, whilst female competitors are reduced, figuratively and bodily, to little more than toned beauty queens.

For those women who nevertheless insist on creating hypermuscular bodies, other suspicions emerge. Allegations of illicit substance abuse surface, based on the assumption that women are incapable of building their bodies without pharmacological assistance and technological manipulation (Heywood 1998). The muscular woman is thus imagined to rely on 'unnatural', masculine means to achieve her 'unnatural' physique, such as the ingestion of various chemicals and hormones, which threatens to produce an unrecognisable creature that is neither wholly female nor wholly male, yet terrifyingly both. Sportswear manufacturer Skins, exploited these fears in an advertising campaign that featured women, digitally altered to resemble men, complete with a flat, masculine, muscular torso, and a hirsute chest, stomach and arms. The banner commanded: 'Improve your sports performance without the side effects', and later entreated: 'Don't take steroids. Wear Skins™ for Women' (Skins 2006). Significantly, the same campaign used male athletes, yet did not proffer the same warning. The outcome of women taking masculine hormones is clearly more horrific than when men supplement their stores. Whilst the advertisements warned of the consequences of biotechnological incursions into the body, the application of the Skins technology was presented as a safe and appropriate alternative for women seeking to legitimately enhance their performance without the need to internally manipulate their bodies.

The use of illicit pharmaceuticals, such as androgenic anabolic steroids, threatens more than simply a loss of gendered self, and is grounded in a growing concern that the human organism may come to rely on these substances for not just physical excellence, but simply mere existence. A Luddite despair about the role of technology in contemporary culture is, however, manifestly surpassed by apprehension towards its specific influence within the human body, which is evident in the increasing dependence on technological assistance for everything from the maintenance of erections, to memory, the prolonging of life and even reproduction. Yet, ironically, within discourses surrounding reproduction, the organic and the technical are often constructed as adapting to and balancing each other, literally serving a social and material function by aiding procreation (Braidotti 1994). Conversely, reproductive technologies are also viewed as a means of mastering the female body, pathologising pregnancy and the (in)ability to conceive as an illness, and, through intervention and cure, function as a specific means to control the female body. Whilst feminist critics have acknowledged the degree of essentialism that has crept into the debates surrounding women, reproductive technology and the body (see Cranny-Francis 1995; Braidotti 1994; Haraway 1991), they nevertheless regard the use of technology as a governing mechanism that turns the female body into 'a mosaic of detachable pieces' (Braidotti 1994: 47). Whilst a similar level of control is exerted over the female athlete, the ingestion of technology is not designed to facilitate or improve her culturally prescribed destiny of reproduction. On the contrary, it is specifically the threat to her reproductive ability, and her concomitant relocation from the private to the public sphere, that supports the prohibition of illicit performance enhancement. Furthermore, the administration of pharmaceuticals to otherwise healthy athletes, which contravenes the 'rational' management required to sustain the inherently weak female body, generates anxiety, perhaps over the prospect of a world where women take control of their bodies and their destinies, relegating child bearing to scientists and their test-tubes.

The potential disruption that can be wreaked upon healthy female bodies seems particularly concerning in light of reproduction, yet it is commensurate

100 *'Those girls with sideburns'*

with the more widespread apprehension of improving the body beyond what is 'normal'. Whilst Varda Burstyn (1999: 235) argues that 'the real issue with respect to steroids is not "cheating," but the injury these drugs do to athletes, and, via the symbolic significance of the athletes, to our values and ideals', when discussing steroid ab/use with regard to female athletes, the discussion takes on new and far-reaching imperatives. Not only does the hyper-normal female body challenge male domains and bodies by masculinising the female body (broader shoulders, defined muscularity and, further, larger clitoris, deeper voices, hirsuteness), the new, hyper-normal female body also has the potential to redefine social 'norms' and the boundaries of what constitutes femaleness. This process is activated when the body is visibly refashioned through the incorporation of performance technologies. The point at which 'the body ... encounters science, medicine, and commerce' (Burstyn 1999: 237) is the juncture at which the *monstrous feminine* is created and the media and public respond accordingly. The steroid-enhanced female is Frankenstein's bride incarnate and a further reminder of what rational, scientific and pharmacological experimentation can create. The muscular, bio-technical body of the steroid-enhanced woman becomes an abject figure who is an object of cultural fascination and horror. She is 'both exceptional and ominous' (Braidotti 1994: 85), she is empowered and eroticised, a site, like Frankenstein's monster, of desire and revulsion.

Killing Zoe

In Mary Shelley's novel *Frankenstein*, the emerging scientific reduction of the body to a series of body parts allowed her protagonist, Victor Frankenstein, to literally piece together, and, by harnessing the powers of electricity, bring to life, a male being, a creature, revealing an emerging cultural fear of science's ability to transcend humanity. Yet, it is when the monster desires a female partner, a companion with whom to share his sense of isolation and Otherness, that a more palpable horror is provoked. Whilst Dr Frankenstein agrees to 'make' a female monster, he destroys her before she can be brought to life, deliberately eliminating her potential to procreate a new race of monsters. Significantly, Frankenstein does not hold his male creature responsible for the propagation of a new and threatening species; it is the female he dreads, requiring the pre-emptive erasure of the monstrous feminine and her dark and malignant womb.

It is significant that the monstrous woman is both built and destroyed by Dr Frankenstein; she is not responsible for her creation or demise but rather is an object constructed and, ultimately, rejected by an external, masculine Other. The sporting equivalent is the female bodybuilder, who inspires a similar horror for their deliberately crafted, monstrous forms. Unlike Frankstein's monster, however, these athletes are not merely a threat to conventional gendered identities because their bodies exceed normative feminine physiques, but because the creation of their transgressive

'*Those girls with sideburns*' 101

forms is a deliberate act. They choose to become monsters. Whilst usually employed as a pejorative term, 'monster' derives from the Latin *monstrum* meaning 'portent or warning' (Bates 2005: 12). And just as Shelley's monsters warned against interfering with nature, so too does the monstrous female athlete foreshadow what can happen to those who seek to fabricate or bio-technically enhance human beings. These grotesque beings counsel against transgressing normative boundaries and threatening established gendered identities; they offer a glimpse at the eventual disintegration of not merely the abstract feminine but the actual female body. The fate of these monsters, and any who dare imitate them, is revealed through cautionary tales that gesture towards the consequences of disrupting nature.

One such monstrous warning appeared in the Australian sports magazine *Inside Sport* in 1996. 'Killing Zoe' featured British bodybuilder and former European women's bodybuilding champion, Zoe Warwick, who, after ingesting up to thirty times the normal therapeutic dose of steroids, took her own life as her body slowly disintegrated. Warwick redesigned her body, using rational techno-scientific means to achieve her goals, yet, in 'Killing Zoe', the initial emphasis is not on her triumphs, but on the horrific changes her body underwent as a result of her systematic steroid abuse. The images and text focused on the damage to health, the physical irregularities and the masculinising of women as a result of massive steroid abuse. The list of physical symptoms included cessation of menstruation, increase in size of her larynx, deepening voice, masculinising genitals, road rage, liver/pancreas failure, loss of hair, bloated limbs, fluid around the heart, failing eyesight, skin rashes, amnesia, loss of coordination, mood swings, fits, confirming the 'unnatural' status of testosterone supplements. Author Sally Jones (1996: 42) emphasises most explicitly the physical and emotional changes Warwick endured before her self-inflicted death in an attempt to warn other women about the 'hidden health risks of taking steroids' and the 'particular physical pitfalls which they face'. She further lists twenty-one medical side effects that plagued Warwick and then revealed an additional twenty-one health problems that are potentially caused by steroid abuse.

Jones (1996: 42) reports that as Warwick's body slowly shut down, she 'was in constant pain, requiring 17 different medications to simply live with any degree of normality'. Whilst the irony seems apparent, the medications used to restore her body to some semblance of 'normality' in this instance are considered essential, part of the therapeutic process. The drugs that she ingested for the purpose of enhancing her athletic prowess are described as having a 'shocking effect on health', 'horrific physical and psychological effects' (Jones 1996: 42), 'potentially deadly side-effects', 'appalling medical side-effects' (Jones 1996: 46). In other words, they irreparably altered the 'normally' functioning body. 'Killing Zoe' offered visual confirmation of the abnormal female corpus threatened, manipulated and, ultimately, doomed by the willing consumption of foreign substances. The monster was destroyed.

102 *'Those girls with sideburns'*

The plethora of side effects associated with extreme drug abuse are certainly worthy of concern, yet it is the overt masculinisation of the female body, the deliberate blurring of what constitutes 'femininity' and 'femaleness', that is deeply unsettling. According to Jones (1996: 40), Warwick's 'Adam's apple increased in size, her voice became as deep as a man's and her genitals became increasingly masculine. She described [to Jones] how her clitoris grew to resemble the head of a penis, and she developed a predatory sex drive'. The masculinisation of Warwick's body is catalogued and her transformation into a phallic woman related so as to evoke horror and sympathy in the reader.

Bodies, like Warwick's, not only traverse the border between male and female, but through the process of 'masculinisation', they reveal a range of social and cultural boundaries to be permeable (Haraway 1991). As Doug Aoki (1996: 5) suggests:

the female body-builder cannot look *exactly* like a man, inasmuch as she is still recognized as a woman and still articulated as a 'she' ... [but] it would be more accurate to say she looks *something like* a man, which has the necessary correlate that she looks *something like* a woman.

It is the liminality of these bodies that is challenging, more so when the transgressive form is liberated from not only the visible, but also the internal, markers of femininity. These bodies challenge cultural notions of a womanhood that is firmly marked by procreation, prompting many to wonder whether the appellation 'she' is relevant for, or applicable to, these bodies. Steroids are, however, more alarming than the physical manipulation of the external female body through, for example, extreme training or even cosmetic surgery, as they represent an intrinsic disruption of the very essence of 'femaleness', namely the hormones that regulate reproduction and make women women. Extreme physical activity may temporarily defer menstruation; however, amenorrhoeic bodies have the potential to return to 'normal', whilst hormonally manipulated bodies are feared to prohibit the restoration of 'femaleness' at some later date. In Warwick's case, her periods ceased altogether, and, as such, she became 'unwomaned' and 'unsexed', displaced to the margins of society.

Whilst Jones (1996) emphasises the extreme and serious health risks associated with steroid use for women, the real horror of the article can be located in the descriptions surrounding Warwick's overt masculinisation and her denial of maternity. In this discourse, the technologically adjusted female body is perceived as malformed and thus outside mainstream configurations of femininity, but Warwick is not simply an instance of Frankenstein's female monster brought to life, but the monstrous feminine as well. Like Dr Frankenstein, society rejects this monster by destroying it, yet at the same time allowing the male equivalent to survive. The horror associated with the masculinised female is destabilising and thus untenable.

By allowing scientific substances to invade and, thus, reconstruct her body, Warwick simultaneously denies herself maternity and a feminine appearance. Her clitoris, a signifier of female pleasure and procreation, is radically altered until she is both the castrated and phallic woman all in one (Creed 1993). She is hermaphroditic and androgenous: a liminal figure that redefines boundaries and sets new limits upon cultural and biological definitions of what constitutes femaleness and femininity. Warwick represents death to one version of the female through the ingestion of massive amounts of drugs, representing a 'grotesque series of bodily invasions' (Creed 1993: 205). She gives birth to another and becomes, in a sense, her own point of reference. Warwick needs a masculine Other neither for definition nor for procreation, for she has created her own body, suggesting her ability to spawn a new, similarly transgressive species. She is an abject body where meanings collapse, disturbing identity, system and order (Kristeva 1982). She is monstrous and indefinable, a fe/male who poses a fundamental threat to traditional social, sexual, political and cultural systems.

Saving Samantha

Whilst 'Killing Zoe' explicitly cautioned women about the dangers of chemically transgressing the bodily confines of femininity, other female athletes have been subject to alternative psychosocial and nationalist discourses that render them not freakish spectacles but rather falsely accused and in need of salvation. On these occasions, the female athlete is not regarded as monstrous and masculine, but rather as attractive, desirable and, above all, feminine. The media responses to Samantha Riley's 1995 drug offence reveals how the drug-tainted female body can be employed to recover a hegemonic femininity threatened by the dominant discourses of performance enhancement, drugs and masculinity. Within the same magazine that warned of the consequences of drug abuse, visual and textual techniques contrasted the visually, and thus intrinsically, grotesque bodies of Chinese swimmers, Zoe Warwick and other alleged drug takers with the petite, vulnerable and womanly physique of Riley (Magdalinski 2001a). Not only was Riley's femininity recuperated, but consumers additionally learned that appropriately feminine athletic bodies signify 'hard work' rather than illegal enhancement.

In the mid-1990s, Samantha Riley was one of Australia's most high-profile athletes, enjoying international success and recognition, the support of sponsors and favourable press coverage, when she tested positive to a banned narcotic analgesic, dextropropoxyphene, contained in a headache tablet she had taken at the 1995 World Short Course Championships. She escaped the mandatory two-year ban usually imposed by FINA, swimming's governing body, whilst her coach, Scott Volkers, who had administered the drug, was dealt a two-year ban on coaching that was later 'clarified' so that he could continue coaching in Australia. Despite revelations

104   *'Those girls with sideburns'*

that Riley had tested positive, she received overwhelming public support, led surprisingly by a national media that was notorious for savaging athletic drug abusers. Her pharmaceutical misdemeanour was represented as an 'inadvertent accident' (Jeffrey 1996a: 1) or a 'clumsy mistake' (Editorial 1996: 12), whilst Riley herself was reaffirmed as 'Australia's favourite sportswoman' (Jeffrey 1996a: 1), 'Australian swimming's golden girl' (Overington 1996: 1) and 'the sweet-smiling princess of Australian swimming' (McGregor 1996: 1). Reports and editorials testified that the substance was not a 'performance enhancer' (Editorial 1996: 12; Overington 1996: 1) and in fact was about to be removed from the banned list (Editorial 1996: 12; Jeffrey 1996b: 20). Editorials and sports commentators alike argued that Riley was deserving of a simple warning, for anything else 'would be a punishment out of proportion to the seriousness of the charge' (Editorial 1996: 12). As a result, Riley was redeemed as the epitome of the 'golden girl', particularly by *Inside Sport*, at a time when the magazine engaged in rigorous criticism of 'suspicious', usually foreign, athletes and performances, supported invariably by distorted images and partisan texts.

Riley's positive test led the March 1996 edition of *Inside Sport*, the same issue in which 'Killing Zoe' appeared, yet unlike Warwick, Riley was not presented as a flawed and monstrous female, teetering on the brink of internal collapse. Instead, editor Greg Hunter asked his readership 'Ever had the feeling that you've been wronged ... grossly misunderstood, or seriously compromised through no fault of your own?' Hunter (1996: 6) lamented the 'unfairness' of Riley's case and finally, to stave off criticisms of hypocrisy, he questioned how anyone could equate taking a 'headache pill' with 'systematic hormonal drug abuse'. Hunter's claims that Riley's positive drug test was less problematic than those of other high-profile athletes were supported through a series of feature articles, notations and visual imagery that offered 'evidence' that 'systematic hormonal manipulation' triggered significant physical transformations in the female body that were simply not apparent in Riley. Each of these contributions educated the audience about the 'real' issue of performance enhancement and cheating, as readers were taught to scrutinise and 'read' female bodies in order to identify and condemn those who 'appear' to be chemically boosted. Riley was thus carefully distinguished from a range of other drug takers through images and articles that confirmed her physique simply did not resemble the grotesque bodies of the hormonally manipulated. Once readers had faithfully learned which bodies were unnaturally enhanced, *Inside Sport* could safely profile Riley without generating confusion as to her chemical status (Alexander 1996).

Many of the visuals used to denote drug abuse throughout the magazine were of Chinese swimmers, who had emerged as a potent symbol of technological and chemical advancement, following the demise of the Soviet bloc and its highly scientised sports system. Their enormous, and unexpected, success in the early 1990s prompted many to suspect their rapid improvement was the result of drug abuse rather than a carefully constructed and implemented talent identification and training programme. Chinese bodies, stereotyped as fragile and petite, were demonised as 'grotesque' and 'unnatural', based on their appearance, which was thought to provide incontrovertible evidence of hormonal abuse (Carlile 1995).

Within the pages of *Inside Sport*, these bodies were further distorted, comically portrayed or artistically rendered to overemphasise their masculine, disproportionate and unnatural appearance. The images reinforced an inaccurate assumption that *all* drug use will have an androgenising effect. Not only are many synthetic steroids created without such side effects, but endurance-oriented performance enhancers, such as rEPO, do not alter the physical appearance of the athlete. Nevertheless, *Inside Sport* relied on stereotypes and altered images to ensure that Riley's womanly physique appeared visibly different from those of 'real' drug takers.

Accompanying Forbes Carlile's (1995) article 'Why the Chinese must not swim at Atlanta '96' was a large, digitally manipulated photograph of a Chinese swimmer, which had been deliberately widened to overemphasise the size of the athlete and her musculature. In this image, her shoulders are enormous, and she threatens to almost burst from the confines of her swimsuit. The identity of the swimmer is obscured by her bathing cap and goggles, but then her identity is immaterial, for she simply represents a faceless, centralised, undifferentiated system where individual needs are subsumed to the collective, an oft repeated Western stereotype of communism. In the May 1996 issue, a 'Hall of Fame' cartoon, by *Inside Sport* regular Loebecke, depicts Riley receiving a gold medal on the victory dais, flanked on either side by large, chiselled and, again, unidentified Chinese swimmers. Riley's face is drawn in detail and is thus easily recognised; the Chinese swimmers by contrast have basic features that identify their ethnicity, but nothing further. Again, their identity is inconsequential. These swimmers are almost double Riley's size, suggesting that their bodies must have been chemically altered to reach such massive proportions and that Riley herself is a 'normal' woman, clearly in proportion. Riley is clutching her gold medal and a bunch of wattle flowers, perhaps indicating a desired scene at a future Olympic Games. One Chinese swimmer gingerly grips a similar bunch of flowers between her enlarged thumb and forefinger in one hand and peers at a bronze medal held in the other.

The image of an unidentified, enlarged Chinese body is reinforced in 'The Last Race', written by John Leonard, Executive Director of the American Swimming Coaches Association, which appears in the same issue. Chinese athletes are artistically rendered, dominated by a large image of the Chinese national flag. A single unidentifiable female swimmer in a swimsuit, her shoulders wider than her hips, stands on the dais flanked by a coach in a tracksuit and a man in a white lab coat, both of whom are smaller than the swimmer. All around the platform hundreds of uniformly attired men and women look on. None smile; men are almost indistinguishable from women. The only orator is the scientist. The undifferentiated mass of people ('they all look the same'), and the unidentified swimmer points towards the anonymity of systematic drug abuse and of the communist sports system as a whole. If one is caught, then another will simply step forward to take their place.

To confirm Riley's innocence, the reader needed to participate in the examination of her body, assessing the physical dimension for any evidence of 'unnatural androgeny' and contrasting it with those of 'confirmed' drug cheats. To this end, the July 1996 issue of *Inside Sport* included an extensive feature article outlining Riley's training methods, her personality and her relationship with her coach and family, whilst mentioning the positive drug test only briefly (Alexander 1996). The article concentrated particularly on Riley's training regime, methods, stroke development and coaching style, demonstrating her hard work, discipline and commitment to swimming, confirming, at the same time, that her success is due to factors other than chemicals. Hers is depicted as a finely tuned body that relies on coach Scott Volkers' input. Riley's stroke is 'relentlessly honed to match the prototype model in Volkers' mind that he has taught her to *hear* when she's in rhythm' (Alexander 1996: 102). Her body is thus deemed fragile, in need of the delicate handling that can only be provided by the masculine Other, and Volkers is claimed as crucial for her success, whilst Riley remains dependent on his support.

Finally, Riley is presented as a woman, as a potential mother type and as feminine. Her PR agent gushed 'I just think she's a princess'; her coach argued 'She's your ideal woman, the sort of girl you'd want for your daughter, your son's wife, your friend. She's just a real lady.' Her subjectivity is defined by the (absent) men in her life, particularly in the father/coach role assumed by Volkers. Riley is depicted as dependent on his advice, nurturing and guidance for success reinforced by the camera angles that present Riley as small and vulnerable, her frail body in need of protection. By restoring her femininity through visual depictions of her 'normal' body, slim and appropriately proportioned, and her dependence on men for her identity, she is cast firmly as *female*, which provides the conclusive evidence of her innocence.

Conclusion

As a patriarchal institution, it is clear that sport contributes to the maintenance of essentialised gender categories. Juxtaposed against the strength and vitality of the male body, the female body is positioned as weak, soft and less physically capable. As such, their entry into the masculine arena of sport was regarded as an explicit intrusion that disrupted the boundaries that demarcated male from female. Gradually, however, women have been accepted as athletes, particularly in those events that display poise and grace, less so in those that require brute strength, muscularity and power. Nevertheless, a range of measures has ensured that an essentialised 'femininity' is foregrounded, both on and off the field, often at the expense of female athletes' physicality. The media, for example, have been instrumental in affirming 'heterosexy' images of women that conform to mainstream expectations and stereotypes to the extent that female athletes are necessarily presented as women first and athletes second.

Yet these representations are not fixed, as normative feminine ideals are fractured by the incursion of performance technologies that blur the boundaries between male and female. In particular, the excessive training and ingestion of substances to produce bodies that closely resemble those of men is regarded essentially as a corruption of the 'natural' female body, and concerted efforts are made to render these bodies 'freakish' and return them to a more acceptable, and desirable, femininity. This is particularly evident in female bodybuilding, where the construction of hard, muscle-bound, 'masculine' bodies so deeply disturbs heterosexual feminine norms, that the sport's own regulating body has decreed that female competitors must specifically embody 'femininity'. The 'systematic hormonal manipulation' of the female body creates monsters, androgenous women, whose bodies can only be reclaimed through the application of feminine accoutrements, rendering their external appearance 'softer' and thus more palatable to the mainstream observer. It is clear that, in essence, those technologies that manipulate the body internally or at the cellular level confound our very understanding of gender, rendering a strict dichotomy obsolete as bodies have the potential to shift between the two.

Although most substances manipulate the body internally, the case studies examined in this chapter suggest that detecting the use of unauthorised means of enhancement may be as simple as examining the surface of the body. Bodies that conform to the ideal feminine shape are understood to be 'natural', womanly and acceptable, whilst those that resemble men are rejected as artificially and unnaturally manipulated. As such, an athlete's physical dimensions and the degree to which they deviate from a predetermined, cultural standard reveals the extent to which they are tainted. The 'masculine' and ultimately flawed body of Zoe Warwick is sharply contrasted against that of Samantha Riley, who was presented as beautiful, desirable and, above all, feminine. The hideous distortions of Chinese swimmers were juxtaposed against the almost girlish bodies and demeanours of Australian competitors. In each example, the former is confirmed as corrupted and androgenised, whilst the latter is accepted as undeniably innocent and natural. Clearly, the application of performance technologies to the human body generates concern over issues of nature and artifice. Those that manipulate the body internally confound essentialist gendered identities, yet technologies that are applied to the body's exterior offer only temporary disruptions. In these instances, the body's ability to draw upon technology without specifically embodying it seems a more reassuring approach, as evidenced by the rapid embrace of prosthetic technologies such as the Fastskin swimsuit. For female athletes, these applications are particularly desirable as they facilitate their entry into the 'masculine arena' with a body temporarily modified, whilst at the same time, allowing their 'femininity' to remain apparent. The following chapter examines technologies that are layered upon or attached to the body to create a temporarily enhanced version that does not risk permanent alteration and allows bodies to return easily, and promptly, to their 'natural' state.

7 Enhancing the body from without
Artificial skins and other prosthetics

Introduction

The tears flowed freely when Laure Manaudou finished third in the 400m freestyle at the French Olympic Trials in April 2008. As she left the pool, clothed in last season's Arena swimsuit, Manaudou valiantly searched for reasons for her first loss in this, her pet event, in nearly four years. Rather than considering her form, disrupted preparation or even the emotional stress caused by the release of unauthorised nude photographs, the Frenchwoman set her sights, and her discontent, firmly on the seamless, ultrasonically welded, corseted contours of Speedo's new Fastskin LZR Racer.

The release of this latest elite swimming costume was met, unsurprisingly, by international controversy. Dismissed as 'technological' or 'swimsuit doping', and even 'doping on a hanger' (Lord 2008), swimmers, coaches and journalists revisited the moral panic that arose in 2000, when Speedo first revealed its redesigned racing suits. Appearing more nineteenth than twenty-first century, the neck-to-ankle outfits initially caused an outcry for the promises they made to enhance an athlete's performance in the pool, and, as a result, Fastskin was not unanimously accepted by the international swimming community. Athletes, coaches and administrators were either fervently in favour of the new design or questioned its legality in the face of FINA's, the international governing body, rules that stated no 'device' that aids 'speed, buoyancy or endurance' may be used (Hiestand 2000: 10C). Concerns about the suit broadly revolved around issues of 'natural' versus 'unnatural' enhancement and replicated, in style, discussions throughout the 1980s and 1990s about performance enhancing drugs.

Whilst 'skins', in their various guises, are applied to the body to effect an improved performance, other technologies with more specific functional purposes can also be attached to competitors. Athletes with missing limbs, for example, are retrofitted with artificial replacements to enable their participation in events designed for bodies with full mobility and functionality. Amputees can affix 'running feet', swimmers can replace their missing hands with 'fins' and those with limited lower body function can race in a custom-designed chair. Whilst some may argue that these 'devices' provide an 'enhancement' to

110 Enhancing the body from without

the disabled athlete, they have not, until recently, been subject to the same level of controversy as those applied to the able-bodied athlete.

Given concerns about 'unnatural' enhancement in sport, is may seem extraordinary that both Fastskin and prosthetic devices are, to a large degree, embraced by the sports community as necessary and, indeed, desirable technologies. Whilst the artificiality of both are clearly apparent – prosthetic limbs are not designed to resemble the fleshy original and the swimsuits are not fashioned after the human sheath – they are nevertheless regarded as a kind of natural artifice: a suitable and acceptable stand-in for the real thing rather than an inappropriate extension of the body's natural capacity. Each of these technologies clearly offers competitive advantages to the user; an amputee would certainly be incapable of running a 200m race without a prosthetic leg, whilst swimmers hope to shave split seconds off their times costumed in an artificial skin. Yet neither is regarded universally as an illegal enhancement, and is instead welcomed as suitable applications of technology to the exercising body. Their status as prosthetic devices, supplements that add to, but do not fully integrate with, the body, allows these technologies to reside comfortably alongside the body without any threat to its integrity or to the legitimacy of the resulting performance.

Despite the acceptance of both, there is, nevertheless, a material difference between wearing various 'skins' and affixing replacement limbs or utilising racing chairs, for 'enhancing what is already nearly perfect and repairing what is seriously damaged are qualitatively different undertakings' (Hood 2005). The former offers the wearer an advantage over their competitors, whilst the latter provides the very means to compete. In this instance, according to Shilling (2005: 178), the body is not simply enhanced, because prosthetic limbs and similar technologies are thought to 'restore rather than extend people's capacities', and are thus less confronting than those that seek to go beyond what the 'natural' body is capable of. Technologies that mimic the form and function of missing limbs or a heart, for example, do not confound our understanding of the body, whilst the replacement of body parts by higher order technologies (The Bionic Man/Terminator) provide a fearful foray into the realm of science fiction's cyborg. Athletes who utilise artificial limbs are not usually conceived as 'unnaturally' enhancing their bodies, and are not vilified in the same way as athletes who take drugs, as long as they remain within the confines of their own arena. Instead, the use of even radically enhancing prostheses that mimic the movement of wild cats, for example, can still be regarded as returning the body to a state of 'normal functioning'. Yet, as these artificial appendages become more advanced and augmented with bionics, there is the potential for them to be regarded as more than simply bodily restoration, reaching a point where they cease enabling participation and begin producing performances beyond the expected physical capacity of the athlete.

Unlike performance enhancing substances, apparel or prosthetics provoke fewer concerns that the boundary between nature and artifice is being irreconcilably blurred. Whilst the ingestion of banned pharmaceuticals is thought to disrupt the purity of the athletic body, the application of technologies to its surface does not threaten the body's integrity in the same way. It would seem that the very externality of these devices confirms the discrete athletic body as legitimate and, above all, natural. In a sense, then, the purity of the body is ensured by the stability of its exterior border, the site where inside and out is established, where the body simultaneously begins and ends: its skin. Protecting the integrity of the skin is paramount, for skin represents the border between outside and in (Connor 2004). It is simultaneously a site of containment, the physical casing that prevents our body from falling apart and a barrier preventing contamination from without. As a recent British advertisement for petroleum jelly confirms: 'skin is amazing ... it's your waterproof barrier. A defence against disease' (Vaseline 2007). Within the context of sport, skin, then, becomes the final line of defence in the vigilant maintenance of an athlete's purity, but may also conceal the chemical and technological turbulence within. Occasionally though, the skin is insufficient to mask the 'true' nature of the body it encases and reveals the inner workings of the body. At the same time, the surface of the body may be marked from the outside, as subjectivities are inscribed onto the body. Skin, in this sense, functions as a kind of tabula rasa that is filled with the changing ideological frames of the culture in which the body finds itself (Benthien 2002). The application of alternative skins onto the body is thus significant, as it not only covers the body's own exterior boundary but delivers an additional surface that is ideologically laden.

This chapter contrasts the application of external technologies to the surfaces of athletes with concerns about the material integrity of the body. Using Fastskin and athletic prostheses as examples, it probes fears of bodily penetration that reside in efforts to maintain a natural, pure sporting body through the application of artificial body parts to 'optimise' sporting performance. It offers insight into the conception of technologies that are applied to the surface, rather than ingested into the body. Finally, it examines the insecure relationship between the pure body and the technologically enhanced cyborg as evidenced through the potential dissolution of borders between able-bodied and disabled sport.

Wearable skins

In many respects, swimming appears to be an 'authentic' sport that simply requires athletes to churn through the water, pitting their bodies against nature's elements. Traditionally immune from the technological advances and attendant controversies that have plagued other elite sports such as cycling and athletics, swimming has instead offered a forum where performance seems to be a pure 'human v water contest' (Brown 2008), where swimmers are 'equal' when they strike the water, with only 'them, a thin strip of [swimsuit] and the wall up the other end' to help determine the

112   Enhancing the body from without

winner (Colman 2000: 159). The swimmer's body, increasingly exposed as the rules of modesty relaxed and the laws of physics were applied, visibly confirmed that the performance was untainted. Of course, the reality is certainly different as swimming has experienced extensive technological innovation. Through the development of, for example, low wash lane dividers, deep gutters that control turbulence, moveable floors and bulkheads that adjust the depth and length of a pool, uniform recirculation of water, temperature regulation and air and lighting systems (Masters 2007), 'fast' pools are modified and adapted to ensure that the environment's impact on performance is negligible. Similarly, swimmers' bodies are technologically constructed as they are biomechanically, physiologically and psychologically analysed and modified to maximise their output. Nevertheless, in the popular mind, technology first seemed to intrude into swimming when Speedo released its Fastskin swimsuit, a radical outfit that was applied directly and visibly to the swimmer's body with the sole purpose of improving performance.

The Fastskin controversy initially began in late 1999 when it was revealed that elite swimmers had begun testing Speedo's new racing costume, described simply as an 'evolution' of the company's Aquablade swimsuit that had been released, and approved, just prior to the 1996 Atlanta Olympics (Cowley 1999). Whilst many were initially impressed with the design and the potential to gain a competitive advantage over their rivals, others remained unconvinced. Debate raged amongst coaches, athletes, administrators and journalists alike in a moral panic that was largely founded on the same concerns about the body, the level playing field and the integrity of sport that had dominated public discussion of elite performance sport throughout the 1990s (Magdalinski 2000c). In short, there was confusion about which side of the nature/artifice binary this 'device' should reside, a debate that was reignited with the release of Speedo's Fastskin LZR Racer in 2008.

On both occasions, 'fairness' emerged as a critical issue, with a number of leading swimmers and coaches arguing that the bodysuits were simply 'unfair', whilst others were more cautious, fearing legal challenges from swimmers who did not wear the new technology. Few, however, were essentially concerned with idealistic notions of 'fair play' or with ethical concerns about a swimsuit that promised an advantage to its wearer. Swimmers were certainly keen to obtain these suits in order to secure an edge over their competitors, but when open access to customised suits was in doubt, only then were many alarmed at the possible violation of sport's 'level playing field'. USA Swimming initially banned the use of Fastskin suits at their 2000 National Trials, citing 'fairness to all participants' rather than a concern over technology, and US swimmer Lenny Krayzelburg agreed suggesting, confusingly, that 'the fair way to make the Olympic team is everyone racing on even ground' (*Sports Illustrated* 2000). Australian coach Don Talbot hedged his bets, indicating that it might be unfair if all athletes

Enhancing the body from without 113

were not entitled to this swimwear, but nevertheless confirmed that 'if there is an advantage we want it' (Lingard 1999).

Although the futuristic design of Speedo's 2008 version prompted greater discussion about the role of technology in swimming, it is significant that the primary concern about fairness again focused on the 'level playing field' in terms of access. To this end, Swimming Canada forbade the use of the reengineered suits in individual events at their national trials (Longley 2008), and the Italian national body, contracted to a rival sportswear company, similarly prohibited Speedo's swimwear. Whilst some certainly decried the prohibitive cost of the new suits and the creation of 'haves' and 'have-nots' in the sport, much as they did in 2000 (FitzSimons 2008; Lord 2008), this time there appeared to be more anxiety about the impact that exclusive sponsorship deals would have on the swimmers' ability to acquire the new technology (Brown 2008; Linnell 2008). The head of French Swimming, Claude Fauquet, suggested that 'the inability of certain partners to supply equipment to athletes creates unfair situations' (Linnell 2008), as coaches around the world encouraged athletes to abandon 'the money' in favour of 'the gold medal' (Lord 2008). Athletes agreed that 'the choice ... between Olympic success or lucrative rival sponsorships' was a 'no-brainer' (Williams 2008), and rather than waiting impatiently for their sponsor to match the performance promises of Speedo's latest offering, several swimmers announced their decision to swim in the Fastskin LZR. South Africa's swimming captain, Gerhard Zandberg, declared he was 'not going to sacrifice performance' and noted that 'Olympic gold is worth much more' than the monetary fine he faced from his sponsor (*Sports Illustrated* 2008), whilst Frenchman Fabien Gilot declared his intention to switch on the basis that he did not 'work hard to be beaten by technology' (Williams 2008).

Although intense debate is reignited each time a new design is released, these typically calm once gold medals and world records, particularly in an Olympic year, are secured. As such, few have questioned the broader relationship between sport and technology and what it may signify within the context of Fastskin. One journalist wondered about the legitimacy of an outcome when results are 'divided by technological rather than athletic prowess' (Le Grand 2000). Whilst content to accept the Fastskin advantage, Talbot was also certain that he did not 'want to see technology becoming the basis on which you win and not the ability of an athlete' (Lingard 1999). Some athletes did not 'fear that credit for ... future achievements would be attributed to the suit rather than to [their] performance', some did not want 'the suits to take the credit for their hard training', whilst others chose not to risk such criticism and elected to contest their sport 'unassisted' (Jeffrey 2000). Journalist Peta Bee (2004) was more forthright in her suggestion that the 'unfair advantage' gained through the suits was 'comparable with taking an illegal substance', and further confirmed her position that 'at the elite level, sports competition is almost as much a battle of technological expertise amongst sports manufacturers as it is of human endeavour' (Bee 2008).

114 *Enhancing the body from without*

Despite isolated efforts to link Fastskin technology with performance enhancing drugs, the fundamental concept of the suits has not been interrogated in the same way that chemical or hormonal manipulation regularly is. Although designed to enhance athletic performance by variously reducing drag and assisting 'grip' in the water, the swimwear has been dissociated from drugs through the construction of a clear distinction between the internal actions of drugs and the external application of suits. As such, Fastskin is typically depicted as a function-specific enhancement of the body's 'natural' ability and form rather than a molecular, and therefore, 'unnatural' bodily manipulation. Speedo confirms the centrality of the body in its mission to 'only focus on the management of existing forces' to 'more effectively make use of the talents an athlete already has' (Speedo 2006a). Fastskin is thus designed to deliver wearers an 'optimum streamlined shape' to 'reduce muscle oscillation and skin vibration' (Speedo 2008a) thereby 'enabling them to cut through the water with more speed and agility' (Speedo 2008b). Fastskin represents a temporary addition to the athlete that does not contaminate the natural body, nor transgress its borders. The spectator is taught to recognise it as a transient addendum: the suits are clearly external, they obviously do not aesthetically resemble human skin and, as such, do not pretend to the category of 'natural'. The Fastskin bodysuit and its performance enhancing potential are thereby presented and legitimated as an acceptable application of human scientific endeavour to the improvement of athletic achievement.

Whilst the suits arguably improve performance, the mode of that enhancement is typically rationalised as maximising natural potential. Even though they are regarded as a performance technology, it is made clear that the suits themselves do not project swimmers through the water; the athletes are still fundamentally responsible for their own performance and still require vigilant physical discipline in order to succeed. When Ian Thorpe noted that his new swimsuit 'optimised' rather than 'enhanced' his performance (Channel 10 2000), he tacitly acknowledged the role of technology in his athletic successes, yet at the same time resituated the body squarely in the centre of his performance. He admitted that technology supports his body but that ultimately it is his body that performs. The fact that he was clear to state that the suit did not 'enhance' his performance confirms that his racing attire was to be understood as no more than an aid, and certainly not the driving force behind his achievements. Other swimmers confirm that 'suits are suits' and 'don't perform miracles' (Dillman 2008), whereas others are more circumspect in their assessment. US swimmer Michael Phelps certainly suggests that the Fastskin suit merely 'enables' him to 'swim at [his] best', but later qualifies that the costume will 'contribute to [his] overall performance' (Speedo 2006b), and Australian Grant Hackett similarly insists that the athletes themselves 'deserve credit' for their 'hard work' before admitting that 'of course, the suit contributes to performance. That's why they are there' (*Sports Illustrated* 2008).

Enhancing the body from without   115

Communicating Fastskin as a 'natural' technology that simply heightens a swimmer's own natural (trained) ability is critical. To this end, the manufacturer's media releases and product descriptions have carefully linked the suits to a swimmer's physical attributes and stress the close relationship between the swimwear and natural products from the animal kingdom. The suits are 'like a second skin' (Lingard 1999); the fabric is said to 'mimic shark skin' (Purcell and Moore 2000) and is 'specifically designed to match ridges on a shark's skin' with 'panels and seams [to] increase co-ordination of muscles', inner forearms that 'feature gripper fabric ... that mimics skin', and the suit allegedly reduces 'muscle vibrations, increasing energy efficiency and limiting fatigue' (Colman 2000). In other words, it produces a superior version of the human body without the sinister overtones of performance enhancing drugs, though with a curious cross-reference to the predatory shark. In this way, Fastskin can be framed as a legitimate technology, one that helps the body to perform more efficiently, as indeed some drugs also do. But its acceptability resides in its externality. It can be donned and cast off as needed, thus the hyperhuman, the more efficient body, does not threaten to cross from the confines of the playing field and challenge established bodily norms. The temporarily grotesque body is contained, in contrast to the permanently altered body, manipulated from within. Fastskin suits do not seek to transform the body, merely assist, and, as such, are effortlessly incorporated into the modulating 'level playing field'.

As discussed, the horror of the hyperhuman body is particularly acute when female athletes threaten to exceed normative dimensions and begin to resemble the proportions of their male counterparts. As evidenced by bodybuilder Zoe Warwick, this is most apparent when their bodies are internally augmented. The impermanence of the external Fastskin, however, effectively extends female athletes a means to access a more efficient athletic body, by 'wearing' a masculine body that does not irreparably alter their essentialised femininity (Budd 1997: 67). It provides something of a masculine drag, whereby the female body is momentarily transgenderised. Drag is necessarily impermanent, a temporary external guise that mimics the opposite sex through hyper-performance and exaggerated, gendered attributes. The body is not permanently altered as through transsexualism, thus the performance is transitory, gesturing to the fluidity of gendered signifiers (Butler 1993). Despite the external layers, the audience remains aware that what lies beneath is a differently sexed body. With the Fastskin, a masculinised body can be slipped on or discarded at will, providing female athletes an opportunity to avoid permanent androgeny, allowing their bodies to conform to feminine norms so they can safely enter the masculine arena of sport. Despite her enhanced contours, the audience is reassured that a 'real' woman hides beneath her provisional skin. *Sports Illustrated*'s August 2000 photograph of a topless US swimmer Jenny Thompson, wearing little more than patriotic hotpants and red ankle boots, contrasted with the aggressive figure she cut in her Fastskin, confirming that underneath was an attractive,

116 *Enhancing the body from without*

feminine physique that in no way could have been hormonally modified (McCallum 2000). Her transformation from strong, efficient and powerful athlete to heterosexually desirable cover girl and back again confirms that her athletic dress offers a fluid, though temporary slide, between gendered signifiers.

Dressing in a faster skin

It is not surprising that Fastskin operates as a meaningful garment beyond its functional application, for dress, more broadly, is more than simple decoration. It communicates broader political and social concerns, gestures towards the wearer's class and occupation and reveals much about the significance of the body and the location of its boundaries within society (Entwistle 2001; Evans *et al.* 1998). It is thus curious that dress, by contrast, has been noticeably absent from studies of the body until recently, given that a body noticeably absent dress is assuredly noticeable. Indeed, studies on the body cannot help but consider that which clothes it, for dress 'embellishes' a body, offering layers of meanings through each fold of the fabric and carefully placed stitch. Dress 'transform[s] flesh into something recognizable and meaningful' (Entwistle 2001: 33), yet even within sports studies where the body is primary and its clothing functional, sporting apparel has been discussed more rigorously in terms of its economic production and distribution rather than in its role as symbolic marker (Benzecry 2008; see also Rothenberg-Aalami 2004). This is certainly an area that requires more attention, given that wearing a uniform alters an athlete from individual to representative of a broader community. Sporting a national uniform, for example, locates the athlete within identifiable political and ideological structures; adorning the body in a specific brand reveals the athlete's economic arrangements and corporate loyalties; and, for the purposes of this chapter, wearing a particular swimsuit can be read as part of a gendered, performance-oriented and technologised endeavour that uncomfortably dwells within dominant frames of amateurist fair play.

But Fastskin is more than mere dress, it is self-consciously a skin, the first to embed the body's largest organ in its name. No longer simply a bodysuit, FSII was renamed a 'bodyskin', gesturing directly to its role as an artificial sheath. The notion of a 'fast' skin suggests that one's own human skin is slow, perhaps cumbersome, certainly inadequate for the performances demanded of elite swimmers or, indeed, other athletes, who can now access a wide range of wearable Skins™. Whilst these artificial skins may structurally resemble the body's own covering, snugly following the contours of the wearer, it is nevertheless not inconsequential that they are likened to skin. Skin is not simply a biological casing that contains the body's internal components and processes. As the outermost layer, it is a kind of 'corporeal dress', the site where 'boundary negotiations' are staged (Benthien 2002: vii, ix). As such, skin is the body's most basic and visible border, a covering that symbolically and physically delimits the body, demarcating its edges, ensuring its integrity (Benthien 2002). Skin is a deliberately malleable surface, one that is neither fixed biologically nor metaphorically. As an organic reality, skin shifts and adjusts as the body moves, ages and cracks with time, colours, fades, erupts and peels. It can be flayed, cut, scarred and pierced, tattooed, stretched and decorated. Skin is also a fluid symbol, at different times a solid, impenetrable boundary, at others a porous, insecure margin. It is essentially incomplete, for various openings allow the body to ingest sustenance or rid itself of waste (Kristeva 1982). Skin thus becomes a site of material exchange between the inner and the outer, betwixt the pure and the potential contaminant, disrupting the integrity of the body and exposing it to invasion from without. This is the interface that technology, for example, can traverse, irreparably altering the body and triggering apprehension about its authenticity.

Not only vulnerable to external threats, skin also conceals the body's interior, provoking anxiety about disruptions that might otherwise remain hidden (Connor 2004). Like golf courses, where the 'natural' facade obscures a technological network, so too skin may provide a 'natural' landscape that masks the toxicity of the body underneath (Magdalinski 2004). Yet despite its ability to conceal, skin has paradoxically been understood as a 'mirror of the soul', the surface upon which the 'invisible inside' is projected (Benthien 2002: ix), and, as such, can be closely examined for evidence of internal disorder or contamination. Skin that is stretched beyond appropriate proportions may indicate hormonal tampering. The distended, 'ripped' form of the bodybuilder, for example, barely contains the hypertrophied musculature underneath; the thick veins visible just below a surface denuded of subcutaneous fat, as well as the prominent striated muscle – both expose an 'unnatural' development. Eruptions on the skin, and particularly the face, attest to the lethal brew simmering below the surface, which occasionally bursts through the body's outermost layers to betray its presence.

Enhanced bodies, and thus performances, can, however, be generated through the application of new, faster, drier or more streamlined skins; technological alternatives that happily eliminate any need for irreversible physical adaptations. Fastskin, Skins^{TM}, XD skin^{TM} or any of the other 'skin suits' offer athletes a secondary membrane that encases the body, reinforcing the body's borders and providing an additional armour to protect against contamination from outside. The technology is thus visibly resident on the skin, rather than beneath it, and unlike real skin, there is no need to permanently graft the artificial variety onto the body. It is deliberately and delightfully impermanent.

Whilst the impermanence of artificial skins contrasts starkly with the intransience of the body's own skin, they nevertheless bear surfaces that are as rich with meaning as the original. It is upon skin, whether real or synthetic, that various cultural, social, gendered and other ideologies are inscribed.

118   *Enhancing the body from without*

From deliberate and permanent markings through to temporary adornments of clothing, make-up and jewellery, identities are written and communicated on and through the skin (Featherstone *et al.* 1991). The artificial, faster skin is similarly marked with subjectivities, including gender or ethnicity. Although the audience may be aware of the sexed body underneath, Fastskin suits are themselves gendered, ensuring that masculine and feminine bodies remain visible and easily identified, even whilst armoured in suits, caps and goggles. Fastskins are produced with male and female variations; the female Fastskin emphasises a normative feminine body, boasting delicate panelling that contours an assumed hourglass figure, whilst the male version presents a more streamlined appearance with straighter and bolder lines. Furthermore, the suits themselves have become emblematic of the dominant technological discourses that underpin Western conceptions of elite sport, initially functioning importantly as a civilising technology, highlighting the binary and hierarchical relationship between oriental and occidental sporting bodies and providing a moment in which the technologically advanced West was mirrored against the primitive Other.

Fastskin as civilising tool

During the 100m swimming heats at the Sydney 2000 Olympic Games, Equatorial Guinean swimmer Eric Moussambani garnered international attention as he struggled to complete his heat alone, after his two competitors were disqualified for false starts. Moussambani finished his race over one minute slower than eventual gold medallist Pieter van den Hoogenband, and the resulting media circus drew upon colonial and paternalist discourses to present Moussambani as an oddity who somehow embodied the 'true' meaning of Olympism (Nauright and Magdalinski 2003). Moussambani's questionable swimming style was reflected in his choice of swimwear. Unlike the full-length Fastskins worn by more 'serious' competitors, Moussambani, who was without access to this device, was left wearing little more than a loincloth, an 'old-fashioned' pair of Speedos, in which his near-nakedness was plainly visible to the spectator.

Whilst flesh unadorned may on one level signify the authentic body (Benthien 2002), on the other, the naked body has been read as 'lacking or unfinished' (Evans *et al.* 1998: 3). Moussambani's exposed flesh was, in essence, a reminder of his unsophisticated technique, whilst his underdeveloped body visibly conflicted with the strong, fit, white male bodies of Western swimmers, revealing not just a lack of preparation and training for this event, but, indeed, any rational approach to modifying the body. Richard Dyer (1997: 165) suggests that

> the built body and the imperial enterprise are analogous. The built body sees the body as submitted to and glorified by the planning and ambition of the mind; colonial worlds are likewise represented as

Enhancing the body from without   119

inchoate terrain needing the skill, sense and vision of the coloniser to be brought to order.

Moussambani's body needed to be 'brought to order', to be landscaped in accordance with Western ideals about masculine athleticism and elite Olympic performance. To this end, Moussambani was presented with a Fastskin suit at a Speedo press conference. He was paraded around in his technologically progressive outfit for a photo shoot, genuinely expressing his desire to compete at the 2004 Athens Olympics. Accepting the Fastskin was the first step towards Moussambani's dream of competing on an even par with the other swimmers and was tacit acknowledgment that his own near-nakedness symbolised a primitive, and thus inappropriate, state. The attention afforded Moussambani demonstrates the totalising force of modern sport incorporating the exotic Other into a Western hegemonic, sportised body culture. His donning of the suit represented the colonisation of the 'primitive' form with civilising technological accoutrements, in a subtle, rather than aggressive, act of imperialism.

The use of clothing as a colonial disciplining technology is well established (Cohn 1989). Dress was considered to be a marker of both civility and morality, and indigenous bodies were taught to perform Europeanness through the adoption of appropriate clothing. Veit Erlmann (1998: 126) argues that: 'By restyling the outer shell of the "heathen", [European missionaries] reasoned, they would reform and salvage the inner self of the newly converted'. Nakedness signified an essential primitive state, whilst clothing demarcated European cultural and moral superiority. Yet, at the same time, nineteenth-century photographers, often on the instruction of ethnographers, took images of naked indigenous bodies 'so that the peculiarity of various races within the British colonies could be recorded' (Skotnes 2001: 311). In novels, such as *Robinson Crusoe*, Roxann Wheeler (1995) suggests that natives were clearly defined by their bodies whilst Europeans were recognised by their clothing. Indeed, there was a 'symbolic value of clothing as a sign of difference from savages' (Wheeler 1995: 860), a 'social skin' as Erlmann (1998: 127) describes. In this way, the Fastskin suit was at once a signifier of difference between Western athletes and Moussambani as well as a disciplining technology that provided the African swimmer with an entrée into the Western world of Olympic sport.

Just as female swimmers could dress in a figurative masculine sheath, Moussambani's embrace of the bodysuit allowed him, temporarily, to 'restyle' his own body and assume the body of Western technological progress. This can only be, however, momentary, for the instant he removes the 'social skin', his colonial drag, he is once again revealed as African, as primitive and as simply imitative of the Western cultural norm. It is clear, then, that the colonialised Other is governed by contradictory demands: they must be mimetically identical at the same time they remain totally other (Bhabha 1984). They are invited to civilise, to embrace technological prowess,

120   *Enhancing the body from without*

but through public, spectacular failures are ultimately revealed to be nothing more than imitations of the 'real' thing. Of course, as Michael Taussig (1993: 250) argues, the relationship between mimesis and alterity is not unidirectional and 'the power of the copy to influence what it is a copy of' suggests that mimicking the colonial Other may function as a form of cultural resistance, a moment where the Self can appropriate some measure of power within the colonial order. Moussambani dreams of being like the Australian or American swimmers, but he is told that 'only in his dreams' will he be able to get even near the victory dais by the next Olympics. He dreams of winning an Olympic medal, when the complicit 'we' already know that he is a mere moment, a passing fad, a useful tool in the reestablishment of Olympic values. When he wears a Fastskin suit, he imitates the other swimmers, but 'we' all know that he is not, and never will be, the other swimmers. Like the designer rip-offs that flood markets all over the developing world, Moussambani, and the primitive world he signifies, can only be a poor imitation of the 'genuine' Western article.

Athletic prosthetics

Just as the Fastskin swimsuit allowed Moussambani to temporarily resemble his Western competitors, some athletes attach devices to their bodies to replicate as far as possible the 'normally' functioning body. Whilst prosthetics were initially designed to resemble the missing limb, within the context of elite performance sport, aesthetic congruence has been superseded by functionality and performance, with a host of technological innovations, including artificial arms, hands, legs, feet and other equipment, providing the opportunity to participate in a variety of recreational and elite sports. Sports are adapted to suit the varying abilities of their participants, and alternative athletic forms emerge where body and machine are fused to create a kind of cyborg competitor. New generation technologies are now creating devices that bear little visual relationship to the body part they replace, whilst the bionic man of science fiction materialises on the para-sporting field through the use of cybernetic and bionic components. Whilst some of these advanced prosthetics prompt speculation about whether science has exceeded the boundaries of the natural body, and, by association, sport, it is significant that despite intensive research and engineering to produce these devices, technological augmentation of the disabled body is not typically rejected as an inappropriate 'enhancement'. Instead, the application of such technologies is framed as 'restoring' the body to something approaching 'normal' rather than extending them beyond normal (Shilling 2005); in other words, 'deficient' bodies are returned to a neutral position through the use of various technologies, the missing or damaged parts replaced, readying the athlete for combat in the sporting arena.

The idea of 'restoring' bodies with disabilities is not an uncommon cultural trope, particularly within the bioscientific model of disability. Yet, no

Enhancing the body from without 121

matter what the intervention, these bodies are never fully returned to 'normal'. A replacement limb might offer both an aesthetic and functional resemblance to 'normal' bodies, yet disabled bodies remain conceptually flawed, incomplete and constructed through a 'normalcy system' that 'devalu[es] bodies that do not conform to cultural standards' (Garland-Thomson 2002: 5). Like other marginalised groups, such as women, people of colour or the insane, bodies with physical impairments are defined against a standard or 'norm that is assumed to possess natural physical superiority' (Garland-Thomson 1997: 19), implying, by contrast, that disabled bodies are inherently weak and inferior. Disabled bodies are thus hierarchically allied with able bodies through a binary relationship where each can only exist in concert with the Other. There is, therefore, no such thing as a disabled body in and of itself; its identity is relational, regarded not 'for what it is, but for what it fails to be' (Shildrick 2005: 756). It is only recognisable when located on the fringes of that which is considered able, and, like other marginalised bodies, disabled bodies offer a mirror through which health, beauty and competence can be assessed and appreciated (Garland-Thomson 2002), but at the same time, they are unsettling, an uncomfortable reminder of the frailty of the 'normal' body.

Furthermore, Sandahl and Auslander (2005: 8) suggest disability cannot be defined merely in terms of the body for it is more accurately a 'disjuncture between the body and the environment'. A blind person who stands before a text in Braille is not impaired; only when s/he is presented with written words does a 'disability' become apparent. Similarly, elite sport reveals disability as mainstream sporting practices are predicated on comprehensive physical and mental functionality, embedded in rules that specify appropriate physical engagement and reject those who cannot comply. A swimmer, for example, unable to rest both feet flat on the starting blocks owing to a shortened right leg, is repeatedly disqualified from her able-bodied competition (Andrews 1999). Whilst her minor disability is largely immaterial to her performance, it is nevertheless exposed through a regulation that assumes physical symmetry and eliminates imperfection.

In many ways, then, disabled bodies are positioned uncomfortably within competitive sport, where skilled bodies strive to push themselves beyond established limits through rigorous physical activity, training and competition, and where the 'less competent' body, whether disabled, overweight, unfit or merely poorly coordinated, is juxtaposed against the strength, agility and proficiency of the rationally trained elite. Whilst athletes with disabilities are similarly engaged, their endeavours and achievements are measured against those of able-bodied competitors, with the former typically appearing second best, for 'obviously ... Paralympians cannot hope to equal the performances of Olympians' (Cowley 1999: 14). Yet, the able and disabled are rarely compared directly with one another in competition, as disabled bodies are pushed to the fringes, marginalised in their own events

122 *Enhancing the body from without*

and only occasionally included as 'demonstration' sports in 'mainstream' competitions, an oddity or novelty rather than a serious competitive event. Instead of representing strong, aggressive and powerful bodies striving to achieve success whilst pushing themselves to the limit, the para-athlete is more commonly framed by a mixture of pity and courage, portrayed as 'brave' souls, competing for the 'love of sport' (Goggin and Newell 2005; 2000), perpetuated in part by the origins of disability sport, which was initially conceived as part of a broader physical and social rehabilitation programme for those suffering spinal cord injuries (de Pauw and Gavron 2005).

Despite efforts to mitigate paternalistic and patronising media coverage (Smith and Thomas 2005), athletes with disabilities nevertheless become reminders of the 'true spirit' of athletic competition, one in which participation is more highly regarded than performance. Such discourses are clearly evident in the shock reactions to revelations that Paralympians engage in various performance enhancing, or 'boosting', strategies. Not only are positive drug tests returned at Paralympic events, but various practices designed to elicit a performance response from the body also surface. Wheelchair athletes, for example, may deliberately sit on pins or tacks, tie piano wire around their testicles or block their catheters to fill their bladders till bursting, each of which cause no physical discomfort, but provoke the sympathetic nervous system to increase blood pressure and the release of adrenalin. Some estimate that the subsequent performance could be improved by up to 15 per cent (Reilly 2000; Holtz 1996). Whilst it is not surprising that, like any elite athlete, Paralympians will try to solicit whatever competitive edge is available to them, the differentiation between 'enhancement' and 'boosting' is noteworthy not just for the inference that only whole bodies can be 'enhanced', but particularly for replicating the broader paternalistic, even cringe-worthy, implication that damaged bodies just need a little extra 'helping hand'. Both confirm that these defective versions are unlikely to exceed 'normal' capacity in the same way that able bodies are encouraged.

The cyborg athlete

Although early prostheses were designed to mimic the function and aesthetically resemble the missing limb (Ott 2002), these ungainly, awkward and heavy artificial body parts were ill suited to athletic competition. Through the latter part of the twentieth century, various innovations in engineering heralded the creation of bionic arms, legs and other devices modelled after the biomechanics of wild cats and a variety of other technologies (Shilling 2005). Whilst those applied to athletic bodies were increasingly designed to do much more than simply provide a replacement limb, as the twenty-first century progresses, biomechanists and engineers are delving further into murky borderlands, designing prosthetic devices to exceed an athlete's 'normal' performance, allowing the wearer to 'close the

Enhancing the body from without 123

gap' on their able-bodied counterparts. This brave new world of prosthetic limbs has prompted further disquiet about technology's role in creating fair and unfair 'advantage' in sport (Longman 2007; Hood 2005), and has revealed concerns about those technologies that interact with the body's internal systems or replace flawed or missing parts, which jeopardise not only bodily purity but create cyborgs.

Cyborgs, short for 'cybernetic organisms', are those part organic, part mechanistic creatures that transcend bodily limits to internalise and incorporate technologies. They assimilate nature and artifice, spawning a bionic body that relies more intimately on technology than on biology for its functioning (Gray 2002; Haraway 1991). More terrifying than the pieced together monster of Dr Frankenstein, cyborgs obliterate normative identities, offering a glimpse into a future where the organic is subsumed by technology, where humanity is shattered and where the hyperhuman predominates. Nevertheless, cyborgs are everywhere; bodies with pacemakers, artificial organs or iPods seem commonplace yet are examples of the body/ machine interface. Populating science fiction narratives are cyborgs of all descriptions, and the *Terminator* series, for example, reveals the 'horrors of intelligent machines' (Morus 2002: 1) whilst the myriad androids that appear in *Star Trek* or *Dr Who* suggest that the human body is increasingly superfluous. Whilst cyborgs are 'boundary crossers' that dwell on the 'frontiers of the social order', destabilising the authentic body and gesturing to the posthuman, like disabled bodies, cyborgs are never fully Other, too much like us yet too different for comfort (Nishime 2005: 34). Similarly, athletic cyborgs are hybrid bodies that resist categorisation within the essentialised binary categories of nature/artifice, organic/inorganic. They are liminal, both, yet neither/nor natural/synthetic, their chemically/technologically/artificially enhanced bodies retaining the organic qualities of the human body despite being augmented beyond what their body should normally be capable. These bodies are upsetting but are contained, separately, in their own event to prevent them disrupting the integrity of the sporting body. Not surprisingly, suggestions to create 'drugged' and 'drug free' sporting events replicate the Olympic/Paralympic segregation by advocating separate spaces for 'natural' and 'unnatural' bodies.

Whilst the conception of the cyborg is not new, the presence of prosthetic limbs, wheelchairs or other devices traditionally signified the body as deficient, rather than inappropriately enhanced, which, within the context of sport, legitimated the relegation of these bodies to a separate athletic sphere. Although other forms of discrimination have been addressed in, though typically not eliminated from, sport, disabled bodies remain deeply unsettling. Disrupting conceptions of the body as organic and natural, delimited by the skin, these bodies generate anxiety for they happily derive their functionality from a body/machine interface that exposes the body as vulnerable, open and impure. Despite their presence on, rather than in, the body, prosthetic limbs blur the edges of the corpus to which they are attached

124 *Enhancing the body from without*

(Wilson 1995) and, with the construction of state-of-the-art dissipative prosthetic knees or energy-storing prosthetic feet, usher in the dawn of a 'new age when [orthotic and prosthetic] appendages will no longer be separate, life-less mechanisms, but will instead be intimate extensions of the human body, structurally, neurologically and dynamically' (Herr *et al.* 2003: 133). Thus, borders will further disintegrate, collapsing the body and machine into the feared cyborg. In this new era, prosthetics will no longer simply be a supplement to the body, whose 'operating system [is] different from the body's organic processes' (Wilson 1995: 243), but rather a fully integrated and integral part of those organic processes, allowing the wearer to 'more readily accept their new artificial appendages as part of their own body, rather than foreign objects that must simply be tolerated' (Herr *et al.* 2003: 133).

Though some may argue that the addition of prostheses to a body may not constitute a fully integrated cyborged body (Wilson 1995), within the Paralympic arena, the attachment of prosthetics to the flawed body renders the cyborg athlete visible, for para-athletic performances rely on the relationship between body and machine. Nevertheless, these cyberathletes do not usually provoke the same kind of horror as science fictive cyborgs, for they do not seek to displace the human body; the technology merely renovates damage wreaked by accident, misadventure or genetic anomalies. Furthermore, these cyborgs are unlikely to jeopardise essentialised categories for they are rendered largely invisible as a result of their usual location in a separate athletic arena. As such, para/cyber/athletes are not directly compared to the able-bodied athlete, remaining contained, thereby, limiting their potential to disrupt normative bodies. It is only when these body/machine hybrids threaten to cross into the able-bodied sporting arena and exceed the performance of 'normal' bodies that they generate alarm, escalating measures to restrict their participation and invoking regulations to categorise their bodies as inappropriately enhanced. At this point, the technologies formerly thought to restore the body to a neutral and level playing field are dismissed as offering an 'unfair' advantage that creates an 'extra-abled' rather than disabled athlete.

Whilst there are a few instances of Paralympians competing in Olympic events (de Pauw and Gavron 2005), as prosthetic technologies become increasingly advanced, there may be a steady stream of athletes seeking to abandon the Paralympic in favour of the Olympic arena. Having already demolished twenty-six world records, most of them his own, South African sprinter Oscar Pistorius, hailed as the 'Fastest Man on No Legs', was poised to crack the 200m and 400m qualifying times for the 2007 IAAF World Championships and the 2008 Beijing Olympic Games. He had already performed impressively in non-para-sporting events, including a second placing in the 400m at the 2007 South African Senior Track and Field Championships. Running on adjustable carbon fibre, heel-less, and perhaps unfortunately nicknamed, 'Cheetah' legs, Pistorius' quest to compete in able-bodied events

Enhancing the body from without 125

by the 2008 Olympics seemed possible, until a decision rushed through by the International Association of Athletics Federations (IAAF), track and field's governing body, brought it all to a grinding halt. In March 2007, the IAAF Council decided to implement an immediate rule change that, according to the final wording, prohibited the use in competition of 'any technical device that incorporates springs, wheels or any other element that provides the user with an advantage over another athlete not using such a device' (IAAF 2008a), which, though already the subject of legal challenges from footwear manufacturers, was primarily designed to preclude the use of a prosthetic device, effectively disqualifying athletes such as Pistorius.

The timing of this rule change is particularly telling, given that, at the same meeting, the council had examined over 100 other proposed amendments and had developed a set of recommendations to be circulated to member federations for consideration at the IAAF Congress just prior to the 2007 World Championships. That this was the only rule change that was implemented with immediate effect, and without discussion by delegates, indicates that the IAAF believed it needed to move swiftly to 'protect' the World Championships. According to Elio Locatelli, the IAAF's director of development, the regulation was a matter of 'purity', which was imminently threatened by 'something that provides advantages', including his prediction that, without a specific rule to prevent it, athletes might be tempted to try 'another device where people can fly with something on their back' (Longman 2007). Although the technology to enable people to fly has certainly been in place for quite some time, its potential incorporation into track events did not seem to be much of a concern to the IAAF only two years previously.

In 2005, when questioned specifically about the eventuality that Pistorius may qualify for mainstream competition, the then general secretary of the IAAF, Istvan Gyulail, indicated explicitly that 'it would seem inhuman and against the sport to say "go away and compete in events for the disabled"' (Hood 2005). Given the recent change of heart, it would seem, then, that the practice of excluding athletes was really only ever 'inhuman' or 'against the sport' when it was highly unlikely that those with disabilities would ever actually try to gain entry. Clearly, as the hypothetical scenario became more of a reality, the IAAF felt compelled to prevent a situation that they had never before seriously considered would arise, namely, the legitimate inclusion of a defective body into an arena that celebrates only perfection. To shatter the carefully constructed able/disabled, and by extension, perfect/imperfect binaries, Pistorius would need only defeat one able-bodied runner. To avoid such an eventuality, the IAAF took the specific decision to preclude the double amputee from able-bodied competition after an independent study concluded that 'Cheetah' blades were assuredly 'technical aids' that provided 'clear mechanical advantages' to the wearer (IAAF 2008b). In response, the IAAF determined the prosthetics were in contravention of Rule 144.2, and Pistorius was deemed ineligible to compete in events run under IAAF rules, including, of course, the Olympic Games

126 *Enhancing the body from without*

(IAAF 2008b), a decision that was overturned on appeal by the Court of Arbitration for Sport in May 2008.

It is significant that Pistorius generated a mainstream media storm only after he seemed set to dismantle the border between able and disabled bodies (Longman 2007); however, his running legs had already generated controversy within the Paralympic arena for several years. His ability to 'manipulate [his] anatomical structure' by artificially adjusting the length of his legs to create a greater stride had prompted the implementation of an anatomical formula, based on a competitor's armspan, to determine the 'true height' of double amputees. These are designed to counteract the 'unfair' advantages gained through prosthetic developments and to ensure that the artificial limb really only restores, rather than enhances, the body (Hood 2005). Whilst intended to regulate 'fairness' within Paralympic sport, as Marlow Hood (2005) observes, rather than trying to 'level' the playing field, this measure may in fact prevent double amputees from ever racing as fast as able-bodied athletes. He suggests that the 'the underlying and unspoken prejudice may be that if a disabled sprinter is able to match the times of the world's best able bodied runners, then, almost by definition, he must somehow have an "unnatural" advantage' (Hood 2005). The zeal with which the 'unfair' and 'advantaged' labels have been applied in this case seems, ironically, to overlook the fact that regardless how efficient his prosthetics may be, Pistorius is still missing his two lower legs.

Conclusion

By the opening refrain of the 2008 Olympic opening ceremony, the hysteria surrounding the Fastskin LZR Racer had largely dissipated, just as the initial controversy over the revolutionary swimsuits had all but died by the 2000 Sydney Games. On that occasion, the level playing field was reestablished in an event that relied on the pure physical performance of the athletes, despite their attire, and with the absence of successful Chinese swimmers, interest turned to the technology of the 'fast' pool and speculation on the swimmers' ability to break world records. The bodysuits were normalised as a new and accepted technology, augmented by an enthusiastic media campaign against performance enhancing drugs that effectively presented the bodysuit as a legitimate and effective mechanism to optimise physical output without the concomitant physical changes. Whilst each redesign of the Fastskin prompts momentary tensions between athletic output and technological innovation, which are typically resolved quickly within both sport and the wider community, the construction of athletic cyborgs with bionic limbs who threaten to outperform 'able-bodied' athletes is only now emerging. These hybrid bodies disrupt the integrity of the natural body by visibly strapping their enhancements to their bodies. Their position on the exterior, however, suggests that this is merely a temporary augmentation and is not designed to permanently alter the debilitated body.

Enhancing the body from without   127

What wearable skins and other athletic prosthetics reveal is that technology is differentially interpreted in terms of its potential to threaten the nature of sport, performance and the body. Technologies that remain external to the athlete may initially provoke anxiety over their relationship to the corporeal; however, these are eventually assimilated into a definition of 'natural' enhancement, for ultimately they do not contaminate the body by passing through its unsettlingly porous borders. For this reason, wearable skins layered upon the body's surface are not thought to jeopardise its integrity, whilst the genetic modification required to produce the same dermal denticles on the skin would be met with widespread condemnation (Miah 2004). Although international sporting federations are working valiantly to ensure sport remains free from genetic engineering, sports apparel companies may yet be looking to such permanent physical modifications in the future. In Speedo's 'Aqualab', a mock, online quest to 'discover' the secrets of Fastskin, the visitor is encouraged to 'rifle' through waste-paper baskets, view 'confidential' files and sneak through various 'laboratories' to piece together information on the innovation. A note attached to the back of one file laments: 'if only we could somehow genetically engineer these very characteristics into the athletes themselves ... ' (Speedo 2007), acknowledging that an artificial skin may assist the performance, but that significant improvements can only happen at the level of the body itself. If we thought that the athletic cyborg provoked fear and dread, just imagine how a fastskinned human might be received.

8 Drugs, sport and Australian identity

Introduction

In early 2007 it was reported that an Australian company had designed a commercial DNA test to assess a person's 'athletic potential'. Designed to analyse the genes governing cardiovascular ability, muscular development, fat burning and recovery, the test prompted immediate concerns over the potential misuse of such technology, especially in its application to younger participants. Its supporters countered that it was merely 'cutting-edge science that can help people achieve their goals', offering children, in particular, a 'real edge from an early age' (Burke 2007: 30). Recognising talent as early as possible is a serious undertaking, and for this reason, evaluating athletic potential at the sub-cellular level seems little more than an addition to the already extensive battery of tests designed to ensure future Australian sporting success. Yet, at the same time that it has sought various scientific 'edges', the Australian elite sports community has also regarded itself as particularly dedicated to the 'essence' and integrity of sport and the cleanliness of competitors. It has been specifically within the realm of performance enhancing drugs that Australian governments, coaches, administrators and athletes have been vocal, despite their enthusiastic embrace of other kinds of performance technologies such as the Fastskin swimsuit.

Since the 1990s, Australia has positioned itself as a leader in the international fight against drugs in sport (ASC 2004; DISR 1999). Government strategies designed to prevent drug use among young athletes confirm Australia's 'leading' position in this 'campaign' (ASC 2004; DISR 1999), whilst former and contemporary athletes are forthright about the presence of illicit drugs in international elite sport. The policy of 'Pure Performance', launched at a conference of the same name in 1999, supported Australia's 'war' on performance enhancing drugs, underpinning, for example, outreach and educational programmes delivered by the Australian Sports Anti-Doping Authority (ASADA 2007a). Such programmes have been designed to warn young athletes of the risks and consequences of doping and to reinforce Australia's status as a principal advocate for 'clean sport'. The authority to protect Australia's sporting integrity has thus been invested in

Drugs, sport and Australian identity   129

a statutory body that proclaims 'the most important sporting record is a clean one' (ASADA 2007b). Yet, it is not only the government that has presented a vigilant and coherent approach towards this 'scourge' of sport. Television news, current affairs programmes and the print media have been consistent in their efforts to present the nation as united in its abhorrence of chemical performance enhancers. The public are encouraged to scrutinise bodies suspected of relying on illicit substances, and those found to be suspicious are dismissed as illegitimate cheats (Magdalinski 2001a). Prior to major events, opponents are often accused of drug taking, national coaches reaffirm that Australian athletes are unequivocally 'clean', and the media implore international sporting federations to do more to clean up sport's 'tarnished' image. Such widespread and frequent debate about performance enhancing drugs in the public domain suggests that its importance lies less in the discussion of sporting integrity and more in understanding Australia's self image within the international arena.

Examining Australia's response to performance technologies, both legal and illicit, reveals how an accepted or singular national identity can be generated through sport, and more specifically, through the relative purity of a nation's athletic representatives. Sport, in this sense, becomes an important, though not exclusive, site where nationalist discourses are generated, and in Australia this is particularly critical. Sport is important to the national psyche, where expressions of Australian identity are popularly located within a sporting context. Athletes are revered as true representatives of Australianness, frequently receiving accolades, such as the Australian of the Year award; international sporting events are used to showcase Australia and its way of life to the world; and politicians at all levels flock to be seen with the latest sports star, shoring up their relationship to 'everyday' Australians. Sport is ever present in Australian society, such that Australians declare themselves to be the most sports-mad people in the world, as a nation 'drunk' on sport. By simultaneously presenting the nation as in love with sport as well as 'one of the most vocal crusaders in the war against drug abuse' (Magnay and Korporaal 1998: 1), Australia is imagined as clean, healthy and virtuous, whilst its rivals are constructed, by contrast, as dirty and despicable. For a country so heavily invested in sport, both financially and emotionally, threats to the perceived purity, innocence and naturalness of sport, and of those who compete in it, have the potential to rupture one of the foundations upon which its identity rests.

Although much of the fervour surrounding drugs in sport emerged in the 1990s, throughout the 1970s and 1980s, there were growing concerns about the presence of illicit substances in elite international sport. Whilst the scandals at the 1988 Seoul Olympics and the Australian Senate Inquiry into Drugs in Sport were landmarks in anti-doping debates during the late 1980s, by the 1990s the discourse had shifted from one of censuring drug cheats within Australia to identifying 'cheats' outside the nation's borders. Australian athletes were confirmed as undeniably pure, whilst athletes that threatened 'our' victories were suspected of cheating as a matter of course. Despite the fact that Australian athletes have also been found guilty of taking illicit substances, the popular perception of untainted Aussies losing their deserved medals to cheats from other nations remains. By juxtaposing 'clean' Australia against 'unclean' nations, a binary relationship is established between 'us' and 'them', where Australia is located clearly on the positive side of the equation. The construction of such a relationship provides certainty that regardless of the outcome of a sporting contest, Australia as an unarguably 'pure', 'natural' nation will always win a moral, if not a material, victory.

Of course, Australia is a theoretical concept, so ascertaining its integrity rests more in its physical representatives, such as athletes, so that natural bodies are important indicators of national cleanliness. In this way, the purity of the athlete symbolises the purity of the nation, for geographic borders are mirrored in biological ones. National difference is thereby fixed through the preservation of unpolluted bodily boundaries, and internal political, psychosocial or cultural fractures are elided as the nation is reproduced through the body of the strong, fit and untainted athlete. In this case study, polarised images of 'clean' and 'unclean' athletes, and by association 'clean' and 'unclean' nations, are able to reinforce boundaries that reassure Australians of their integrity as a nation within a global community continually in flux. Through such a construction, boundaries are maintained by clearly locating the 'loser'/'unclean' nation outside the geographical, political and imagined Australian nation, whilst the corrupted foreign body is considered the antithesis of Australianness.

Significantly, the accepted cleanliness of contemporary Australian athletes is also retroactively applied to former sportsmen and women, such that past athletic non-successes are rehistoricised through allegations of drug abuse levelled at their competitors. An imagined golden sporting tradition is, thereby, recovered through the construction of Australia as a nation of pure/natural athletes, who were defeated not by the superior skill of their competitors, but by the use of performance enhancing substances. Branding foreign athletes exclusively as drug cheats evokes images of the beleaguered 'Aussie battler', the hard-done-by Australian athlete, who, despite a superior moral, is conquered by illicit scientific practices. Australia's image as a champion for clean sport thus reinforces the battler amateurist ethos within which sport and its heroes are entrenched, an image that is currently being historicised as a handful of athletes seek to have Olympic medals awarded or upgraded because they had apparently 'lost to drugs'. The construction of a nostalgic pining for what 'might have been' confirms, if only in Australian minds, that the nation was, and will remain, a leader in international sport.

This chapter argues that the development of a national identity, couched within the conceptual framework of Australia as 'sporty nation', is incomplete without the location of sporting Others on the fringes of that identity.

The construction of 'us' and 'them' through athletic competition, whilst important, is insufficient to reinforce the nation's identity, and the nature/ artifice binary is employed to compare the relative cleanliness of each nation's sporting representatives. A fervent stance against performance enhancing substances constructs the Australian nation and its athletes as incontrovertibly clean, effectively confirming the integrity of both its national and biological borders. These Other bodies, located as they are on the periphery of Australian identity, serve as a referent or yardstick against which the Self can be measured, identified and refined.

Australia as 'sporty nation'

Historians have oft suggested that Australians have a 'passionate attachment' to sport that surpasses any other nation (Farrell 1999: 68). The nation's dedication and funding of sport, support of local, national and international teams and competitions, the overall interest that the average person is thought to display in all matters sporting, as well as the many statements from politicians and other community leaders that remind citizens about their love for sport are each taken as compelling evidence that attest to the fact that Australia is 'drunk' on sport (McKay 1991). Indeed, government policies specify that sport is 'integral to [Australia's] unique culture' and a 'legitimate source of national pride' (DISR 1999), whilst federal ministers profess that 'Australia's national identity is largely defined by the efforts of our ... sportspeople' (ASC 2008). Yet, despite such avowed commitment, on many indicators Australians have not been particularly more sporty than people from many other nations, though the per capita rate of success in some international sports has been relatively high (Booth and Tatz 2000; Vamplew and Stoddart 1994; McKay 1991). Although some observers have begun to partially deconstruct assertions about sporting success, the national (and international) perception that Australians are an outdoor, rugged, athletic breed, encompassed in the 'bronzed Aussie', the Ironman or surf-lifesaver, is perpetuated by the media, particularly leading up to international sporting events (Booth and Tatz 2000; Cashman 1995; McKay 1991). Such representations draw upon a long line of international observers such as Mark Twain, Anthony Trollope and D. H. Lawrence, who each commented on the robust nature of Australians and their interest in sporting activities (Stoddart 1986). The myth of physical prowess has also been reinforced by Australia's long history of successes in several, relatively obscure, British-developed, international sports such as rugby union, rugby league, cricket and netball. Winning the right to host the 2000 Olympics, however, put Australia squarely on the world sporting stage, or, as former prime minister Paul Keating asserted, in the 'swim with the big boys' (Booth and Tatz 1994: 4), and since then Australia has hosted several other notable international sporting events, each confirming that Australia's national and international image rests, in part, on its position as a sporting powerhouse.

132 *Drugs, sport and Australian identity*

Despite Australia's successes in sport internationally, 'Australian' identity has become increasingly fragmented in recent years, a result of the rise of conservative politics, sustained debates about the ethnic, racial and religious make-up of the Australian population and concerns about indigenous relations. As a result, cultural practices that promise unity and clarity of identity, such as sport, have been overemphasised, particularly by the former centrist government concerned with implementing a reactionary social agenda. Nothing appears to be more traditionally 'Australian' than sport, and international competitions remain a forum where the nation can test itself on a global stage and its citizens can bond through shared triumphs. Constructing Australian identity through international sporting achievements means that contentious social issues can be replaced by a different 'us' and 'them' binary. Rather than a nation divided internally along class, race or ethnic lines, Australia is unified in the international arena against a common athletic enemy, and whether one is black or white or left or right, 'Australianness' as a cogent identity can be celebrated as we defeat the 'Poms', 'Kiwis', 'Krauts', or 'Frogs'. For example, soccer, once derided as 'wogball' in Australia, became a measure to inspire national unity through the excitement generated by the Socceroos unexpectedly reaching the second round of the 2006 World Cup. Whilst such a cohesive Australian identity is not uncontested, during periods of social upheaval there are nevertheless rigorous efforts to promote the nation as unified.

The active and deliberate structuring of the nation confirms that national identities are fragile, elusive and rarely fixed. They are constantly (re)negotiated as competing versions are offered, debated and dismissed. Images intended to secure consensus about what the nation is and what it means reside comfortably alongside declarations of what the country is not (Hall 1992). In Australia, nation-building has, for over two centuries, rested on specific efforts to construct oppositional cultural positions, where the Australian nation is contrasted with others to stress its uniqueness (Walter 1992). Australian exceptionalism is evident in not only in its topography, flora and fauna, but also in its development as a nation. The construction of a national history is an important mechanism that contributes to the development of identity, particularly as a fictive nation is more effectively brought to life through historical accounts that present a continuous and inevitable narrative of the nation's maturation. Once agreed, attempts to revise or to tender alternative accounts of the nation's origin and development are typically met with contempt by a public that rejects challenges to the established 'truth' of an agreed past. The generic conventions of history, for example, require that nations 'unfold a glorious past, a golden age of saints and heroes' (Smith 1991: 161), as meanings about the nation are often explained through the personal triumphs of historical figures who become rallying points for the nation and symbolic of its struggle against adversity. Sporting heroes are particularly effective as they rarely represent radical ideological standpoints and tend to epitomise the 'rags-to-riches' myth of

Drugs, sport and Australian identity   133

social mobility. Within Australia, they evoke images of the 'Aussie battler', the ever-present underdog, striving to conquer against the odds. Former sporting 'greats', such as Dawn Fraser, Herb Elliot and Shane Gould, are paraded at national and international sporting events to serve as explicit reminders of the nation's 'golden age'. Their presence allows Australia's athletic prowess, both historically and contemporarily, to form a largely uncontested foundation for a unified national identity.

Whilst a shared past and a pantheon of heroes are critical, the presence of a common territory is an essential element in the construction of national identities. As a discrete geographic entity, the continental perimeter has effectively demarcated the nation, offering a reliable and stable terrain, which is easily recognised as 'Australia', compared with nations with shared or fluid boundaries that feel a greater uncertainty and a sense of being at risk of contamination from beyond. Nevertheless, despite the oceans that divide it from other landmasses, the integrity of Australia's national borders are popularly perceived to be under the threat of penetration by outside forces such as Asianisation, immigration, American popular culture, and, most enduringly, pestilence and disease. Consequently, Australia's shores are monitored with vigilance, confirmed by television programmes such as *Border Security – Australia's Front Line* that allow citizens to consume images of national protection through reality television. A breach of these borders is, first, a national concern and, second, a personal one, as evidenced by unannounced arrivals of boats carrying illegal immigrants. In one instance, the arrival of such 'aliens' on Australia's beaches was announced with great alarm by a newsagent (Meade 1999), confirming that even national citizens police the geo-political borders, establishing a correlation between the macro and micro social: the nation stands for the individual and vice versa. The threat, in the form of the illegal immigrant, is contained and borders both personal and geographical are reinforced. This type of containment is not reserved for illegal immigrants alone. Refugees, particularly after the events of 11 September 2001, were isolated and quarantined in a manner similar to foreign plants, foodstuffs or anything that may cause the introduction of dis/ease and thus threaten the 'health' of the Australian nation and the security of its borders.

Whilst the health of the Australian nation has been a concern since the foundation of a white settler colony in the late eighteenth century, it is significant that national 'health' in this context refers largely to the well-being of individual bodies. The colonial settlers, upon arrival in Australia, encountered a hostile environment, and many observers feared that the colonial British would physically deteriorate as a result of the harsh Australian landscape. Yet, it was the bush and the vigorous outdoors lifestyle that began to distinguish the young, emerging nation from its imperial core, if only in the minds of urban dwellers (Ward 1992). By the early 1900s, there was a belief that Australia and other settler colonies produced healthier, manly specimens, confirmed by post-Boer War reports that

134 *Drugs, sport and Australian identity*

investigated reasons for the poor physical condition of British recruits. The 1904 *Report of the Interdepartmental Committee on Physical Deterioration*, for example, established that young men from Australia, Canada and New Zealand were healthier and made better soldiers (Hardy 2001), and given the successes of these troops in the Boer War and in international sporting events, British leaders recognised that colonial bodies were thriving. In response, physical activities in the form of institutional sport were considered primary in efforts to prevent the 'enfeebling' of the British nation through the strengthening of individual bodies (Wohl 1983), and international sporting contests became moments in which physical national strength could be demonstrated to the world. Success based on physical or sporting performance gradually supplemented, and then replaced, success based on other forms of international competition, and athletic bodies became potent symbols of national strength, unity and health.

International expositions and other such gatherings have provided opportunities for nations to evaluate each other, yet sport has offered an important forum through which nations may be directly, and physically, compared. Individual bodies compete, swathed in national colours and symbols of the nation, offering a material link between the theoretical concept of the nation and its physical expression (Jarvie and Walker 1994). Furthermore, the national character is thought to reside within the individual athletes themselves, so that in this case study, Australian identity is embodied specifically within the bodies of its representatives. Individually and collectively, sporting bodies synecdochally stand in for the nation by representing 'us', the people. In Australia, sports commentators regularly link the nation to its people through the sporting bodies on display:

> Kieren Perkins epitomises the Australian who lives in so many of our hearts. He is the face of Australia. Kieren is the Australian we want to hang on to. The Australian so many of us admire. … Kieren Perkins made me feel not only extremely proud to be an Australian. Kieren Perkins made me feel both privileged and proud to have an Australian of his calibre out there representing me. If the world is going to see what an Australian is like, if there is a picture of an Australian we'd like shown around the globe, Kieren Perkins represents that image.
>
> (cited in *Ironbark Legends* 1997: 46)

In this way, athletic bodies symbolise more than individual achievement. They represent the collective aims and goals, characteristics and ideals of the nation as personal victories become shared victories, signifying national vigour and collective strength.

As the preferred image of Australia as a strong and successful nation is communicated not merely through the performances of the national team, but also through individual athletes, the physical state of those bodies becomes indicative of the state of the nation. For this reason, the bodies of

Australian athletes are policed as stringently as the national perimeter, so that individual biological borders become as impenetrable to foreign contaminants as the conceptual and physical boundaries demarcating the national body. The pure athlete thus signifies the integrity of the nation. Through sport then, Australia as a unified and thriving nation is juxtaposed against 'despicable', 'drug-cheating' nations, further cementing Australian identity and eliding potential ambiguities. The image of a collective stand against drugs, for example, symbolises the desired unity of the nation, and for this reason, it is critical that the bodies of those who represent it be free from contamination, so that the nation itself may remain pure. It is thus of little surprise that Australians have been long engaged in discussions about the appropriate role of technology in sport, confirming that their preferred sports and athletes are 'natural'.

Sport and scientisation

In addition to being a nation in love with sport, Australia further presents itself as a community particularly concerned with the 'naturalness' of physical achievement. Former marathon runner Steve Moneghetti (1999, emphasis added) suggests that Australians seem to be 'particularly good at *natural* sports', those that set body to do battle against nature without the need for extraneous technologies. Popular images of sport present bodies conquering the elements, as, for example, surf-lifesavers power through raging oceans or churn through golden sand. Yet, the concept of 'natural' sport and, more specifically, 'natural' sporting bodies has adjusted over time in Australia, as elsewhere, to accommodate changing training methods, techniques and technological additions. Whilst illicit drug use is the contemporary signifier of the 'unnatural', and therefore illegitimate, athlete, within Australia public debates about natural/unnatural physical activity have, in the past, centred on concerns about the increasing scientisation and professionalisation of sport, particularly as Eastern Bloc nations began dominating Olympic sport in the 1970s, the same time that Australian victories were declining.

Prior to the 1980s, the Soviet model of elite sport was disparaged by Australians as 'shamateurism', a state-run, professional, or 'sham amateur' system that was accused of violating if not the law then the spirit of the Olympic charter. Furthermore, the Soviet system was regarded as an infraction of the very principles of sport itself, and scientific training methods were rejected in favour of a more natural 'amateurist' approach. Australian athletes were generally in employment and trained primarily during their leisure time; talent identification programmes were years away; and the very idea of centralised training programmes conjured propagandistic images of Eastern Bloc babies being ripped from their screaming mothers' arms to be locked away in sports schools by the state. The approach was considered far too serious and far too professional for those clinging to the way of the amateur. These differing training systems epitomised the physical/technological or

136 *Drugs, sport and Australian identity*

natural/artificial binaries, so that despite a lack of international athletic success, particularly in the 1970s, the more ad hoc Australian system of elite sport was justified as more wholesome, more 'natural' and, thus, more legitimate.

Soviet athletes were largely construed as robotic and drugged, to coincide with Western stereotypes of citizens living without freedom in 'totalitarian' states. Fictional Russian boxing 'automaton' Drago, from *Rocky IV*, solidified the 1980s image of the mechanical, not-quite-human athlete produced by overtly scientific training methods employed by dubious political regimes (Prince 1997), whilst female athletes from communist regimes were portrayed as large, bulky and masculine, devoid of any feminine characteristics. Western athletes, on the other hand, were assuredly 'real' or 'natural', even 'authentic', revealing that ideological differences between the two systems were inscribed onto the bodies of their respective representatives.

Nevertheless, despite widespread criticism, Soviet scientific training methods proved to be highly successful in the development of elite sport, which led to rapid international success for the Eastern Bloc. Australia's 'natural' approach, however, was not so prosperous, and following the 1976 Montreal Olympics, at which Australian athletes won no gold medals, 'shamateur' training methods were promptly adopted by the Australian sporting fraternity, frustrated at the lack of systematic organisation at the elite level. Following massive capital investments into elite level sport by the Commonwealth and despite public reticence about the appropriateness of a 'communist'-style system, the Australian Institute of Sport (AIS), founded on the principles of 'scientific' training, opened in 1981 (Daly 1991; Semotiuk 1987). Such a radical shift prompted a thorough reconceptualisation of elite sport in Australia, and scientific training systems were eventually normalised as a 'natural' approach to improving athletic performance. Enhancement through chemical means, by contrast, remained categorically unnatural or artificial.

The adoption of Soviet training and talent identification programmes disrupted the construction of the natural/artificial contrapositions that had firmly categorised scientific training as antithetical to a more natural, Australian approach. Yet such approaches to athletic preparation could no longer be condemned as unnatural, for to denounce it would be to attack Australia's own training schemes and, by association, the Australian nation itself. In this context, the nature/artifice binary could have been disrupted irreparably; however, scientific training was quickly incorporated into a popular understanding of sport. Systematic talent identification, centralised training programmes, sports schools and the application of science to training, each of which had been eschewed a decade earlier, were rapidly accepted as part of the Australian approach to sport. In this way, binary categories reveal themselves to be fluid, rather than fixed, shifting to incorporate emerging ideological positions, such that, in this case study, scientific training could be reconfigured as an honest and legitimate pursuit designed to enhance pre-existing natural talent. Yet, despite these shifts, the nature/artifice binary remains intact as 'natural' methods of enhancing performance are still juxtaposed against 'unnatural' methods, namely illicit drugs, which were now 'universally' understood as an 'artificial' means of enhancing performance. In other words, both sides of the binary were reconstituted so that scientific training was accepted as a natural method of extending the body's abilities, whereas physical enhancement through drugs remained synthetic. The adoption of these training methods did not, however, correspond with an acceptance of rival nations, thus the process of 'Othering' communist bloc athletes shifted from a focus on training to a focus on drug-taking and, in particular, the policing of drug-taking. As such, the 'unnatural' manipulation of the body was examined at a cellular rather than gross anatomical level, and to protect the new Australian scientific approach to sport, a vigilant stance against illegal and immoral performance technologies was taken.

Australia as crusader against drugs

In Australia, there has been increasing public awareness and debate about the presence of drugs in sport, particularly in the latter part of the twentieth century as the nation prepared to host a range of high-level sporting events, including the 2000 Olympic Games and the 2006 Commonwealth Games. Australia is presented as especially concerned about safeguarding sport, and regards itself as a global crusader agitating for reform within sport. The ASADA's (2007b) mission statement confirms that it is working 'to protect Australia's sporting integrity through the elimination of doping', boasting that it represents the 'most fully integrated anti-doping framework in the world', whilst the Australian Sports Commission's (ASC) (2004) *Anti Doping Policy* categorically states that 'as a leader in the fight against drugs in sport, Australia's antidoping programs have helped set the standard for the world sporting community'. It is clear that Australia positions itself as internationally significant in the fight against doping, a role that protects the stated 'essence' and integrity of Australian sport (ASC 2007).

For over two decades, Australian sports officials and media outlets have focused on the relationship between drugs and sport. The drugs scandals at the 1988 Seoul Olympics and the Australian Senate Inquiry into Drugs in Sport revealed an urgency, in the late 1980s, to expel cheats from within the national borders. More recently, however, there has been a shift in focus, and during the 1990s, discourses of drugs in sport have varied from one of identifying drug cheats within Australia to identifying cheats outside the national border. Whilst drug-taking in sport is widespread and is not limited by political or ideological positions, within Australia there was a concerted focus on Chinese swimmers, although others, including former Eastern Bloc athletes, remain reviled as both current and former athletes, coaches and administrators came under public scrutiny.

Sustained criticism of the Chinese swimmers began in earnest at the 1994 World Swimming Championships held in Rome. China's female swimmers won twelve of the sixteen events and broke several world records. Leading

138 *Drugs, sport and Australian identity*

Australian sports coaches remarked that one only required minimal intelligence to suspect something illegal was afoot (Carlile 1995: 23), and the image of Le Jingyi climbing from the pool, her massive shoulders emphasised by the cut of her swimsuit, which now accompanies almost every media report on drug-taking in sport, became irrefutable evidence of the systematic administration of banned substances in China. The vehement attack on the Chinese was, in part, owing to Australian expectations that following the end of the communist reign in women's swimming Australia's athletes would dominate; however, all predictions for international success and glory in the pool were thwarted by the ascendancy of China's swimmers. Despite the shift in focus to the Chinese, the demise of the Soviet bloc did not prevent the scrutiny of Eastern European athletes and officials, particularly when many coaches, athletes and administrators relocated to the West.

In Australia, the appointment of former East German athletics coach Ekkart Arbeit to the position of head coach of Australian track and field fuelled heated debates about Eastern European training methods, and, more importantly, their systematic doping of elite athletes. His appointment earned Athletics Australia, the national governing body of track and field, the title 'Buttheads of the Month' from *Inside Sport* (1997). The magazine argued that such an appointment of an 'admitted cheat' to 'perhaps the most important athletics position in the land' was out of step with Australian attitudes, and feared that Australia's 'public anti-drugs stance' would be held up to 'international ridicule' (*Inside Sport* 1997: 15). Athletes and officials were outraged that their reputations might be besmirched by Arbeit's presence and were forthright in their opposition.

The Arbeit incident provided further incentive for those athletes who had petitioned the IOC to have medals previously 'stolen' by 'drug cheats' 'returned' to them (Black 1998; Kitney 1997). Swimmer Lisa Curry-Kenny and sprinter Raelene Boyle both argued that they had been 'robbed' of their rightful Olympic medals by 'steroid-fuelled' athletes from East Germany in the 1970s and 1980s (Black 1998; Kitney 1997). Taking up the cause, Australian current affairs programme *Sixty Minutes* accompanied Curry-Kenny and Boyle to Germany to pursue evidence against, and then hunt down and confront, the women who had 'stolen' *their* medals (Channel 9 1997). Raelene Boyle, who believes she 'lost to drugs', was defeated by GDR sprinter Renate Stecher in the 100m and 200m in the 1972 Munich games, and Lisa Curry-Kenny finished fifth behind three East Germans in the 100m butterfly in Moscow in 1980 (Evans 1997; Gatt 1997). These former athletes demanded that their opponents admit their victories were drug-induced, and, armed with their confessions, hoped to rewrite the record books and reclaim the medals that were 'rightfully' theirs.

The Arbeit 'scandal' was followed three months later by the 1998 World Swimming Championships held in Perth, Australia. Rumours concerning the illicit taking of banned substances abounded, and both German and Chinese swimmers were caught in the crossfire. Upon arrival in Perth, former East

German swim coach Winfried Leopold had his credentials revoked by FINA for his participation in the 'doping' of East German swimmers during the 1970s and 1980s, a 'crime' for which he had already served a two-year ban from coaching in Germany. Allegations of Chinese drug-taking already dominated media reports of the swimming championship well before the event had started, and Australia's head coach, Don Talbot, with the support of elite Australian swimmers, pre-emptively branded the Chinese 'cheats' (Magnay 1997). The media frenzy intensified following the discovery by Australian Customs officers of thirteen vials of somatropin, a growth hormone, in the suitcase of Chinese breaststroker Yuan Yuan, and calls by athletes and coaches to have the Chinese team banned in its entirety followed as coverage of the events made front-page news headlines around the nation (Evans 1998). Even the discovery of a syringe filled with a 'mystery liquid' nearly ten years on at the 2007 World Swimming Championships was reason enough to revisit Yuan Yuan's transgression, despite the fact that Chinese swimmers were not implicated in this recent controversy (Magnay 2007a).

Whilst there had been little confirmed evidence of widespread drug-taking by the Chinese, their 'grotesque bodies' were demonised and labelled 'unnatural' by Australian competitors and commentators alike and were thought to offer explicit evidence of illicit doping. Part of the reason that these bodies appeared 'grotesque' was because of the obvious gender confusion their external appearance generated. As Chinese swimmers appeared neither wholly male nor wholly female, they were regarded as objects of fear for Australia's female swimmers, as these 'anabolic Amazons' represented what their own bodies could become: masculine women. Furthermore, these forms represented threats to the clear boundaries between East and West bodies, for the Chinese swimmers obliterated the traditional stereotype of the small, petite, fragile oriental body. Only occidental bodies were considered to be large and strong. These swimmers were the yellow peril manifest, a particularly potent threat in light of Australia's cultural history and anti-Asian hysteria. As a prophylactic to the anxiety the Chinese athletes augured, Australian swimmers publicly announced their victories in the pool prior to races being held, such as swimmer Elli Overton, who suggested that if she were to finish third behind two Chinese swimmers at the 1996 Atlanta Olympics, she would know that she had 'really' won the race. This type of announcement functions as a recovery for the lost or threatened Self as the Other invades and penetrates by winning and taking the glory that rightfully belongs to the nation/Self. Australian athletes were thus ensuring that after a drought of Olympic swimming medals over the past two decades, the Chinese would not 'rob' them of their 'rightful medals' as the communists had previously done.

Constructing Australian identity

Australia's obsession with establishing its place in the international arena through sport may be explained by reference to Lacan's theories of identity

140 *Drugs, sport and Australian identity*

formation discussed in Chapter 3. Whilst his theories typically refer to the development of the subject, in many respects, Australia can be read as a Lacanian 'infant', which seeks its discrete and whole identity within the global Symbolic Order. Lacan suggests that the whole/pure Self is only possible prior to the Imaginary stage of psychosocial development, so that the introduction into the Symbolic Order means that a person's search for identity focuses on the search for the whole, unfragmented self. Australia in the Imaginary stage is Australia in isolation, yet the nation's foray into the international arena, into the Symbolic Order, obliterates the illusory feeling of unity. Borders are exposed as the nation comes to know its edges and limits. The search for Australian identity thus becomes a search for a sense of wholeness, and, through the mirror stage, Australia is 'able to imagine itself as a coherent and self-governing whole' (Sarup 1992: 64), yet this whole conflicts with feelings of fragmentation, of an 'Australia-in-bits-and-pieces'.

Debates about Australia's 'maturity' as a nation searching for independent status and efforts to position the nation within the international hierarchy can be strengthened through its (re)presentation as a successful nation on the world sports stage. Success in international sport is held up as an indicator of national worth and as a way of differentiating 'us' from 'them'. Australia's self-perception as a nation at the pinnacle of world sport is effectively reinforced by a sports media that provides the national self with an artificial, external image of the nation that comes to represent Australian identity. Thus, Australia believes itself to be a great sporting nation, yet when looking in the 'mirror' of international sport, past and present, the image reflected back to Australia is that of a moderately successful sporting nation, and certainly a nation in which physical fitness levels and sports participation are declining. The mirror reveals Australia's identity as a 'sporty nation' to be an artificial construct, and Australia's identity as a unified nation with an excellent sporting tradition is undermined by the reality of a fragmented social body with an average sporting record (Magdalinski 2000b).

At the same time, the sporting culture cannot provide a pure, whole self, for the sporting body is impure, contaminated by the presence of undesirable enhancement. The source of this contamination must therefore be ejected before the whole identity can be obtained. Australia's struggle to purify sport is, thus, an attempt to purify the nation and the ideals to which it holds. Yet, the futility of this process is clear. By closely linking Australian identity with sport, and particularly through the issue of performance technologies, the search for a pure Australia will never end. The Australian nation has been constructed as a vigilant crusader against drugs, which offers it a sense of purpose and identity, differentiating it from 'weaker' or 'impure' nations. As such, Australia as a discrete entity is protected by metaphorical boundaries that distinguish it not just from the Other, but also from possible contamination by the Other. As Sibley (1995: 15) points out, 'the self is associated with fear and anxiety over the loss of control' and these fears and anxieties are 'projected onto bad objects', onto

Drugs, sport and Australian identity   141

the Other. Thus, 'stereotypes serve to maintain the boundaries of the self' in relation to both the self and the Other (Sibley 1995: 15), for essentially, the maintenance of this identity, of the illusory unity, is paramount. Yet, confirmation of Australia's identity through the relentless crusade against drugs could unravel if all drug use was removed from sport. An 'Aussie battler' only exists if there is something against which to battle. Yet despite this, increasingly sophisticated efforts are made to rid the sporting body of the scourge of drug use.

The preoccupation with the drug-taking of foreign athletes reveals how social anxieties are projected onto a concern with the body (Shilling 1993). By focusing attention on the *abuse* of foreign athletic bodies, the correct use of Australian athletic bodies is emphasised. This displacement and Othering of those who take performance enhancing drugs locates them outside not only a national discourse, but outside the boundaries of a shared international moral code. By injecting her/his body with a forbidden substance the athlete incorporates, or makes part of her/his body, the Other, and thus contaminates her/his Self/national identity. When this occurs, a destabilisation of the boundaries between Self/Other or nation/Other occurs, introducing a state of dis/ease and creating national and global uncertainty, opening up a liminal space that reveals the fragility of essentialised binary categories. The process of identifying drug abusers thus requires strict monitoring and a surveillance that moves across individual, physical and national borders to ensure that liminal zones are removed and the binary positions are restabilised.

In this context, the manufacturing of a specific 'natural' Australian identity and associated nation-building becomes important. The relationship between the nation as an imagined community and the sporting body as a manifestation of this construct signifies the relevance of sport and athletic competition to a nation's sense of self. Focusing the construction of a 'natural' and healthy self upon performance enhancing drugs suggests that the elimination of the drug threat functions as a way of excising the 'unnatural' and grotesque from the nation/self. Those who are found to have, or merely are suspected of having, taken drugs are demonised by the media, the public and their fellow athletes. These campaigns seek to specifically Other a variety of sporting bodies and nations, such as the East Germans and Chinese, displacing them outside of, and as a justification for, a moralistic discourse tinged with nationalistic fervour. This displacement and Othering continues the 'us' and 'them' binary in which the 'us' is configured as clean and proper and the 'them' as grotesque and improper. The use of these binary oppositions to support and enhance national identity functions to displace the bodies that 'abuse' outside mainstream configurations of national and sporting identity and, in this case study, reaffirm the purity of the Australian nation/body.

Yet, the very basis of such a construct is threatened when Australian athletes are themselves accused or found guilty of taking illicit substances. Despite

142   *Drugs, sport and Australian identity*

their hardline, public stance, Australian coaches and scientists have not been averse to using a range of substances to boost their athletes' performances. Yet when accusations of illegal drug abuse have been levelled at Australian athletes, officials and administrators have responded curiously, carefully reconfiguring performance enhancing substances as 'health-restoring' supplements. Samantha Riley's 'headache' tablet, for example, was carefully contrasted against the 'systematic hormonal manipulation' of her Chinese competitors (Magdalinski 2001a), thereby dismissing allegations that she had sought an 'unfair' advantage, whilst swimmers Richard Upton (ear infection) and Natasha Bowron (chronic bowel inflammation), as well as the Australian cycling team (immune system) were all essentially excused by a public that understood the restoration of health to be a legitimate reason for ingesting banned substances (Schlink 1998; Smith 1998). Perhaps the most useful revelation, however, was the response by team officials to suggestions, in the late 1990s, that Australian cyclists were using banned substances, a scandal that was to pre-empt similar allegations in 2004.

At the 1998 Commonwealth Games in Kuala Lumpur, the head of the British Sport Council's drug unit revealed that Australian cyclists were taking colostrum, a product that contains the banned substance Insulin Growth Factor-1 (IGF-1) (Schlink 1998). These allegations had come soon after Australian cyclist and Festina team member Neil Stephens had been accused of taking rEPO during the 1998 Tour de France, and the Australian cyclists were subsequently branded 'drug cheats'. Such allegations threatened to invalidate Australia's claim to take the toughest stance on illegal performance enhancing drugs and expose the fragility of constructing 'us' as inherently clean. Without the presence of a definite Other, the security of Australian identity was in jeopardy, thus colostrum was firmly recast as a 'natural' product that represented an advance in scientific training to boost the immune systems of Australia's representatives. Thus, colostrum could not be equated with artificial or synthetic products, and the performance enhancing properties of IGF-1 were negated by the 'natural' ingestion of colostrum tablets. According to Australian Commonwealth Games medical director, Brian Sando, if colostrum is taken in tablet form, the IGF-1 is '*denatured* in the stomach and cannot be absorbed into the body. ... The only way it can be absorbed is by injection' (Schlink 1998, emphasis added). Colostrum tablets are thus assuredly 'natural', for all sustenance must come through the mouth; however, the injection of this same substance represents an illegitimate penetration of the body's boundaries.

Whilst negating the performance enhancing aspects of IGF-1, the Australian cycling team doctor Peter Barnes further explained that colostrum was a 'dairy product' rather than a drug and confirmed that colostrum is 'produced *naturally* at the moment of birth' (Schlink 1998, emphasis added). The 'naturalness', and thus legitimacy, of the product is validated through associations with 'Mother Nature'. Barnes thereby links colostrum with the purity of life and the innocence of children by equating athletic performance enhancement with the life-giving properties of mother's milk. Thus the (national) body is strengthened by 'natural' substances that prevent the penetration of infection, and the nation takes on the role of motherhood in the managing of health and well-being of 'her' athletes.

The presence or even suggestion of drug-taking Australian athletes is unsettling for it opens up the liminal space that confounds strict binary categories. These spaces provoke anxiety for they are neither one nor the other, lying between, for example, 'us' and 'them'. For this reason, liminal zones are rapidly reabsorbed as binary opposites expand and contract, incorporating and thus eliminating these threats to their essentialist categories. John Boultbee's, then executive director of the AIS, suggestion in April 1998 highlights the mechanisms used to ensure the integrity of binary categories and to elide any ambiguity. In a letter sent to the IOC Medical Commission, Boultbee recommends removing all substances from the banned list with the exception of steroids, human growth hormone and rEPO (Magnay 1998b). On the surface, this may appear to be a clumsy attempt to simply allow those banned substances that Australian athletes have been guilty of ingesting, but what it actually does is collapse the liminal zones between both clean us/drug-tainted them and clean us/drug-tainted us. Boultbee further suggests that only those drugs that are 'clearly used by cheats' be banned, and that only '*real* cases of substantial cheating' (emphasis added) be investigated in order to catch the 'real cheats' (Magnay 1998b). This need to establish 'real' cheats compared with 'accidental' or 'innocent' cheats forcibly re-essentialises the binary categories cheat/non-cheat and again tries to deny the uncertainty of liminal space.

Conclusion

The Australian sports community has been vocal in its crusade against performance enhancing drugs. From all levels of government through to sports administrators and the media, an awareness of, and disdain for, synthetic enhancement has been well entrenched. Foreign athletes who are suspected of taking illicit substances are criticised openly, whilst Australian athletes are presented as incontrovertibly clean. The ASC's 'Essence of Australian Sport' appears to confirm that, for this nation in particular, the abuse of performance technologies is categorically rejected, and is something of a slight on the national character. Yet, to view such fervent protest as simply part of a desire to protect the spirit and sanctity of sport would be to miss important ideological implications. In essence, the Australian response to, and its self-proclaimed status as a world leader in, the war against doping effectively generates a sense of Australianness founded on the mythical image of the nation as exceptionally sporty and incontrovertibly clean.

Given that identity is founded more concertedly on describing what one is not, rather than what one is, it is clear that the construction of Australian identity through the forum of sport requires sporting Others against which

144 *Drugs, sport and Australian identity*

Australians can be measured. Whilst the competitive nature of sport readily provides bodies against which Australia's representatives can be contrasted, the presentation of 'our' athletes as pure, compared with the 'impure' Other, creates an effective binary arrangement that privileges 'us' over 'them'. Yet, the notion of 'pure' shifts to accommodate technological innovation in training systems, clothing and supplementation. The overtly scientised training regimes of the Soviet bloc were initially rejected as inauthentic, their cyborgian athletes regarded as a 'shamateur' infringement on the true spirit of amateur sport. Following Australia's poor performance at the 1976 Montreal Olympics, and the subsequent foundation of centralised training systems, sports science was, however, embraced as part of a decidedly 'natural' approach to the preparation of athletes. The notion of authenticity, however, remained critical and focused primarily on the use of artificial supplementation and its eradication.

Imagining Australia as particularly vigilant against performance enhancement, and the fervour with which Australian innocence is assumed, suggests that the purity of individual bodies is indicative of the broader integrity of the nation. When Australian athletes fail or return 'suspicious' drug tests, such as Ian Thorpe did in early 2007, the nation responds with shock and outrage at even the mere suggestion that an Australian 'legend' could be accused of such crimes, whilst determined efforts are made to recover their tarnished reputations (Dick 2007; Magnay 2007b). To charge an Australian athlete with illicit enhancement is to indict the nation as a whole, for the individual embodies the national character.

Not only do athletes serve as national representatives on an ideological level, but the bodies of Australian athletes are closely aligned to the national landscape, whereby the untouched geographical terrain is replicated in descriptions of athletic bodies, which are similarly essentialised as natural and uncontaminated. In the chapter that follows, the relationship between the landscape, body and nation is explored with specific reference to the Sydney 2000 Olympics, an event that was an opportunity to showcase Australia, through its landscape and its athletes, to the world. The site of the games, Homebush Bay, can be read as a potent symbol of not only Australian, but Olympic, purity that is discovered through the land and in the bodies of those who competed there.

9 The performance of nature at the Sydney 2000 Olympics

Introduction

In Australia, the distinctive national body, produced by a hostile and foreign environment, modified and improved in battle, tested against the imperial centre in sporting contest and cemented in a 'love affair' with the great outdoors has become central to an understanding of the nation. Whether it is the rugged outdoorsman or the bronzed lifesaver, Australian identity has been located largely within an understanding of nature, the natural body and the interaction between the two. Given Australia's self-declared love for sport and its significance in the construction of national identity, it is no surprise that sport is similarly grounded in conceptions of nature and that the natural athletic body is idealised as the epitome of 'Australianness'. Yet, the relationship between 'nature' and sport and their contribution to 'Australianness' is not reduced to corporeality alone. When Sydney was awarded the 2000 Olympic Games in 1993, its success was, in part, based on its commitment to an 'environmentally friendly', 'athletes' games', an event that was unpolluted and unpolluting (McGeoch and Korporaal 1994). The 'freedom to play' in a healthy, natural environment formed the basis of efforts to 'clean up' not only the dioxin-contaminated Homebush Bay Olympic site, but also the wider Olympic movement through the removal of the corrupting influence of various tainted IOC members as well as other 'scourges' such as performance enhancing drugs (Lehmann 1999; Magnay 1999a). By removing these 'snakes' from the Olympic 'Garden of Eden', the unpolluted home/bush was, in turn, reproduced in assurances about the purity and naturalness of Australian bodies that occupied the site. By constructing the nation as 'clean/sed' and 'natural', Australian athletes were signified as rightful heirs to the utopian, psychosocial space of the home/bush.

The extensive marketing of Sydney relied on images that presented Australia as a wild landscape with extremes of both climate and geography: 'Australia. A country of contradictions. Vast and uncrowded. Modern and highly urbanised. ... Parched red desert and endless golden summer grasses. Lush primeval green rainforest adjacent to sparkling sandy beaches. Rugged

146 *The performance of nature*

blue mountains and dazzling white snowfields' (SOGC 1991). At the same time, the emphasis on environmental restoration was mirrored in attempts to reclaim a lost Olympic innocence and to ensure the legitimacy of the athletic contest. Such a pristine location was considered an appropriate site for the games, predicated as they are on 'healthy' bodies engaging in wholesome 'play'. To this end, the Sydney Olympics were promoted as the 'green' games at the same time that Australian sporting authorities assured the public that stringent doping controls would be applied. Consumers were thereby reminded that the natural/Olympic environment was being recovered whilst the sporting results were guaranteed to be the sole outcome of an athlete's pure bodily performance.

The representation of 'natural' bodies, competing in 'natural' activities in a 'natural' landscape was primary to the Sydney 2000 Olympic Games. Within official Sydney Organising Committee for the Olympic Games (SOCOG) Image Guidelines, related merchandising and the televisual media, the Australian landscape played a dominant role in Olympic promotional activities. Australia was popularly conceptualised as an environmental paradise in which healthy play could be guaranteed, whilst the vocal, national stance against 'unnatural' intrusions into elite athletic competition meant that SOCOG could provide the requisite assurances that the games would remain pure and untainted on a number of levels. Within the production of these landscapes, the relationships between the body, the Olympic site and the Australian nation were revealed. What is important in this analysis is the way that the construction of an uncontaminated athletic body was mirrored in the manufactured 'nature' of Homebush Bay, which in turn was represented as a microcosm of the national environment. In this way, the athletic body came to symbolise the national body, and the purity of each was mutually reinforcing.

Analysing the relationship between space, sport and the body in this context reveals a plethora of cultural assumptions about the nature of 'nature'. The presence of natural bodies in a natural site was a paramount concern in not only Olympic advertising, but amongst sporting bodies themselves, and the success of the event hinged on selling the games as a return to traditional values that eschewed extreme bodily modifications. 'Nature', as embodied in the 'natural athlete' or the 'environment', thus became central to an understanding of not just the Sydney games, but of modern sport itself. Neil Smith (1996: 41) argues that 'the authority of "nature" as a source of social norms derives from its assumed externality to human interference, the givenness and unalterability of natural events and processes that are not susceptible to social manipulation'. The success of sport rests upon the pure physical performance unaffected by any kind of external interference. The body, in this instance, is isolated from social construction, alone in its pursuit of physical proficiency. The irony here is that neither the body, the site nor the nation is free from manipulation; each is subject to both discursive and physical interference and interpretation.

The performance of nature   147

By contrast, the notion of landscape embodies the 'natural' world as well as its interaction with human influences. Paul Groth (1997: 1) states that 'cultural landscape studies focus most on the history of how people have used *everyday* spaces ... to establish their identity, articulate their social relations, and derive cultural meaning'. An analysis of Homebush Bay acknowledges how the Olympic site produced meanings about the Australian landscape, thereby contributing to a reaffirmation of several foundations of Australian identity, at the same time that it confirmed broader Olympic ideals and philosophies. Although nature is privileged in the sporting world, the relationship between nature and culture is more revealing, and, as such, the concept of 'landscape' denotes a geographical realm (Homebush Bay) as well as a bodily terrain (athletes). Landscape, in this sense, refers neatly to the organic 'natural' quality of both body and site, whilst remaining cognisant of their cultural constructedness. As Nadia Lovell (1998: 6) suggests, 'landscapes are inscribed onto bodies through the mutual positioning of humans within nature and nature within society', so that both spaces and bodies represent surfaces onto which a multitude of meanings can be mapped.

John Bale's (1994: 13) assertion that 'sportscapes' are always subject to interpretation as they are 'mythical landscapes' proves instructive, as meanings embodied in a sportscape are as much a construction as the venue itself. His further suggestion that sportscapes are ideologically informed is particularly useful, for, after all, it is the mythical Olympic landscape that is central to this chapter. Homebush Bay offers an excellent example of the way that athletic spaces can be imbued with iconic meanings that extend beyond the bounds of the stadium and encompass not just an athletic, but a national typology. In this case study, the environmental ideology embodied in Homebush Bay was promulgated through the surveillance and regulation of Olympic bodies.

This chapter argues that the discourses surrounding Homebush Bay as a remediated environmental site had a dual function: spectators were reminded that Australian Olympic authorities had constructed an Olympic site in, and as, a broader natural paradise, at the same time that they had implemented stringent processes designed to restore the 'natural' athlete to its rightful place. It is clear that the presentation of both site and body as natural rested upon broader assumptions about the integrity of sporting performance and the naturalness of competitors, which essentially negates the 'construction' of sporting abilities through training and other bodily modifications. At the same time, assurances about 'natural' competition suggest an underlying confidence in the notion of 'fair play', an ideal central to 'Olympism' but one that ultimately disregards the structural elements of competition, achievement and success that are fundamental to contemporary sport. This chapter thus examines the performance of nature through both the bodies and site of an international sporting event, whereby nature, as a technologically constructed achievement, is celebrated and idealised as innate and immutable. By focusing on Homebush Bay and the Sydney Olympics, it is possible to identify a synecdochal relationship between the athletic body and the Australian

148   *The performance of nature*

nation for which it stands, such that the bodily purity of the athletes is mirrored in assurances about the environmental cleanliness of Homebush Bay.

Building a natural landscape: Homebush Bay

Selling the 2000 Olympic Games as the 'Green Games' linked athletic bodies through sport to a mythology that regards the 'Australian spirit' as intimately connected with the bush and thus with the natural/national environment. For over two centuries, the landscape, and people's interaction with it, has been at the centre of non-indigenous Australia's search for a distinctive identity (Dunlap 1999). The Olympic vision, promulgated by the Sydney Bid team, was of Australia as a natural and unpolluted environmental paradise, an 'ancient and mysterious land', where the youth of the world could gather to play without the threat of contamination (SOBL 1993). This ideology was celebrated in an opening ceremony that depicted Australia's natural landscape as conquered and tamed by European progress, which is an integral part of the nation's 'pioneering legend' (Hirst 1992) and contributed to the official corporate 'image' of the Sydney Olympics. This branding of the Olympics confirmed the presence of clean, pure, natural bodies in clean, pure, natural sites:

> In the cities, parks, forests and valleys, seas, lakes, rivers and pools, athletes relentlessly train. Fresh oxygen powers through their blood. Pure water quenches their thirst. A clean environment provides them with their most precious asset – the opportunity to excel.
>
> (SOCOG 1998)

Despite representing Sydney, and by extension Australia, as a pristine environment, the Olympic site at Homebush Bay was built on a toxic waste dump, the result of decades of unfettered pollution by heavy industry. Although the level of environmental degradation was known prior to the games – indeed, staging the Olympics was integral to the bay's 'regeneration' – the event remained steadfastly and popularly 'green'.

The restoration of Homebush Bay sought not only to develop 'environmentally sustainable' sporting facilities but to rejuvenate the surrounding 'natural' habitats, thereby providing a 'legacy' for the people of Sydney. The city's civic boosters and local councils had identified the Olympic Games in the early 1970s as a vehicle to promote the city's profile on a 'world stage', presenting Sydney as a centre for Asia-Pacific commerce and a destination for tourists. Originally targeting the 1988 Olympics to coincide with the Australian bicentennial celebrations, the New South Wales state government initially selected a site in Sydney's eastern suburbs; however, after protests from affluent residents, it was determined that Homebush Bay would serve the government's Olympic strategy instead (Weirick 1999).

Homebush Bay was an ideal site. It was located in the heart of Sydney, close to public transport, and was a state-owned parcel of land, which meant that the construction of a sporting precinct did not require the resumption of parkland and homes, as had been suggested in the previous proposal (Weirick 1999). Whilst it was a suitable location for sporting facilities, the site's history as variously an abattoir, brickworks and munitions dump meant that the ground was unstable as well as highly polluted. According to Greenpeace (2000), around 9 million cubic metres of waste had been dumped in the area, which filled over 160 hectares of natural wetlands in both Homebush and Wentworth Bays. Homebush Bay subsequently became the only waterway in Australia where fishing had been banned as a result of the high levels of dioxin poisoning (Greenpeace 2000). Despite the significant outlay required to remediate Homebush Bay, its waters were portrayed in Bid documents as 'serene' and 'glistening', and the site was ratified as the venue for a future Olympic Games.

Sydney's bid for the 2000 games was launched amidst a growing awareness of the potential links between sustainability and sporting endeavours, as well as at a time when environmental issues were gaining greater exposure through the world's media. The IOC was under enormous pressure to adopt environmentalism as a 'third arm' of the movement's philosophy of Olympism, along with sport and culture. The 1992 Albertville Winter Olympics had been soundly criticised for the destruction wreaked upon the pristine alpine village, and protesters insisted that the 1994 Lillehammer games be organised according to 'green' principles (Cantelon and Letters 2000; Lenskyj 2000). Environmental advocates increasingly pointed out that sporting and leisure pursuits, particularly those designed to take advantage of the 'outdoors', were having a devastating effect on natural areas, both in terms of actual physical degradation, as well as the polluting effects of large numbers of participants and spectators (Allison 1993).

Sydney Olympic Bid Limited, the company established to bid for the games, quickly recognised the expediency of relying on 'green' rhetoric, and what was originally dubbed the 'Athletes' Games', also acquired the 'Green Games' epithet. After winning the bid in 1993, however, many of the evironmentally sustainable initiatives that had been proposed were shelved in favour of more cost-efficient construction methods and materials (Lenskyj 2000). Whilst the proposed 'eco-village' all but disappeared, the perception of the 'Green Games' remained, reinforced by a plethora of 'environmental factsheets' on the webpages of the Olympic Coordination Authority, SOCOG and a host of other Olympic-related organisations. In addition, the image of the 'Green Games' was strengthened by SOCOG's relentless imagery of the unparalleled beauty and 'purity' of the Australian landscape.

Landscape and Australian identity

The desire to showcase Australia's natural beauty as part of the Olympic bid is not without precedent. Since European occupation, the Australian land has been subject to different interpretations that have said more about

150 The performance of nature

the observer than the terrain. Europeans had long imagined a 'Great South Land', an Antipodean 'Other', whose landscape was regarded, after settlement, as variously a 'pastoral Arcadia, as a bushland for utopian reverie, and as refuge for romantic escapists', each of which contributed to the presentation of Australia as 'an unproblematic exotic essence' (Hoffie 1997: 69). By the late nineteenth century, writers, poets and artists, influenced by an emerging nationalism, sought to define Australianness and saw a distinctive national identity embodied in an outback lifestyle that was narrated as quintessentially Australian (Dunlap 1999; Turner 1986). Harsh and uncompromising, the land was represented as a virgin territory in need of conquering, taming and modifying, and popular images of the outback portrayed a hostile environment, ready to swallow the intrepid explorer should he, and it was always a he, stand still even for a moment (Turner 1986). The landscape has thus provided a point of reference for Australians, a means of distinguishing themselves from both the imperial centre and other colonial territories and as a way of forging an identity based on their responses to the challenges of the outback (Dunlap 1999). Since the late nineteenth century, Australians have celebrated their native flora and fauna as a marker of difference and as a source of national collective identification (Dunlap 1999; Hoffie 1997; Turner 1986), and these versions of Australia find resonance in contemporary tourist campaigns that reproduce an image of the nation as an exotic refuge, an empty land filled with geological and climatic wonders.

Confirmed by the success of movies such as *Crocodile Dundee*, the Australian landscape has come to dominate the popular global conception of Australia and, as such, the concept of a green, environmentally friendly Olympic Games was not far removed from many of these oft-displayed images. In North America and elsewhere, images of a rugged outback sparsely peopled with laid-back Aussies, are coupled with images of the rainforest, Great Barrier Reef and coastal and tropical regions. Australia is still represented a *terra nullius*, a land largely empty of people but replete with expansive and varied terrains, open to consumption by both touristic and televisual voyeur. These images contributed to a popular understanding of Australia by global audiences as an environmental paradise and were reinforced by Olympic advertising, tourist strategies and popular entertainment, such as *Survivor II: The Australian Outback* or *The Crocodile Hunter*.

The primacy of the landscape in constructing a suitable national vision of Australia was evident at the opening ceremony of the 2000 Olympic Games, where the spectacular diversity of Australia's flora and fauna was gradually tamed under the yoke of industrial progress. From the ethereal Barrier Reef to the harsh landscape destroyed by fire and the reemergence of flowers and bushland thereafter, Australia's topography was stylised and inhabited with appropriate iconic beasts. Thomas Dunlap (1999) reveals that traditionally Australian flora and fauna was used to delineate the nation from its northern hemisphere counterparts; however, more recently, as native plants and

The performance of nature   151

animals are increasingly globalised, wattle can be purchased in Berlin and koalas reside in San Diego, indigenous cultures are used to represent national difference and distinction (Godwell 2000; MacCannell 1999). Thus, Aboriginal Australians in the opening ceremony appeared together with other national 'natural' emblems and were thereby confirmed as merely 'inhabitants' or even 'custodians' of the land rather than citizens of the nation. Indigenous Australians were embedded in the natural realm and featured as part of an ancient land, an historic people 'linked to the dawn of man'. Yet after thoughtfully 'moving aside' to facilitate European occupation, indigenous Australians had little role to play in the ceremony. Akin more to the kangaroo than the white settler, their status as a distinctive 'feature' of the Australian landscape reaffirmed the status of the 'Great South Land' as an empty space that had waited for centuries to be peopled.

The montage of images and sounds, voiced-over by American actor James Earl Jones and presented at the start of the opening ceremony on US network NBC set the immediate tone for the international consumer of the Sydney Olympics:

> Terra Australis incognita. The unknown Southern land. An island continent where all around the sea tumbled the shore with a beautiful fury. With beaches guarded by towering rocks carpeted by the whitest sands, a place where there was a reef more than a thousand miles long, sheltering a jungle among the wildlife, a place where geography was made gigantic, where there stood a monolith, one hundred million years old, a seemingly infinite wilderness, a land of living fossils, occupied by a proud culture, linked to the dawn of man. A land where a city would be settled among sheltering coves, where a spectacular metropolis would wrap itself around a glistening harbour. Where a daring structure, perched on the waters, announced the none-too-subtle ambitions of a bold, restless people.
>
> (NBC 2000)

Despite the preponderance of landscape images in Olympic marketing during the preparations for the games, Australia's reputation as a natural environment was juxtaposed against the reality of its highly urbanised culture. The enduring images of Australia's landscape would certainly sell 'Brand Australia' to an international audience of travellers, but the additional mission for the Sydney games was to present Australia as a desirable location for regional, if not global corporate headquarters. Bid documents, thus, depicted Australia as a technologically competent nation capable of staging this and other global events. To satisfy the demands of both the corporate and tourist industries, the nation was summarised, binarised even, as simply a land of contrasts between 'sand and sea, land and sky, city and outback' (SOCOG 1998), which continued through to SOCOG's official corporate image and which featured in the opening ceremony celebrations.

152   *The performance of nature*

Furthermore, in the months immediately preceding the games, the Olympic torch relay became a powerful symbol of a nation unified as it traversed the land, visiting natural geographical features, such as Uluru, the Great Barrier Reef, a billabong and farmland, as well as urban scapes. In a sense, through the journey of the flame, the imagined nation materialised (Anderson 1983). The torch was always coming from somewhere and, never stopping, always continued on its journey to somewhere else. Daily televised accounts of the flame's progress gave a sense of space to the nation and supported our imaginary national conceptions. And as the flame gradually made its way to Stadium Australia, it provided the necessary link between the nation, its population and the opening ceremony. The flame's journey through the land was only concluded as it was used to light the new Olympic cauldron, but the journey through Australian landscapes was not over.

Restoring the land and the body

The site of the Sydney 2000 Olympics at Homebush Bay was replete with contradictions. It was the home of an event that celebrates health and competition in a natural state, yet the environment was one that required immediate remediation and intervention if it was to conform to the glistening images presented through the bidding process. It was a sporting venue that gestured to the natural authentic realm, yet it symbolised the convergence of culture and nature, and artifice and environment. It was constructed as a sporting space that offered respite from urban life, yet was engineered to meet the complex demands of international sport. In essence, Homebush Bay was not a natural space in which athletes were invited to take recreation, but was regulated and controlled to meet the rational standards of an activity that requires 'geographical "sameness"' (Bale 1994: 63). Nevertheless, sport is popularly conceived as some kind of return to nature, and sportscapes are often named for organic spaces, such as parks or gardens, which themselves are not pure wilderness areas but are cultivated and manipulated to produce a version of nature that is neat, tidy and, above all, unthreatening. The interface between nature and culture, embodied in the garden, is evident within both sports stadia, like Homebush Bay, as well as the athletes that come to such spaces to compete. Each are caught between nature and culture, representing both the site of unbounded play and the strict regulation of codified sport; both body and site are symbolic of a location where nature is contained (Bale 1994).

Homebush Bay epitomises the liminality of the garden; it is not quite wild, but not completely controlled either. Indeed, the ambiguity of the site is embedded in its name, Home/Bush/Bay, which offers multiple readings as to its 'true' nature. 'Home' represents cultural spaces, 'a place of return, an original settlement where peace can finally be found and experienced' (Lovell 1998: 2–3), which contrasts with the 'mysterious and undiscovered' Australian continent (SOBL 1993: 6), signified by the 'bush'. The 'bay', on

The performance of nature   153

the other hand, offers us a site where the two reside side by side, where a 'spectacular metropolis' is 'settled among [the] sheltering coves' of a 'glistening harbour' (NBC 2000). The imaging of Homebush Bay as a safe 'home' for the Olympics was critical in efforts to reform the movement's ailing reputation. Throughout the 1990s, the movement had stumbled from one allegation of corruption to the next, from Vyv Simpson and Andrew Jennings' (1992) initial charges through to later investigations of improprieties within the bidding process, and the celebration of 'serenity', 'peace, harmony and understanding' in a restored natural wonderland was a welcome respite from these indictments (SOBL 1992: 19). Locating the games in such a landscape provided the Olympic movement with an opportunity to regenerate from corrupt movement to pure ideal, just as the site itself had been restored from industrial toxicity to unpolluted paradise. After several years of turmoil, then, the Olympic movement itself was returned 'home' to a calm 'bay' and an unblemished 'bush'.

The contradictions inherent in the Home/Bush/Bay site, and within the Australian landscape more generally, were mirrored in representations of athletic bodies. At the same time that the built environment was projected as reclaiming nature, the Sydney games sought to recover the 'natural' athlete, free from the influence of illicit performance technologies. To this end, Australia had positioned itself as a world leader in the fight against performance enhancing drugs and as a nation particularly concerned with preserving the organic body. The Sydney games were predicted to be the 'most tested' games, reinforcing initial promotional efforts to reaffirm the unity of 'nature' and the 'natural athlete' within the Olympic movement, thereby restoring innocence and purity to the tarnished event. Of course, within the Olympic arena, and certainly in terms of Australian athletes, such strategies were clearly at odds with the presence of one of the most efficient technological systems of elite sport training. In other words, just as the environment was merely a mimesis of a statically defined 'natural habitat', so too did athletes only appear to be free from scientific manipulation.

As discussed in the previous chapter, Australia's objective for preserving the integrity of the athletic body is supported by the nation's quest to locate its identity upon and within the bodies of its athletes. Whilst an athlete's physical performance has often been regarded as indicative of national strength and vitality, it is at the level of the body that the nation is also visible. As soon as athletes are attired in the national uniform, they become national bodies, yet signifying the nation also takes place beneath the layers of clothing that, to varying degrees, conceal the sportsman or woman. Ideologies are inscribed directly onto the body itself, such that its physical contours are construed to reflect broader national ideologies that are similarly embedded in the landscape. Athletic bodies are thereby revealed to be a kind of geographical terrain that are inscribed with the same ideologies as the nation's topography. The body's surfaces thus mirror interpretations of the landscape, such that its very size, shape and dimension are as meaningful

154 *The performance of nature*

as the terrain. The athlete's external appearance and its conformity to expected physical ideals indicate national strength and vitality, whilst bodies that exceed normative dimensions imply unnatural enhancement, fracturing the mythology of untouched nature.

The athlete, in essence, exposes the point where the sporting body and nation intersect, confirming that its surfaces are subject to scrutiny in the same way that the geographical terrain is. This was particularly evident in the case of the Sydney Olympics. Images of the Australian landscape as boundless, free and untouched by technology, culture or civilisation, which underpinned Olympic promotional efforts, were effective in reinforcing Australian claims to produce exclusively healthy, clean competitors. The bodies of athletes, like the nation itself, were fit, strong and healthy, essentially beyond reproach and assuredly pure and unaffected by inappropriate technological intervention. In this way, an athlete's physical state signifies not only the integrity of their performance but also, more broadly, the state of the nation. Thus, the purity of Australia's athletes, reflected through the uncontaminated natural landscape, confirmed the nation's own integrity, suggesting that the borders of both body and country are closely regulated and secured from unnatural penetration.

The protection of the nation and its identity rests on the maintenance of physical and imaginative borders that delimit the territory and establish the margins of the national terrain. Those seeking entry must cross borders at the appropriate place with the appropriate documentation, and unauthorised entry (or departure) is strictly controlled to ensure that there is no illegal infraction of the nation's borders. In some instances, explicit physical barriers, such as the Berlin Wall or the proposed structure on the USA/Mexico border, are erected to ensure entry is strictly regulated, whilst exposed points are monitored to ensure the nation is protected. Establishing and patrolling the limits of the Australian nation is simplified by the geographical coherency of the national terrain as well as its relative isolation, though rendered difficult by its sheer size. As an island, Australia shares no direct physical borders with another country, which allows a national identity to be confidently formed around its geography. The margins of the land seem permanent, fixed and secure, unlike the more fluid borders of, for example, European states, where invasion seems omnipresent.

The body, like the nation, seems secure. It is isolated from unauthorised penetration through metaphorical and physical boundaries that distinguish it not just from the Other, but also from possible corruption by the Other. In this conception, the skin is thought to function as a protective shield that secures the integrity of the body as discrete at the same time it fortifies the body against external contaminants. Although it appears to be a pristine and continuous whole (Benthien 2002), the physical limits of the body are not fixed and are easily traversed. Nutrition enters through the mouth, air through the lungs, and waste is excreted as a host of other natural functions crosses the body's borders. Foreign bodies enter, take up residence in and

The performance of nature   155

are expelled from both the individual and the nation, confirming that although each imagines itself to be a discrete whole, the fluidity across their margins reveals each to be permeable.

Whilst some breaches of its borders are required for the body's normal functioning, others are used to augment the body and enhance its capacity for physical output. Within the context of sport, it is now widely accepted that the natural body must be exposed to technological intervention through systematic training and preparatory regimes. Lawful supplements are taken to boost nutrients and minerals in the body, and customised diets are designed to ensure that the most valuable combination of foodstuffs is consumed. Each of these is evidently an appropriate way of enhancing the body's capacity, whilst other external influences are regarded as a disruption to the body's inherent 'naturalness'. The ingestion of performance enhancing substances or other synthetic agents provokes anxiety as it represents an artificial contaminant that endangers the integrity of the athletic body. Injecting substances into the body pierces the body's outer protective layer, introducing contamination through an unauthorised point that essentially compromises the body.

Given that the athlete's skin serves as a proxy national border (Williams and Bendelow 1998), it is clear that unlawful transgression of the body jeopardises the nation as a whole and efforts to repair the breach are intensified in response. To ensure the integrity of both the athlete and nation, it is not merely the exterior that is significant as the body's interior is also subject to scrutiny. Rigorous testing procedures plumb the body's depths for fluids that will reveal impurities at the same time that bodily surfaces are popularly inspected for evidence of unnatural enhancement. Manipulation of the inner workings is thus assumed to be visible upon the outer surfaces as internal toxicity distorts the margins of the body, creating 'unnatural', even monstrous, forms that betray illicit enhancement.

More terrifying than the appearance of distorted and disfigured monsters is the potential for an athlete to be encased in a skin that obscures the degree to which their body has been chemically manipulated. Despite concerns about disruptions to national or bodily landscapes, it is the visible surface that must conform to normative standards, which allows any underlying contamination to remain concealed. Golf courses famously present themselves as a kind of manicured nature (Bale 1994), whilst just below the surface is a labyrinth of watering and drainage systems that are required to sustain the garden above. Below the surface of Homebush Bay throbbed a similar level of toxicity, whilst athletic bodies are contained in a skin that elides the degree to which the human form has been chemically manipulated in its pursuit of sporting glory. In the case of Homebush Bay, the poisons that lie beneath the surface threaten to leach out and pollute the Olympic host. The skin of 'environmental restoration', which demarcates inside and out, is all that contains the contamination. Athletic bodies, by contrast, are regarded as 'natural' entities under threat from contamination

156   *The performance of nature*

from without; their skin represents the final line of defence in the vigilant maintenance of their athletic purity. Yet, at the same time, they resemble the Olympic site. Their skin is all that prevents the modern Olympic athlete from exposing the chemical and technological manipulation within.

Conclusion

The landscape remains central to constructions of Australian identity, both internally and externally. The promise of an untouched outback, pristine coastal regions and rainforests, which once inspired intrepid explorers to cross oceans, now appears extensively in advertising campaigns to market Australia as an attractive tourist destination. Internally, the landscape serves as a candid reminder of what differentiates Australia from its peers, and the bush mythology that informed early stirrings of Australian nationalism continues to resonate within popular representations of Australia and Australianness. The performance of nature was nowhere more explicit than during the 2000 Sydney Olympics, where the Australian landscape played a critical role in both securing and promoting the games, and in convincing the watching world that those who were invited to compete were, like the land, undeniably natural.

What has been significant for this analysis is the multiple ways in which nature and landscape were embedded within both Olympic and Australian rhetoric. From an emphasis on natural landscapes to the preservation of natural athletes, nature was central to the Sydney games, offering not only an attractive backdrop but a philosophical reminder that the integrity and morality of the Olympic movement could be, and would be, restored. Through the depictions of Homebush Bay as a glistening harbour and an environmental showcase, international audiences were offered a haven within which the corrupted Olympic movement could regenerate. It was a redemptive site that championed both the environmental restoration of Homebush Bay and the return of biological integrity and pure, untainted athletic performances.

Within these landscapes, it was thus possible to identify a relationship between the body, the Olympic site and the Australian nation, such that the construction of an uncontaminated athletic body was mirrored in the manufactured 'nature' of Homebush Bay, which in turn was represented as a microcosm of the national environment. In doing so, this relationship revealed the explicit tensions between culture and nature, and artifice and environment that were reflected in both the body and the site of the 2000 Olympics. It revered environmental sustainability, yet the Olympic precinct was built on a toxic site that required extensive remediation. It celebrated the biological integrity of its participants yet had to develop an intrusive system of drug detection to ensure it. The nature/artifice binary inherent in the Home/Bush Bay site, and within the Australian landscape more generally, was thus replayed in and on the body.

10 Conclusion

Modern sport is a paradox. It seeks to surpass established records with astonishing performances that push the body beyond its current limits. Entire industries are dedicated to its development as national governments and international corporations annually invest billions to sustain an industry they feel serves their diverse interests. At the same time, sport adheres to strict, and, for some, archaic, principles that rely on conservative notions of chivalry, amateurism and gentlemanliness. These are seemingly at odds with the realities of contemporary elite and professional sport, and the conflict between these priorities has generated a series of moral panics. The lament over an increasingly commercialised industry, where top players command more in a day than most earn in a year, or the dismay over sports administrators who allow the corrupting effects of 'politics' into the game, highlights, for example, the critical discord between sport's 'noble' ideals and 'grim' realities. The antagonism between these ideological positions, as expressed through an aversion to performance technologies, is addressed in this book, as substances and techniques, applied directly to the athletic body or utilised within the conduct of sport for the sole purpose of enhancing performance, represent, for many, the most exigent crisis currently facing sport. To use any and all measures to enhance a performance is thought to privilege winning over participation and, potentially, cheating over morality. Embracing the pursuit of excellence and playing for intrinsic reasons is, however, to uphold sport's values by rejecting behaviours that may tarnish its reputation. Indeed, the fundamental conflict appears to be between the 'essence' and 'spirit' of sport.

Categorising sport's various qualities and characteristics as part of either its 'essence' or 'spirit' is to reduce the athletic experience to a simple binary, an either/or scenario where participants compete for the win or for the love. But it is a problematic construct because we know, perhaps from personal experience, that sport is never merely about one or the other of these. Motivation to play can be, and often is to varying degrees, a combination of both, or, indeed, neither. An elite athlete does not spend significant portions of their life preparing their mind and body merely for the joy of 'just being there' nor simply for the 'love of the game'; however, this

158   Conclusion

is not to suggest that they derive no pleasure from their training schedules or competitive events. By contrast, a casual participant may join a team to socialise or improve fitness without the explicit desire to win or an expectation of a material reward, but equally, this does not mean they would not be rather chuffed with a victory or trophy. Though it might beget more problems than it solves, abbreviating sport into the simple shorthand of 'essence' and 'spirit' was a deliberate strategy to establish, with the specific intention of collapsing, a rudimentary, yet encompassing, binary that could represent the myriad others present in sport. Drawing attention to this construct serves to identify and dismantle the natural/artifice couplet, perhaps the most critical to this discussion, by using it as an interrogatory device to illustrate how it creates, and sustains, tense relationships between sport, the body, performance and technology.

Within sport, nature and artifice are explicitly and implicitly juxtaposed to design a series of binaries that both reinforce the essentialist natures of health, the body and the 'spirit' of sport and inform contemporary attitudes towards performance technologies. As binaries are necessarily hierarchical, the nature/artifice couplet foregrounds nature as privileged, which is supported by a range of ideological positions that regard it as an unadulterated concept that can both inspire and instruct humankind. Nature is, at once, a moral touchstone, a sublime space that reminds of the consequences of technical progress, and a mirror through which human culture can be studied. In such a paradigm, nature is axiomatic, represented as an immutable, trans-cultural and trans-historical reality that informs a wide variety of social frameworks and institutions. Sport is firmly situated within a discourse of 'nature', where talent and ability are thought to be firmly embedded in the body. Furthermore, sport is imagined to be an expression of freedom, an opportunity for the weary soul to be refreshed, and an activity traditionally conducted amongst the fields and forests of the natural realm. The reality of sport is, certainly, quite different, yet appeals to its 'natural' origin are evident in the names of the 'parks' and 'fields', which are engineered for competition, and in the determination to protect the sporting body from technological corruption. What is feared to be a gradual easing of the nature/artifice distinction is embodied in the apprehension and despair directed towards the increasing reliance on performance technologies.

Although illicit enhancements are proscribed for many reasons, and though there are countless ways that these might have been organised, for the purposes of this book, the conceptual categories 'health' and 'morality' were identified as the primary reasons that particular performance technologies are prohibited. Critically, I arrived at this broad classification not because I find no value in the detailed taxonomies that philosophers of sport have already established, but because health and morality encompass the most pressing, and public, concerns, confirmed by anti-doping agencies around the world that typically stress that protecting the integrity of both sport and the body are core to their mission. Similarly, within popular discourses, illicitly enhanced athletes are generally thought to damage both their physical well-being and their honour. Yet, whilst appealing to both health and morality might appear to serve the prohibitionist strategy twice as effectively, this analysis confirms that, far from being discrete or independent, health and morality are intimately related. They are both embedded in a discourse of nature that constructs each as an organic concept that is exposed to contamination by external, and, more terrifyingly, internal contagion. Furthermore, health cannot be regarded as simply an individual concern and is located within broader moral discourses of civic and national well-being, at the same time that morality is not simply a social issue, but a personal responsibility, which starts with the protection of the body and its integrity.

Dismantling the nature/artifice binary reveals health, morality, the body and sport to be interconnected rather than independent and, like all analytical frameworks, flexible rather than fixed. What are initially presented as enduring categories withstand only a cursory interrogation before they crumble, exposing a fluidity that points towards a continual process of modification that corresponds to the ebb and flow of ideology. Health is not, for example, a strict or immutable biological phenomenon, but rather an amorphous concept that relies on disease, injury and illness for its identity. Furthermore, it embodies critical aspects of morality, civic order and national well-being, confirming that health is not merely a personal but a collective concern. Nature, too, proves to be a slippery concept, defined in terms of its relationship with culture to serve as a mirror through which rational and technical progress can be audited. The body, though it has a material dimension, is similarly elusive, conceived as mechanical or natural, fluid or fixed, and abject and liminal as its depths are plumbed and its surfaces surveilled to verify its degrees of 'organicity' and 'inorganicity'. It is clear, then, that each of these percepts can only ever be constructed against, and is visible only in the presence of, its presumed opposite. In this way, nature, health, the body and morality serve not merely as discursive strategies to interrogate nature/artifice, but are metaphors of one another.

It is, of course, the body that is central to constructions of nature and artifice, and, in particular, the 'natural' body appears to require specific protection from the corrupting influences of technology. Various health practices and interventions, for example, eradicate toxins and contagions, which enter and disrupt the body, whilst the spectre of Frankenstein's monster is a reminder of the horrifying consequences of amalgamating technology and the body. It is the ever-present exposure to corruption and disorder that reminds us how precious and precarious the body is as well as the steps required to secure its integrity. These constructions are particularly critical to discourses of sport, which position the natural body firmly at its core. In this context, the surfaces and depths of the natural sporting body are carefully scrutinised, both literally and figuratively, for signs of the illicit intrusion

160 *Conclusion*

of unnatural substances or the use of forbidden methods and techniques. Bodies that exceed normative expectations, then, are transgressive and threatening, embodying an alternate subjectivity that conflicts with the nature of sport. Female bodies are particularly vulnerable. Zoe Warwick's excessive frame obliterated heterosexual and feminine norms, whilst the lithe physique of Samantha Riley or the girlish figure of Andreea Raducan offer reminders of what a 'true' woman is, regardless of her status as a 'drug cheat'. Flo-Jo, Michelle Smith, Marion Jones and a host of others are similarly constructed in the public eye as either guilty or innocent, using physical markers to support their assessments.

It is curious, however, that even though 'performance' technologies or 'performance' enhancement are considered to be the fundamental threat, 'performance' itself is typically omitted from analyses. Its absence is certainly remarkable, given it is not the actions of a sedentary body that are of interest in sport, but rather those of the performing body. This exclusion, in part, prompted the inclusion of 'performance' in the title of this book, because it was critical to signal its centrality to, and remove it from the margins of, the debate. Analysing this concept is essential not merely because it is foregrounded in the name of that which is most feared, but because establishing the nature of performance illustrates precisely what is potentially disrupted by proscribed technologies. It is not merely the body, its health or the more nebulous 'spirit' of sport that are corrupted by these substances or methods, but performances, which are, in essence, the central feature of sport. What a discussion of performance reveals is a distilled narrative of integrity, unobscured by health, the body or even morality, which represents the primary characteristic that differentiates sport from other staged events.

Whilst performance might be overshadowed by the more seductive and emotive discourses of health and integrity, the importance of authenticity is clearly evident. The rules and regulations that govern sport and its conduct focus largely on removing ambiguity from the field of sport so that the performance is an accurate reflection of the competitor's actual bodily capacity. Extraneous influences, including climatic conditions, environmental vagaries and even subjective interests, are either eliminated or mitigated as far as possible to ensure that nothing other than the body itself contributes to the final outcome. Critically, the purpose of athletic competition is not merely to test bodies against one another, but to establish the absolute limit of human capacity. Clearly, the body must have a threshold that it simply cannot exceed no matter how well prepared it might be; athletes cannot, physics reminds us, traverse one hundred metres in absolutely no time at all, but that does not stop speculation on what might be the absolute fastest that a human can run this distance. Is it the current world record of 9.69 seconds or is 9 seconds physically achievable? If we reach 9 seconds flat, would an athlete be able to shatter that milestone if the track were slightly modified, their uniform made more conducive or the air quality improved? These are the questions that drive the performance sciences, prompting John Hoberman's (1992: ix) contention that sport might best be regarded a 'vast, loosely coordinated experiment upon the human organism', as elite athletes unwittingly submit their bodies to this research.

It is for this reason that the decision by the IAAF to outlaw the use of 'technological aids' in competition, effectively preventing disabled athletes from mainstream events, is not altogether surprising. Some have suggested that the IAAF rule change, in response to the event that double amputee Oscar Pistorius qualifies for mainstream track and field meets, reveals an intrinsic fear that the perfect athletic body could be surpassed by a less perfect version. Whilst the cultural privileging of the 'normal' body may appear to be threatened, I would argue that the rule change does not represent a fear of the consequences or implications should disabled bodies outperform able bodies; indeed disabled athletes sitting on motorbikes can already do that. Instead, the rule change protects the 'purity' of sport, in terms of its quest to determine the absolute most the human body can do. Anything added to the body, even if it is just to enable mobility, simply does not help establish those outer limits. What is critical is that, regardless how accomplished the athlete might be and despite the number of able bodied athletes they may outshine, the fundamental fact is that a disabled body restored to functionality reveals nothing about the human body's limits; it only demonstrates what a defective body can be made to do with prosthetic assistance. In terms of Hoberman's 'experiment' of sport, it is a second-class body and a second-class performance that has no value outside comparisons that can be drawn with similarly disadvantaged specimens.

Clearly, then, it is not merely the nature of performance, but rather the nature of the pure human performance that is of critical import in this discussion, and it is here that performance and the body intersect. Performances are created by bodies; pure performances, consequently, are created by pure bodies. For this reason, performances do not easily tolerate threats to their integrity, and, as indicated above, institutional measures ensure the authenticity of athletic performances, as evidenced by the strict monitoring of the body to reaffirm the nature/artifice binary. But disruptions to this binary can only occur if these concepts are thought to be fixed. If they are shown to be malleable, then the binary collapses, revealing an exciting, unexplored territory.

By dismantling the nature/artifice binary, I wanted to demonstrate explicitly that fixed categories do nothing to unravel the paradox of sport but rather it is at their margins that the discord between natural and unnatural is revealed. Binaries, though compelling, create an inadequate, limiting and unsatisfying framework that cannot account for diversity or difference without trying to reduce these anomalies back into an either/or construct. As such, it is neither the 'either' nor the 'or' that is terribly interesting, but rather the '/' in-between, for this is the point where two essentialist categories are forced to confront one another. When the binary is disrupted by

162   *Conclusion*

a confounding variable, it is the border between that deteriorates to reveal a hazy or liminal space where we are neither/nor but both. At this moment, ideologies not only intersect, but interfuse, thereby collapsing binaries to offer enticing glimpses into the nature of Self and Other from a third perspective. It is here, in this intermediary zone, betwixt and between the unabashed pursuit of victory and a conservative philosophy, that performance technologies, for example, reside.

Within this study, I focused specifically on Australian examples to offer a sustained reading of the nature/artifice binary within a single national milieu. Yet case studies, by their very nature, are limited even though they are useful tools to explore and apply theoretical perspectives and suppositions. Future studies might examine the construction of this binary in other athletic contexts to determine the limits, or margins, of this theoretical approach. These settings do not need to be national as in the final two chapters of this volume, rather the nature/artifice relationship can be interrogated within any framework in which collective identities are asserted through sporting competition to distinguish us from them, Self from Other.

Whilst this analysis has focused on performance technologies and the nature/artifice construct as a way of illustrating the problems of binarism, it could be equally and successfully applied to other concerns within sport to illustrate, for example, reductive categories of 'ability' and 'disability'. Understanding the body not simply as able or disabled would, for example, mean athletes such as Pistorius would not represent any kind of threat to sport, its purity or the chances of athletes. He would simply be an addition to an already diverse field of competitors. Epithets of 'special' or 'para' would be rendered meaningless, cast out of an athletic paradigm that recognises and celebrates diversity, rather than one that tries to contain and eliminate it.

In essence, then, this book respects the fluidity and role of the liminal space of practice and performance to interrogate and unravel the essentialist binaries that constitute modern sport. The apprehension over performance technologies and their potential to disrupt the 'natural' body and the 'integrity' of sport exposes the limitations and the ideological power and role of the nature/artifice binary within constructs of the body, health, morality and nature.

Bibliography

Adam, B. (1998) *Timescapes of Modernity: the environment and invisible hazards*, London: Routledge.

Adirim, T. A. and Cheng, T. L. (2003) 'Overview of injuries in the young athlete', *Sports Medicine*, 33(1): 75–81.

Aitchison, C., Macleod, N. E. and Shaw, S. J. (2000) *Leisure and Tourism Landscapes: social and cultural geographies*, London: Routledge.

Alexander, R. (1996) 'The deep end', *Inside Sport*, 55: 98–105.

Allison, L. (2001) *Amateurism in Sport: an analysis and a defence*, London: Frank Cass.

—— (1993) 'Sport as an environmental issue', in L. Allison (ed.) *The Changing Politics of Sport*, Manchester: Manchester University Press.

Allmark, P. (2005) 'Health, happiness and health promotion', *Journal of Applied Philosophy*, 22(1): 1–15.

Anderson, B. (1983) *Imagined Communities: reflections on the origin and spread of nationalism*, New York: Verso.

Anderson, R. (2004) *Second Stage Report to the Australian Sports Commission and Cycling Australia*, 27 October. Available at www.ausport.gov.au/fulltext/2004/feddep/Anderson_report_secondstage.pdf (accessed 10 January 2007).

Andrews, M. (1999) 'Blood, sweat and well-earned tears', *The Newcastle Herald*, 17 July.

Aoki, D. (1996) 'Sex and muscle: the female bodybuilder meets Lacan', *Body and Society*, 2(4): 59–74.

Armstrong, T. (ed.) (1996) *American Bodies: cultural histories of the physique*, New York: New York Press.

Arnold, P. J. (1990) 'Sport, the aesthetic and art: further thoughts', *British Journal of Educational Studies*, 38(2): 160–79.

Aron, C. (1999) *Working at Play: a history of vacations in the United States*, Oxford: Oxford University Press.

Arthur, L. B. (1999) 'Introduction: dress and the social control of the body', in L. B. Arthur (ed.) *Religion, Dress and the Body*, Oxford: Berg.

ASADA (Australian Sports Anti-Doping Authority) (2007a) 'ASADA reaches out to the next generation of Olympians', media release, 11 January. Available at: www.asada.gov.au/news/releases/current/asada_release_070111_next_generation_olympians.pdf (accessed 16 March 2007).

—— (2007b) *ASADA Homepage*. Available at: www.asada.gov.au/ (accessed 16 March 2007).

—— (2006) 'About ASADA'. Available at: www.asada.gov.au/about/role.htm (accessed 14 July 2006).

164   *Bibliography*

ASC (Australian Sports Commission) (2008) 'Crossing new frontiers in sports science'. Available at: www.ausport.gov.au/ais/news/cutting_edge_sports_technology_showcased (accessed 24 March 2008).

—— (2007) 'The essence of Australian sport'. Available at: www.ausport.gov.au/asc/teoas/index.asp (accessed 16 March 2007).

—— (2004) *Australian Sports Commission Anti-Doping Policy 2004*. Available at: www.ausport.gov.au (accessed 25 November 2005).

Ashworth, W. J. (2002) 'England and the machinery of reason, 1780 to 1830', in I. R. Morus (ed.) *Bodies/machines*, Oxford: Berg.

Auslander, P. (2004) 'Postmodernism and performance', in S. Connor (ed.) *The Cambridge Companion to Postmodernism*, Cambridge: Cambridge University Press.

—— (1999) *Liveness: performance in a mediatized culture*, London: Routledge.

Baldwin, P. (1999) *Contagion and the State in Europe, 1830–1930*, Cambridge: Cambridge University Press.

Bale, J. (1994) *Landscapes of Modern Sport*, Leicester, UK: Leicester University Press.

Barilan, Y. M. and Weintraub, M. (2001) 'The naturalness of the artificial and our concepts of health, disease and medicine', *Medicine, Health Care and Philosophy*, 4(3): 311–25.

Bates, A. W. (2005) *Emblematic Monsters: unnatural conceptions and deformed births in early modern Europe*, Amsterdam: Rodopi.

Bauman, R. (1989) 'American folklore studies and social transition: a performance-centered perspective', *Text and Performance Quarterly*, 9(3): 175–84.

BBC (2004) 'Cyclist Dajka loses appeal', *BBC News Website*, 9 August. Available at: www.news.bbc.co.uk/sport1/hi/Olympics_2004/cycling/3935897.stm (accessed 14 August 2004).

Beamish, R. and Ritchie, I. (2005) 'From fixed capacities to performance-enhancement: the paradigm shift in the science of "training" and the use of performance-enhancing substances', *Sport in History*, 25(3): 412–33.

Bednarek, J. R. D. (2005) 'The flying machine in the garden: parks and airports, 1918–38', *Technology and Culture*, 46(2): 350–73.

Bee, P. (2008) 'It's not what you do, it's what you wear', *Guardian*, 19 February. Available at: www.guardian.co.uk/sport/2008/feb/19/thegear.petabee (accessed 30 April 2008).

—— (2004) 'On the skin of under it, a cheat is still a cheat', *Guardian*, 15 March. Available at: http://sport.guardian.co.uk/news/story/0,10488,1169512,00.html (accessed 18 March 2004).

Beilin, R. (1999) 'Cultivating the global garden', *South Atlantic Quarterly*, 98(4): 761–80.

Bell, D. and Holliday, R. (2000) 'Naked as nature intended', *Body and Society*, 6 (3/4): 127–40.

Benthien, C. (2002) *Skin: on the cultural border between self and the world*, New York: Columbia University Press.

Benzecry, C. E. (2008) 'Azul y Oro: the many social lives of a football jersey', *Theory, Culture and Society*, 25(1): 49–76.

Berlin, N. (2006) 'Traffic of our stage: boxing as theatre', *Massachusetts Review*, 47(1): 22–34.

Berryman, J. and Park, R. (eds) (1992) *Sport and Exercise Science: essays in the history of sports medicine*, Urbana: University of Illinois Press.

Bhabha, H. (1984) 'Of mimicry and man: the ambivalence of colonial discourse', *October*, 28: 125–33.

Bibliography 165

Birchard, K. (2000) 'Past, present, and future of drug abuse at the Olympics', *The Lancet*, 356: 1008.

Black, R. (1998) 'Cheated duo calls for action', *Sydney Morning Herald*, 25 October.

Black, T. and Pape, A. (1997) 'The ban on drugs in sports: the solution or the problem?' *Journal of Sport and Social Issues*, 21(1): 83–92.

Boorse, C. (1977) 'Health as a theoretical concept', *Philosophy of Science*, 44(4): 542–73.

Booth, D. and Tatz, C. (2000) *One-Eyed: a view of Australian sport*, St Leonard's: Allen & Unwin.

—— (1994) 'Swimming with the big boys?: the politics of Sydney's 2000 Olympic bid', *Sporting Traditions*, 11(1): 3–24.

Bordo, S. (1993) *Unbearable Weight: feminism, western culture, and the body*, Berkeley: University of California Press.

Bordreau, F. and Konzak, B. (1991) 'Ben Johnson and the use of steroids in sport: sociological and ethical consideration', *Canadian Journal of Sport Science*, 16(2): 88–98.

Bose, M (2005) 'Verifying drug tests make take years', *The Telegraph*, 12 December. Available at: www.sport.telegraph.co.uk/sport/main.jhtml?xml=/sport/2005/12/12/sobose12.xml (accessed 15 December 2005).

Braidotti, R. (1994) *Nomadic Subjects: embodiment and sexual difference in contemporary feminist theory*, New York: Columbia University Press.

Brandt, A. M. and Rozin, P. (1997) *Morality and Health*, London: Routledge.

Brohm, J. M. (1978) *Sport: a prison of measured time*, London: Ink Links.

Brown, A. (2008) 'Belief in purity of human v water contest a snag for super cossie', *Sydney Morning Herald*, 26 April. Available at: www.smh.com.au/news/beijing2008/belief-in-purity-of-human-v-water-contest-a-snag-for-super-cossie/2008/04/25/1208743249142.html (accessed 30 April 2008).

Bryson, L. (1990) 'Sport, drugs and the development of modern capitalism', *Sporting Traditions*, 6(2): 135–53.

Budd, M. A. (1997) *The Sculpture Machine: physical culture and body politics in the age of empire*, London: Macmillan.

Burke, E. (2007) 'DNA test for talent: unfair on kids, say critics', *Sunday Mail*, 4 February.

Burke, M. (1998) 'Drugs and postmodern female "identities": a response to Tara Magdalinski', *Bulletin of Sport and Culture*, 15: 25–9.

Burstyn, V. (1999) *The Rites of Men: manhood, politics and the culture of sport*, Toronto: University of Toronto Press.

Butcher, R. B and Schneider, A. J. (2001) 'Fair play as respect for the game', in W. J. Morgan, K. V. Meier and A. J. Schneider (eds) *Ethics in Sport*, Champaign: Human Kinetics.

Butler, J. (1993) *Bodies That Matter: on the discursive limits of 'sex'*, New York: Routledge.

—— (1990) *Gender Trouble: feminism and the subversion of identity*, New York: Routledge.

Cahn, S. K. (1993) 'From the "muscle moll" to the "butch" ballplayer: mannishness, lesbianism and homophobia in US women's sport', *Feminist Studies*, 19(2): 343–68.

Caine, D., DiFiori, J. and Maffulli, N. (2006) 'Physical injuries in children's and youth sports: reasons for concern?', *British Journal of Sports Medicine*, 40(9): 749–60.

Callahan, D. (1973) 'The WHO definition of "health"', *The Hastings Center Studies*, 1 (3): 77–87.

Cameron, P. (1998) 'Aussies' Olympic apathy', *Sunday Mail*, 24 April.

166 Bibliography

Cantelon, H. and Letters, M. (2000) 'The making of the IOC environmental policy as a third dimension of the Olympic Movement', *International Review for the Sociology of Sport*, 35(3): 294–308.

Carlile, F. (1995) 'Why the Chinese must not swim at Atlanta '96', *Inside Sport*, 47: 18–29.

Carlson, M. (2004) *Performance: a critical introduction*, 2nd edn, London: Routledge.

Cashman, R. (1995) *Paradise of Sport: the rise of organised sport in Australia*, Melbourne: Oxford University Press.

Chandler, T. J. L. (1996) 'The structuring of manliness and the development of rugby football at the public schools and Oxbridge', in J. Nauright and T. J. L. Chandler (eds) *Making Men: rugby and masculine identity*, London: Frank Cass.

Channel 9 (1997) *Sixty Minutes*, 23 November.

Channel 10 (2000) *Channel 10 News*, 25 September.

Choi, P. Y. L. (2003) 'Muscle matters: maintaining visible differences between women and men', *Sexualities, Evolution and Gender*, 5(2): 71–81.

CNN/Sports Illustrated (1999) 'Giant strokes: Hingis faces muscular Mauresmo for women's title', *CNN/Sports Illustrated*, 29 January. Available at: http://sportsillustr ated.cnn.com/tennis/1999/australian_open/news/1999/01/28/womens_advance/ (accessed 15 June 2005).

Cohn, B. (1989) 'Cloth, clothes and colonialism', in A. B. Weiner and J. Schneider (eds) *Cloth and the Human Experience*, Washington DC: Smithsonian Institution Press.

Colman, M. (2000) 'Let's play fair – it has to suit 'em all', *Sunday Mail*, 19 March.

Connor, S. (2004) *The Book of Skin*, London: Reaktion.

Conrad, P. (1994) 'Wellness as virtue: morality and the pursuit of health', *Culture, Medicine and Psychiatry*, 18(3): 385–401.

Cooke, J. and Magnay, J. (1998) 'No test available to detect hGH cheats', *Sydney Morning Herald*, 8 January.

Cowley, M. (1999) 'O'Neill, Thorpe may be next to cover up in go-fast "scoot suit"', *Sydney Morning Herald*, 3 August.

—— (1998) 'China's long day's journey into drugs nightmare', *Sydney Morning Herald*, 9 January.

Crane, M. T. (2001) 'What was performance?', *Criticism*, 43(2): 169–87.

Cranny-Francis, A. (1995) *The Body in the Text*, Melbourne: Melbourne University Press.

Crawford, R. (2006) 'Health as meaningful social practice', *Health*, 10(4): 401–20.

—— (1994) 'The boundaries of the self and the unhealthy other: reflections on health, culture and Aids', *Social Science and Medicine*, 38(10): 1347–65.

—— (1984) 'A cultural account of "health"', in J. B. McKinlay (ed.) *Issues in the Political Economy of Health Care*, London: Tavistock.

Creed, B. (1993) 'The monstrous feminine: film, feminism and psychoanalysis', in B. Ashley (ed.) *Reading Popular Narrative: a source book*, Leicester: Leicester University Press.

Crozier, M. (1999) 'After the garden?', *The South Atlantic Quarterly*, 98(4): 625–31.

Curtis, V. (2001) 'Dirt, disgust, and disease: is hygiene in our genes?', *Perspectives in Biology and Medicine*, 44(1): 17–31.

Daly, J. (1991) *The Australian Institute of Sport in Canberra*, Canberra: AGPS.

Davis, L. and Delano, L. (1992) 'Fixing the boundaries of physical gender: side effects of anti-drug campaigns in athletics', *Sociology of Sport Journal*, 9(1): 1–19.

Dawson, R. T. (2001) 'Drugs in sport – the role of the physician', *Journal of Endocrinology*, 170(1): 55–61.

de la Peña, C. T. (2003) *The Body Electric: how strange machines build the modern American*, New York: New York University Press.

De Pauw, K. P. and Gavron, S. (2005) *Disability Sport*, Champaign: Human Kinetics.

Dick, B. (2007) 'Thorpe questions need answering', *Courier Mail*, 1 April.

Dillman, L. (2008) 'The suit that's turned the swim world on its head', *Los Angeles Times*, 27 March. Available at: www.latimes.com/sports/la-sp-swim27mar27,0,360 2017.story (accessed 30 April 2008).

DISR (Department of Industry, Science and Resources), Sport and Tourism Division (1999) *Tough on Drugs in Sport: Australia's anti-drugs in sport strategy 1999–2000 and beyond*, Canberra: DISR.

Dolan, J. (1993) 'Geographies of learning: theatre studies, performance, and the performative', *Theatre Journal*, 45(4): 417–41.

Donald, J. (1988) 'How English is it?: popular literature and national culture', *New Foundations*, 6: 31–47.

Duncan, Margaret C. (1994) 'The politics of women's body images and practices: Foucault, the panopticon, and *Shape* magazine', *Journal of Sport and Social Issues*, 18(1): 49–65.

Dunlap, T. R. (1999) *Nature and the English Diaspora: environment and history in the United States, Canada, Australia, and New Zealand*, Cambridge: Cambridge University Press.

Dunn, W. R., George, M. S., Churchill, L. and Spindler, K. P. (2007) 'Ethics in sports medicine', *American Journal of Sports Medicine*, 10(10): 1–5.

Dworkin, S. (2001) '"Holding back": negotiating a glass ceiling on women's muscular strength', *Sociological Perspectives*, 44(3): 333–50.

Dyer, R. (1997) *White*, London: Routledge.

Editorial (2004) 'Drugs in sport: the mud gets stickier', *The Age*, 14 July.

—— (1996) 'Riley deserves a warning, not a ban', *The Australian*, 15 February.

Eichberg, H. (1998) *Body Cultures: essays on sport, space and identity*, eds J. Bale and C. Philo, London: Routledge.

Eitzen, D. S. (2006) *Fair and Foul: beyond the myths and paradoxes of sport*, Lanham: Rowman & Littlefield.

Entwistle, J. (2001) 'The dressed body', in J. Entwistle and E. Wilson (eds) *Body Dressing*, Oxford: Berg.

Erlmann, V. (1998) '"Spectatorial Lust": the African Choir in London, 1891–93', in B. Lindfors (ed.) *Africans on Stage: studies in ethnological show business*, Bloomington: Indiana University Press.

Evans, L. (1998) 'Perkins: FINA must act to save our sport', *Sydney Morning Herald*, 10 January.

—— (1997) 'Anger as East German gets top sport job', *Sydney Morning Herald*, 3 October.

Evans, M., Cavallaro, D. and Warwick, A. (1998) *Fashioning the Frame: boundaries, dress and the body*, Oxford: Berg.

Evans, N. (2004) 'Current concepts in anabolic-androgenic steroids', *American Journal of Sports Medicine*, 32(2): 534–42.

Fainaru-Wada, M. and Williams, L. (2006) *Game of Shadows: Barry Bonds, BALCO, and the steroids scandal that rocked professional sport*, New York: Gotham Books.

Fairchild, D. L. (1989) 'Sport abjection: steroids and the uglification of the athlete', *Journal of the Philosophy of Sport*, 16(1): 74–88.

168   Bibliography

Farrell, F. (1999) 'Australian identity', in R. Cashman and A. Hughes (eds) *Staging the Olympics: the event and its impact*, Sydney: University of New South Wales Press.

Featherstone, M., Hepworth, M. and Turner, B. S. (eds) (1991) *The Body, Social Process and Cultural Theory*, London: Sage.

Feezell, R. M. (2004) *Sport, Play and Ethical Reflection*, Urbana: University of Illinois Press.

Finch, C. F. and Owen, N. (2001) 'Injury prevention and the promotion of physical activity: what is the nexus?', *Journal of Science and Medicine in Sport*, 4(1): 77–87.

Fisher, J. W. (2003) 'Erythropoietin: physiology and pharmacology update', *Experimental Biology and Medicine*, 228(1): 1–14.

FitzSimons, P. (2008) 'Should only rich kids get fancy togs?' *Sydney Morning Herald*, 29 March.

Forbes, M. (2000) 'IOC rejects CJ's "impossible" excuse', *Sydney Morning Herald*, 26 September.

Foster, H. (1997) 'Prosthetic gods', *Modernism and Modernity*, 4(2): 5–38.

Fotheringham, R. (1992) *Sport in Australian Drama*, Cambridge: Cambridge University Press.

Foucault, M. (1977) *Discipline and Punish: the birth of the prison*, trans. Alan Sheridan, New York: Pantheon Books.

Frank, A. W. (1991) 'For a sociology of the body: an analytical review', in M. Featherstone, M. Hepworth and B. S. Turner (eds) *The Body: social process and cultural theory*, London: Sage.

Franko, M. and Richards, A. (2000) 'Actualizing absence: the pastness of performance', in M. Franko and A. Richards (eds) *Acting on the Past*, Hanover: Wesleyan University Press.

Frew, M. and McGillivray, D. (2005) 'Health clubs and body politics: aesthetics and the quest for physical capital', *Leisure Studies*, 24(2): 161–75.

Gardner, R. (1989) 'On performance-enhancing substances and the unfair advantage argument', *Journal of the Philosophy of Sport*, 16: 59–73.

Garland, J. and Rowe, M. (1999) 'War minus the shooting: jingoism, the English press and Euro '96', *Journal of Sport and Social Issues*, 23(1): 80–95.

Garland-Thomson, R. (2002) 'Integrating disability, transforming feminist theory', *National Women's Studies Association Journal*, 14(3): 1–32.

——(1997) *Extraordinary Bodies: figuring physical disability in American culture and literature*, New York: Columbia University Press.

Garnier, A. (2007) 'An open letter to those promoting the medical supervision of doping', *Play True*, 1: 17–18.

Gatt, R. (1997) 'Aussies line up for retrospective honours', *The Australian*, 12 September.

Gelder, K. (2005) *The Subcultures Reader*, London: Routledge.

Godwell, D. (2000) 'The Olympic branding of Aborigines: the 2000 Olympic Games and Australia's indigenous peoples', in K. Schaffer and S. Smith (eds) *The Olympics at the Millennium: power, politics and the games*, New Brunswick: Rutgers University Press.

Goffman, E. (1956) *The Presentation of Self in Everyday Life*, New York: Doubleday.

Goggin, G. and Newell, C. (2005) *Disability in Australia: exploring a social apartheid*, Sydney: University of New South Wales Press.

—— (2000) 'Crippling Paralympics? Media, disability and Olympism', *Media International Australia*, 97: 71–83.

Bibliography   169

Gould, S. J. (1981) *The Mismeasure of Man*, New York: W. W. Norton.

Gray, C. H. (2002) *Cyborg Citizen*, London: Routledge.

Greenpeace (2000) *Environmental Report*. Available at: www.greenpeace.com.au (accessed 10 November 2000).

Grosz, E. (1989) *Sexual Subversions*, St Leonard's: Allen & Unwin.

Groth, P. (1997) 'Frameworks for cultural landscape study', in P. Groth and T. W. Bressi (eds) *Understanding Ordinary Landscapes*, New Haven: Yale University Press.

Guinness, R. (1999) 'Chemically-enhanced cheats destroying fable of sport', *The Australian*, 9 June.

Gusfield, J. R. (2000) 'Sport as story: form and content in athletics', *Society*, 37(4): 63–71.

Guttmann, A. (1978) *From Ritual to Record: the nature of modern sports*, New York: Columbia University Press.

Hall, S. (1992) 'The question of cultural identity', in S. Hall, D. Held and T. McGrew (eds) *Modernity and Its Futures*, Cambridge: Polity Press.

Haraway, D. (1991) *Simians, Cyborgs and Women: the reinvention of nature*, London: Routledge.

Hardy, A. (2001) *Health and Medicine in Britain since 1860*, London: Palgrave.

Hargreaves, J. (1994) *Sporting Females: critical issues in the history and sociology of women's sports*, London: Routledge.

Hargreaves, M. and Hawley, J. (eds) (2003) *Physiological Bases of Sports Performance*, Sydney: McGraw Hill.

Harris, T. (2000a) 'Drug cheats sour Games', *The Australian*, 28 September.

—— (2000b) 'The cold tablet that tripped the darling of Romanian gymnastics', *The Australian*, 28 September 2000.

Hawkins, M. (2002) '"A great and difficult thing": understanding and explaining the human machine in Restoration England', in I. R. Morus (ed.) *Bodies/machines*, Oxford: Berg.

Herr, H., Whiteley, G. P. and Childress, D. (2003) 'Cyborg technology: biomimetic orthotic and prosthetic technology', in Y. Bar-Cohen and C. Breazeal (eds) *Biologically Inspired Intelligent Robots*, Bellingham: SPIE Press.

Heywood, L. (1998) *Bodymakers: a cultural anatomy of women's body building*, New Brunswick: Rutgers University Press.

Hiestand, M. (2000) 'Full-body swimsuit stirs controversy', *USA Today*, 28 March.

Hill, A. (2005) *Reality TV: audiences and popular factual television*, London: Routledge.

Hill, K. L. (2001) *Frameworks for Sport Psychologists: enhancing sport performance*, Champaign: Human Kinetics

Hillier, L. and Harrison, L. (2004) 'Homophobia and the production of shame: young people and same sex attraction', *Culture, Health and Sexuality*, 6(1): 79–94.

Hirst, J. B. (1992) 'The pioneer legend', in J. Carroll (ed.) *Intruders in the Bush: the Australian quest for identity*, Melbourne: Oxford University Press.

Hoberman, J. (2005) *Testosterone Dreams: rejuvenation, aphrodisia, doping*, Berkeley: University of California Press.

—— (1992) *Mortal Engines: the science of performance and the dehumanization of sport*, New York: The Free Press.

Hoffie, P. (1997) 'Landscape and identity in the 1980s', in G. Levitus (ed.) *Lying about the Landscape*, Sydney: Craftsman House.

Hoffman, J. (2002) *Physiological Aspects of Sport Training and Performance*, Champaign: Human Kinetics.

170 Bibliography

Holmlund, C. A. (1989) 'Visible difference and flex appeal: the body, sex, sexuality, and race in the *Pumping Iron* films', *Cinema Journal*, 28(4): 38–51.

Holt, R. (1989) *Sport and the British*, Oxford: Oxford University Press.

Holtz, A. (1996) 'Paralympic officials keep eye out for "boosting"'. *CNN Website* Available at: www.cnn.com/US/9608/16/paralympics.booster/index.html?eref=site search (accessed 14 August 2006).

Hood, M. (2005) 'Born to run', *IEEE Spectrum Online*, November. Available at: www.spectrum.ieee.org/nov05/2189 (accessed 20 December 2006).

Houlihan, B. (2004) 'Civil rights, doping control and the World Anti-Doping Code', *Sport in Society*, 7(3): 420–37.

Howe, P. D. (2004) *Sport, Professionalism and Pain: ethnographies of injury and risk*, London: Routledge.

Hughson, J., Inglis, D. and Free, M. (2005) *The Uses of Sport: a critical study*, London: Routledge.

Hunter, G. (1996) 'Editorial: Ever had the feeling', *Inside Sport*, 51: 6.

Hutchinson, R. (1996) *Empire Games: the British invention of twentieth century sport*, Edinburgh: Edinburgh University Press.

Hymes, D. (1975) 'Breakthrough into performance', in D. Ben-Amos and S. Goldstein (eds) *Folklore: performance and communication*, The Hague: Mouton.

IAAF (International Association of Athletic Federations) (2008a) *Competition Rules 2008*. Monaco: IAAF. Available at: www.iaaf.org/mm/Document/imported/42192. pdf (accessed 30 April 2008).

—— (2008b) 'Press release: Oscar Pistorius – independent scientific study concludes that cheetah prosthetics offer clear mechanical advantages', *IAAF*, 14 January. Available at: www.iaaf.org/news/kind=101/newsid=42896.html (accessed 30 January 2008).

Ian, M. (2001) 'The primitive subject of female bodybuilding: transgression and other postmodern myths', *Differences: Journal of Feminist Cultural Studies*, 12(3): 69–100.

IFBB (International Federation of Bodybuilders) (2006) *IFBB Rules*. Available at: www.ifbb.com/amarules/IFBBRulebook_2006-7Edition.pdf (accessed 7 December 2006).

Imrie, R. (2004) 'Demystifying disability: a review of the International Classification of Functioning, Disability and Health', *Sociology of Health and Illness*, 26(3): 287–305.

Inside Sport (1997) 'Buttheads of the Month', 71: 15.

Inside Sport (1999) 'This is what they said', 49: 13.

—— (1997) 'Buttheads of the Month', 71: 15.

IOC (International Olympic Committee) (2005) 'Celebrate Humanity', *The Official Website of the Olympic Movement*. Available at: www.olympic.org/uk/index_uk.asp (accessed 20 October 2005).

Irigaray, L. (1985) *The Speculum of the Other Woman*, trans. G. G. Gill, Ithaca: Cornell University Press.

ISC (Irish Sports Council) (2006) 'Antidoping'. Available at: www.irishsportscounci l.ie/supporting-overview.aspx (accessed 14 July 2006).

Ironbark Legends (1997) *Kieren Perkins*, Melbourne: Macmillan.

Jarvie, G. and Walker, G. (eds) (1994) *Scottish Sport in the Making of the Nation: ninety minute patriots?* Leicester: Leicester University Press.

Jeffrey, N. (2000) 'Revolutionary bodysuit on horizon', *The Weekend Australian*, 18/19 March.

—— (1996a) 'Riley's career on the line', *The Australian*, 13 February.

—— (1996b) 'No reprieve for Riley, urges Fraser', *The Australian*, 21 February.

Jenkins, H. (1997) '"Never trust a snake": WWF wrestling as masculine melodrama', in A. Baker (ed.) *Out of Bounds: sports, media and the politics of identity*, Bloomington: Indiana University Press.

Jenkins, P. (2002) 'Doping in sport', *The Lancet*, 360(9327): 99–100.

Jones, S. (1996) 'Killing Zoe', *Inside Sport*, 51: 40–6.

Judovitz, D. (2001) *The Culture of the Body: genealogies of modernity*, Ann Arbor: University of Michigan Press.

Juengst, E. T. (1998) 'What does enhancement mean?', in E. Parens (ed.) *Enhancing Human Traits: ethical and social implications*, Washington DC: Georgetown University Press.

Jutel, A. (2005) 'Weighing health: the moral burden of obesity', *Social Semiotics*, 15 (2): 113–25.

Kayser, B., Mauron, A. and Miah, A. (2005) 'Legalisation of performance-enhancing drugs', *The Lancet*, 366: S21.

Keating, J. (1964) 'Sportsmanship as a moral category', *Ethics*, 75(1): 25–35.

Kelly, F. and Aiken, K. (2004) 'Australia "damaged" by cycling drugs scandal', *ABC Website*, 1 August. Available at: www.abc.net.au/sport/content/200408/S1166440. htm (accessed 10 August 2004).

Kidnie, M. J. (2006) 'Where is *Hamlet*?: text, performance and adaptation', in B Hodgdon and W. B. Worthen (eds) *A Companion to Shakespeare and Performance*, London: Blackwell.

Kirk, D. (1994) 'Physical education and regimes of the body', *Journal of Sociology*, 30 (2): 165–77.

Kirshenblatt-Gimblett, B. (1998) *Destination Culture: tourism, museums, and heritage*, Berkeley: University of California Press.

Kitney, G. (1997) 'Raelene's hopes for gold dashed once more', *Sydney Morning Herald*, 22 November.

Klein, J. (2000) 'Waiting for performance', *PAJ: A Journal of Performance and Art*, 22 (3): 78–87.

Kolcio, K. (2005) 'A somatic engagement of technology', *International Journal of Performance Arts and Digital Media*, 1(2): 101–25.

König, E. (1995) 'Criticism of doping: the nihilistic side of technological sport and the antiquated view of sport ethics', *International Review for the Sociology of Sport*, 34(3/4): 247–61.

Kristeva, J. (1982) *Powers of Horror: an essay on abjection*, New York: Columbia University Press.

Kutt, L. M. (2005) 'Letter to the editor: should altitude simulation be legal for athletics training?', *High Altitude Medicine and Biology*, 6(2): 189–90.

Lacan, J. (1977) *Écrits: a selection*, trans. A. Sheridan, London: Routledge.

Laqueur, T. (1987) 'Orgasm, generation, and the politics of reproductive biology', in C. Gallagher and T. Laqueur (eds) *The Making of the Modern Body*, Berkeley: University of California Press.

Larson, J. S. (1991) *The Measurement of Health: concepts and indicators*, Westport: Greenwood Press.

Le Grand, C. (2000) 'Costume drama', *The Weekend Australian*, 15/16 April.

Lehmann, J. (1999) 'Coles case hurting good name of Games', *The Weekend Australian*, 6/7 March.

172   *Bibliography*

Lenskyj, H. (2000) *Inside the Olympic industry: power, politics, and activism*, Albany: SUNY Press.

—— (1986) *Out of Bounds: women, sport and sexuality*, Toronto: Women's Press.

Leonard, J. (1996) 'The last race', *Inside Sport*, 53: 50–57.

Lester, D. (1998) 'The proof of vial goings-on among Chinese athletes', *Sydney Morning Herald*, 10 January.

Levine, B. D. (2006) 'Should "artificial" high altitude environments be considered doping?', *Scandinavian Journal of Medicine and Science in Sports*, 16: 297–301.

Lewis, S. (2001). 'Approaching the problem of defining "health" and "disease" from the perspectives of evolutionary psychology and Darwinian medicine', poster presented at the Joint Symposium of the Society for the Study of Human Biology and the Human Biological Association, 17–18 September 2001. Available at: www.chester.ac.uk/~sjlewis/DM/Sept01Poster2.htm (accessed 19 December 2006).

Lindsay, C. (1996) 'Bodybuilding: a postmodern freak show', in R. G. Thomas (ed.) *Freakery: cultural spectacles of the extraordinary body*, New York: New York University Press.

Lingard, J. (2000) 'Susie flies into "suss" de Bruijn', *Sydney Morning Herald*, 9 June.

—— (1999) 'Talbot presses suit for all or none', *Sydney Morning Herald*, 2 August.

Linnell, G. (2008) 'Tears of injustice', *Daily Telegraph*, 23 April. Available at: www.news.com.au/dailytelegraph/story/0,22049,23584378-5014104,00.html (accessed 30 April 2008).

Löbbecke (1996) 'Löbbecke's hall of fame', *Inside Sport*, 53: 15.

Lock, M. (1997) 'Decentring the natural body: making difference matter', *Configurations*, 5(2): 267–92

Lock, R. A. (2003) 'The doping ban: compulsory heterosexuality and lesbophobia', *International Review for the Sociology of Sport*, 38(4): 397–411.

Loland, S. (2002) *Fair Play in Sport: a moral norm system*, London: Routledge.

Longley, R. (2008) 'High-tech suit kept in dry dock', *Toronto Sun*, 2 April. Available at: http://torontosun.com/Sports/OtherSports/2008/04/02/5168121-sun.html (accessed 30 April 2008).

Longman, J. (2007) 'An amputee springer: is he disabled or too-abled?' *New York Times*, 15 May.

Lorber, J. and Moore, L. J. (2002) *Gender and the Social Construction of Illness*, 2nd edn, Oxford: Rowman Altamira.

Lord, C. (2008) 'Time to sink or swim', *The Times Online*, 13 April. Available at: www.timesonline.co.uk/tol/sport/more_sport/article3736278.ece (accessed 30 April 2008).

Lovell, N. (1998) 'Introduction: belonging in need of emplacement?', in N. Lovell (ed.) *Locality and Belonging*, London: Routledge.

Lupton, D. (2003) *Medicine as Culture: illness, disease and the body in western societies*, 2nd edn, London: Sage.

McCallum, J. (2000) 'Unflagging', *Sports Illustrated*, 14 August. Available at: http://sports illustrated.cnn.com/features/cover/news/2000/08/14/unflagging/ (accessed 12 July 2006).

MacCannell, D. (1999) *The Tourist: A new theory of the leisure class*, Berkeley: University of California Press.

McGeoch, R. and Korporaal, G. (1994) *The Bid: how Australia won the 2000 Games*, Melbourne: William Heinemann.

McGrath, A. C. and Ozanne-Smith, J. (1998) *Attacking the Goal of Netball Injury Prevention: a review of the literature*, Melbourne: Monash University Accident Research Centre.

Bibliography 173

McGregor, A. (1996) 'Riley puts a brave face on adversity', *The Australian*, 14 February.

McKay, J. (1991) *No Pain, No Gain: sport and Australian culture*, Sydney: Prentice Hall.

McKenzie, J. (2001) *Perform or Else: from discipline to performance*, London: Routledge.

Macnaghten, P. and Urry, J. (2000) 'Bodies of nature: introduction', *Body and Society*, 6(3/4): 1–11.

—— (1998) *Contested Natures*, London: Sage.

Magdalinski, T. (2004) 'Homebush: site of the clean/sed and natural Australian athlete', in P. Vertinsky and J. Bale (eds) *Sites of Sport: space, place, experience*, London: Routledge.

—— (2001a) 'Drugs *Inside Sport*: the rehabilitation of Samantha Riley', *Sporting Traditions*, 17(2): 17–32.

—— (2001b) 'Drugs, sport and national identity in Australia', in W. Wilson and E. Derse (eds) *Doping in Elite Sport: the politics of drugs in the Olympic movement*, Champaign: Human Kinetics.

—— (2000a) '"Excising the cancer": drugs, sport and the crisis of Australian identity', *Avante*, 6(3): 1–15.

—— (2000b) 'Reinventing Australia for the Sydney 2000 Olympic Games', in J. A. Mangan and J. Nauright (eds) *Sport in Australasian Society*, London: Frank Cass.

—— (2000c) 'Performance technologies: drugs and Fastskin at the Sydney 2000 Olympics', *Media International Australia*, 97: 59–70.

—— (1998a) 'Recapturing Australia's glorious sporting past: drugs and Australian identity', *Bulletin of Sport and Culture*, 14: 1, 6–8.

—— (1998b) 'Organized memories: the construction of sporting traditions in the GDR', *European Sports History Review*, 1: 144–63.

Magdalinski, T. and Brooks, K. (2002) 'Bride of Frankenstein: technology and the consumption of the female athlete', *Research in Philosophy and Technology*, 21: 195–212.

Magdalinski, T. and Warren, I. (2004) 'Sport: civil liberties and athletes', *Alternative Law Journal*, 28(1–6): 95–6.

Magnat, V. (2002) 'Theatricality from the performative perspective', *SubStance*, 31(2/3): 147–66.

Magnay, J. (2007a) 'Mystery syringe casts shadow over world titles', *Sydney Morning Herald*, 21 March.

—— (2007b) 'Hue and cry reveals double standard', *Sydney Morning Herald*, 2 April.

—— (1999a) 'Coles accused of disgracing IOC', *Sydney Morning Herald*, 5 March.

—— (1999b) 'IOC backs airport drug test', *Sydney Morning Herald*, 18 June.

—— (1998a) 'Chinese drug disgrace', *Sydney Morning Herald*, 15 January.

—— (1998b) 'Boultbee's plan allows all drugs bar three', *Sydney Morning Herald*, 25 April.

—— (1997) 'Suspicion, accusation, question', *Sydney Morning Herald*, 22 October.

Magnay, J. and Korporaal, G. (1998) 'Cut-off date for drugs', *The Age*, 16 April.

Maguire, J. (2004) 'Challenging the sports-industrial complex: human sciences, advocacy and service', *European Physical Education Review*, 10(3): 299–322.

Malcolmson, R. (1973) *Popular Recreations in English Society 1700–1850*, Cambridge: Cambridge University Press.

Malson, H. (1998) *The Thin Woman: feminism, post-structuralism, and social psychology of anorexia nervosa*, London: Routledge.

Mangan, J. A. (1981) *Athleticism in the Victorian and Edwardian Public School*, Cambridge: Cambridge University Press.

174 Bibliography

Markula, P. (1995) 'Firm but shapely, fit but sexy, strong but thin: the postmodern aerobicizing female bodies', *Sociology of Sport Journal*, 12(4): 424–53.

Massengale, J. and Swanson, R. (eds) (1997) *The History of Exercise and Sport Science*, Champaign: Human Kinetics.

Masters, R. (2007) 'Why faster pools don't necessarily mean faster swimmers', *Sydney Morning Herald*, 27 March.

Mathias, M. B. (2004) 'The competing demands of sport and health: an essay on the history of ethics in sports medicine', *Clinics in Sports Medicine*, 23(2): 195–214.

Mazer, S. (1998) *Professional Wrestling: sport and spectacle*, Jackson: University Press of Mississippi.

Mbaye, K. (1999) *Report of the Working Group on the Legal and Political Aspects of Doping*, Lausanne: World Conference on Doping.

Meade, K. (1999) 'Life's a beach for boatload of intruders', *The Weekend Australian*, 13/14 March.

Merleau-Ponty, M. (1962) *Phenomenology of Perception*, trans. C. Smith, London: Routledge and Kegan Paul.

Messner, M. and Sabo, D. (eds) (1990) *Sport, Men, and the Gender Order: critical feminist perspectives*, Champaign: Human Kinetics.

Miah, A. (2006) 'Rethinking Enhancement in Sport', *Annals of the New York Academy of Sciences*, 1093: 301–20.

—— (2004) *Genetically Modified Athletes: biomedical ethics, gene doping and sport*, London: Routledge.

Michael, M. A. (2005) 'Is it natural to drive species to extinction?' *Ethics and the Environment*, 10(1): 49–66.

Moi, T. (1985) *Sexual/textual Politics: feminist literary theory*, London: Routledge.

Møller, V. (2003) 'What is sport: outline to a redefinition', in V. Møller and J. Nauright (eds) *The Essence of Sport*, Odense: University of Southern Denmark Press.

Moneghetti, S. (1999) 'Sport is big business', keynote address presented to the Business Information and Research Bureau Monthly Meeting, 8 November.

Moore, M. (1998) 'They're bloody liars: Talbot', *Sydney Morning Herald*, 15 January.

Morgan, W. J. (2006) 'Fair is fair, or is it? A moral consideration of the doping wars in American sport', *Sport in Society*, 9(2): 177–98.

Morus, I. R. (ed.) (2002) *Bodies/machines*, Oxford: Berg.

Mottram, D. (2003) 'An introduction to drugs and their use in sport', in D. Mottram (ed.) *Drugs in Sport*, 3rd edn, London: Routledge.

Munthe, C. (2000) 'Selected champions: making winners in the age of genetic technology', in T. Tännsjö and C. Tamburrini (eds) *Values in Sport: elitism, nationalism, gender equality and the scientific manufacture of winners*, London: Spon.

Murphie, A. and Potts, J. (2003) *Culture and Technology*, Basingstoke: Palgrave.

NADA (Nationale Anti-Doping Agentur) (2006) *NADA Website*. Available at: www. nada-bonn.de/nada.html (accessed 14 July 2006).

Nathan, D. (2003) *Saying It's So: a cultural history of the Black Sox scandal*, Urbana: University of Illinois Press.

Nauright, J. and Magdalinski, T. (2003) '"A hapless attempt at swimming": framing Africa through Eric Moussambani', *Critical Arts*, 17(1/2): 106–19.

NBC (2000) *Telecast of the Opening Ceremony of the Games of the XXVIIth Olympiad*, 15 September.

Nishime, L. (2005) 'The mulatto cyborg: imagining a multiracial future', *Cinema Journal*, 44(2): 34–49.

Bibliography 175

Noakes, T. D. (2004) 'Tainted glory: doping and athletic performance', *New England Journal of Medicine*, 351(9): 847–50.

O'Leary, J. (2001) *Drugs and Doping in Sport: socio-legal perspectives*, London: Routledge Cavendish.

Ott, K. (2002) 'The sum of its parts: an introduction to modern histories of prosthetics', in K. Ott, D. Serlin and S. Mihm (eds) *Artificial Parts, Practical Lives: modern histories of prosthetics*, New York: New York University Press.

Overington, C. (1996) 'Minor headache sinks Riley', *The Age*, 13 February.

Palladino, P. (2003) 'Life ... on biology, biography, and bio-power in the age of genetic engineering', *Configurations*, 11(1): 81–109.

Palmer, G. B. and Jankowiak, W. R. (1996) 'Performance and imagination: towards an anthropology of the spectacular and the mundane', *Cultural Anthropology*, 11(2): 225–58.

Parens, E. (1998) 'Is better always good?: the enhancement project', *The Hastings Center Report*, 28(1): S1–17.

Park, R. (1992) 'Athletes and their training in Britain and America, 1800–1914', in J. Berryman and R. Park (eds) *Sport and Exercise Science: essays in the history of sports medicine*, Urbana: University of Illinois Press.

Peacock, J. (1990) 'Ethnographic notes on sacred and profane performance', in R. Schechner and W. Appel (eds) *By Means of Performance*, Cambridge: Cambridge University Press.

Phelan, P. (1993) *Unmarked: the politics of performance*, London: Routledge.

Prince, S. (1997) *Movies and Meaning: an introduction to film*, Boston: Allyn and Bacon.

Pronger, B. (2002) *Body Fascism: salvation in the technology of physical fitness*, Toronto: University of Toronto Press.

—— (1990) *The Arena of Masculinity: sports, homosexuality and the meaning of sex*, Toronto: University of Toronto Press.

Purcell, C. and Moore, M. (2000) 'New suits turn the Dolphins into sharks', *Sydney Morning Herald*, 17 March.

Queensland Department of Tourism, Sport and Racing (1998) 'What is drugs in sport?' Information Paper no. 1.

Reid, H. (2006) 'Sport, education and the meaning of victory', paper presented at Twentieth World Congress of Philosophy, Boston, August 1998. Available at: www.bu.edu/wcp/Papers/Sport/SportReid.htm. (accessed 31 October 2006).

Reilly, R. (2000), 'Paralympic paradox', *Sports Illustrated*. Available at: http://sports-illustrated.cnn.com/inside_the_game/magazine/life_of_reilly/news/2000/12/05/life_-of_reilly/ (accessed 5 June 2006).

Rinehart, R. E. (1998) *Players All: performances in contemporary sport*, Bloomington: Indiana University Press.

Roberts, L. (2004) 'An arcadian apparatus: the introduction of the steam engine into the Dutch landscape', *Technology and Culture*, 45(2): 251–76.

Robertson, A. (2001) 'Biotechnology, political rationality and discourses on health risk', *Health*, 5(3): 293–309.

Robinson, J. (2004) 'Mapping performance culture: locating the spectator in theatre history', *Nineteenth Century Theatre and Film*, 31(1): 3–17.

Rothenberg-Aalami, J. (2004) 'Coming full circle? Forging missing links along Nike's integrated production networks', *Global Networks: A Journal of Transnational Affairs*, 4(4): 335–54.

Sabatini, S. (2001) 'The female athlete triad', *American Journal of the Medical Sciences*, 322(4): 193–5.

176 Bibliography

Sandahl, C. and Auslander, P. (2005) 'Introduction', in C. Sandahl and P. Auslander (eds) *Bodies in Commotion: disability and performance*, Ann Arbor: University of Michigan Press.

Sarup, M. (1992) *Jacques Lacan*, New York: Harvester Wheatsheaf.

Sassatelli, R. (1999) 'Interaction order and beyond: a field analysis of body culture within fitness gyms', *Body and Society*, 5(2/3): 227–48.

Savulescu, J. (2006) 'Justice, fairness, and enhancement', *Annals of the New York Academy of Sciences*, 1093(1): 321–38.

Savulescu, J., Foddy, B. and Clayton, M. (2004) 'Why we should allow performance enhancing drugs in sport', *British Journal of Sports Medicine*, 38(6): 666–70.

Schechner, R. (2002) *Performance: an introduction*, London: Routledge.

——(1988) *Performance Theory*, London: Routledge.

Schieffelin, E. (2005) 'Moving performance to text: can performance be transcribed?', *Oral Tradition*, 20(1): 80–92.

Schlink, L. (1998) '"Drug cheats": games claim rocks Aussies'. *Sunday Mail*, 20 September.

Schneider, A. J. and Butcher, R. B. (2000) 'A philosophical overview of the arguments on banning doping in sport', in T. Tännsjö and C. Tamburrini (eds) *Values in Sport: elitism, nationalism, gender equality and the scientific manufacture of winners*, London: Spon.

—— (1993/4) 'Why Olympic athletes should avoid the use and seek the elimination of performance-enhancing substances and practices from the Olympic Games', *Journal of the Philosophy of Sport*, 10–11: 64–81.

Semotiuk, D. (1987) 'Commonwealth government initiatives in amateur sport in Australia 1972–85', *Sporting Traditions*, 3(2): 152–62.

Senate Standing Committee on Environment, Recreation and the Arts (1992) *Report on Physical and Sport Education*, Canberra: Parliament of the Commonwealth of Australia.

Sheridan, H. (2003) 'Conceptualizing "fair play": a review of the literature', *European Physical Education Review*, 9(2): 163–84.

Sherlock, C. (2004) 'The performative: body-text-context and the construction of tradition', *Studies in Theatre and Performance*, 24(3): 151–61.

Shields, D. L. and Bredemeier, B. J. (1995) *Character Development and Physical Activity*, Champaign: Human Kinetics.

Shildrick, M. (2005) 'The disabled body, genealogy and undecidability', *Cultural Studies*, 19(6): 755–70.

—— (1996) 'Posthumanism and the monstrous body', *Body and Society*, 2(1): 1–15.

Shildrick, M. and Price, J. (1999) 'Openings on the body: a critical introduction', in J. Price and M. Shildrick (eds) *Feminist Theory and the Body: a reader*, Edinburgh: Edinburgh University Press.

Shilling, C. (2005) *The Body in Culture, Technology and Society*, London: Sage.

—— (1993) *The Body and Social Theory*, London: Sage.

Shogan, D. A. (1999) *The Making of High-Performance Athletes: discipline, diversity, ethics*, Toronto: University of Toronto Press.

Showalter, E. (1997) *Hystories: hysterical epidemics and modern culture*, New York: Columbia University Press.

Sibley, D. (1995) *Geographies of Exclusion: society and difference in the West*, London: Routledge.

Simpson, V. and Jennings, A. (1992) *The Lords of the Rings*, Toronto: Stoddart.

Bibliography 177

Skins (2006) *Skins*[TM]. Available at: www.skins.com (accessed 19 October 2006).

Skotnes, P. (2001) '"Civilised off the face of the earth": museum display and the silencing of the /Xam', *Poetics Today*, 22(2): 299–321.

Slattery, L. (1998) 'Steroids: society's quick fix', *The Weekend Australian*, 27/28 June.

Smith, A. D. (1991) *National Identity*, London: Penguin.

Smith, A. and Thomas, N. (2005) 'The "inclusion" of elite athletes with disabilities in the 2002 Manchester Commonwealth Games: an exploratory analysis of British newspaper coverage', *Sport, Education and Society*, 10(1): 49–67.

Smith, N. (1996) 'The production of nature', in G. Robertson, M. Mash, L. Tickner, J. Bird, B. Curtie and T. Putnam (eds) *FutureNatural: nature, science, culture*, London: Routledge.

Smith, W. (1998) 'Coaches join doping battle', *Sunday Mail*, 11 January.

SOBL (Sydney Olympics 2000 Bid Limited) (1993) *Sydney 2000. Share the spirit. Volume 2 Olympic information*, Sydney: SOBL.

—— (1992) *Sydney 2000 Presentation to the IOC Executive Board*, ANOC, Acapulco, Mexico, November.

SOCOG (Sydney Organising Committee for the Olympic Games) (1998) *Sydney 2000 Olympic Games Image Guidelines*, Sydney: SOCOG.

SOGC (Sydney Olympic Games Committee) (1991) *Sydney Olympics 2000*. Sydney: SOGC.

Soper, K. (1996) 'Nature/"nature"', in G. Robertson, M. Mash, L. Tickner, J. Bird, B. Curtie and T. Putnam (eds) *FutureNatural: nature, science, culture*, London: Routledge.

Speedo (2008a) *Fastskin LZR Racer*. Available at: www.speedo80.com/lzr-racer/features/ (accessed 30 April 2008).

—— (2008b) 'Press Release: Speedo "space age" swimsuit set for take off', *Speedo*, 13 February. Available at: www.speedo.com/index.php?option=com_content&task=view&id=822&Itemid=158&lc=en&cc=global (accessed 30 April 2008).

—— (2007) *Speedo Aqualab*. Available at: www.speedoaqualab.com/site.html (accessed 9 January 2007).

—— (2006a) *Fastskin*[TM] *fact sheet*. Available at: www.speedousa.com/index.cfm/fuseaction/content.page/model/nodelID/751a5318-1e1e-4561-9331-999703fd0c0f/ (accessed 6 June 2006).

—— (2006b) *Fastskin FSII*. Available at: www.speedo.com/index.php?option=com_content&task=view&id=19&Itemid=115&lc=es&cc=ar (accessed 6 June 2006).

Sport Illustrated (2008) 'Swimmers face tough choice', *Sports Illustrated*, 12 April. Available at: http://sportsillustrated.cnn.com/2008/more/04/12/speedos.ap/ (accessed 30 April 2008).

—— (2000) '"In the best interest of all": bodysuits banned from US Olympic trials', *Sports Illustrated*, 22 June. Available at: http://sportsillustrated.cnn.com/olympics/news/2000/06/21/bodysuit_ban_ap/ (accessed 6 June 2006).

Stern, R. F. (1998) 'Moving parts and speaking parts: situating Victorian antitheatricality', *English Literary History*, 65(2): 423–49.

Stewart, C. (2000) 'The bitter pill', *The Australian*, 28 September.

Stoddart, B. (1986) *Saturday Afternoon Fever: sport in the Australian culture*, North Ryde: Angus & Robertson.

Stoner, L. J. and Keating, M. (1993) 'Hockey equipment: safety or illusion?', in C. R. Castaldi, P. J. Bishop and E. F. Hoerner (eds) *Safety in Ice Hockey: second volume, ASTM STP 1212*, Philadelphia: American Society for Testing and Materials.

178 Bibliography

Street, C., Antonio, J. and Cudlipp, D. (1996) 'Androgen use by athletes: a reevaluation of the health risks', *Canadian Journal of Applied Physiology*, 21(6): 421–40.

Sweeney, L. (2004) 'Gene doping', *Scientific American*, 29(1): 62–69.

Szerszynski, B., Heim, W. and Waterton, C. (2003) 'Introduction', in B. Szerszynski, W. Heim and C. Waterton (eds) *Nature Performed: environment, culture and performance*, Oxford: Blackwell.

Tamburrini, C. M. (2000) 'What's wrong with doping?', in T. Tännsjö and C.M. Tamburrini (eds) *Values in Sport: elitism, nationalism, gender equality and the scientific manufacture of winners*, London: Spon.

Taussig, M. (1993) *Mimesis and Alterity: a particular history of the senses*, London: Routledge.

Taylor, D. (2003) *The Archive and the Repertoire: performing cultural memory in the Americas*, Durham: Duke University Press.

Terry, J. and Urla, J. (eds) (1995) *Deviant Bodies: critical perspectives on difference in science and popular culture*, Bloomington: Indiana University Press.

Todd, T. (1992) 'A history of the use of anabolic steroids in sport', in J. W. Berryman and R. J. Park (eds) *Sport and Exercise Science: essays in the history of sports medicine*, Urbana: University of Illinois Press.

Tokish, J. M., Kocher, M. S. and Hawkins, R. J. (2004) 'Ergogenic aids: a review of basic science, performance side effects, and status in sports', *American Journal of Sports Medicine*, 32(6): 1543–53.

Treacy, L. (1998) Letter to the sports editor, *Sunday Mail*, 18 January.

Tritos, N. A. and Mantzoros, C. S. (1998) 'Recombinant human growth hormone: old and novel uses', *American Journal of Medicine*, 105(1): 44–57.

Tudor, A. (1992) 'Them and us: story and stereotype in TV World Cup coverage', *European Journal of Communication*, 7(3): 391–413.

Turner, B. S. (2003) 'Social fluids: metaphors and meanings of society', *Body and Society*, 9(1): 1–10.

—— (1996) *The Body and Society: explorations in social theory*, 2nd edn, London: Sage.

Turner, G. (1994) *Making it National: nationalism and Australian popular culture*, St Leonards: Allen & Unwin.

—— (1986) *National Fictions: literature, film and the construction of Australian narrative*, St Leonards: Allen & Unwin.

Turner, V. (1988) *The Anthropology of Performance*, New York: PAJ Publications.

Tuxill, C. and Wigmore, S. (1991) 'Cheating the public? An exploration of some issues surrounding the condemnation of the use of drugs in sport', *Physical Education Review*, 14(2): 119–28.

UK Sport (2006) *UK National Anti-Doping Policy*. Available at: www.uksport.gov. uk/assets/File/Generic_Template_Documents/Drug_Free_Sport/policy_160505.pdf (accessed 14 July 2006).

United States Olympic Team (USOT) (2006) 'Education Center: US Anti-Doping Agency'. Available at: www.Olympic-usa.org/12696.htm (accessed 14 July 2006).

Vamplew, W. and Stoddart, B. (eds) (1994) *Sport in Australia: a social history*, Melbourne: Cambridge University Press.

van Dijck, J. (2001) 'Bodyworlds: the art of plastinated cadavers', *Configurations*, 9(1): 99–126.

Vaseline (2007) Vaseline advertisement. Available at: www.vaseline.co.uk (accessed 30 March 2007).

Vertinsky, P. A. (1990) *The Eternally Wounded Woman: women, doctors, and exercise in the late nineteenth century*, Manchester: Manchester University Press.

Bibliography 179

Voy, R. (1991) *Drugs, Sport and Politics*, Champaign: Leisure Press.

Verroken, M. (2003) 'Drug use and abuse in sport', in D. R. Mottram (ed.) *Drugs in Sport*, 3rd edn, London: Routledge.

—— (2001) 'Ethical aspects and the prevalence of hormone abuse in sport', *Journal of Endocrinology*, 170(1): 49–54.

Waddington, I. (2000) *Sport, Health and Drugs: a critical sociological perspective*, London: Spon.

Waddington, I., Loland, S. and Skirstad, B. (2006) 'Introduction', in S. Loland, B. Skirstad and I. Waddington (eds) *Pain and Injury in Sport: social and ethical analysis*, London: Routledge.

Waitt, G. (1999) 'Playing games with Sydney: marketing Sydney for the 2000 Olympics', *Urban Studies*, 36(7): 1055–77

Wallis, M. and Shepherd, S. (2004) *Drama/Theatre/Performance*, London: Routledge.

Walter, J. (1992) 'Defining Australia', in G. Whitlock and D. Carter (eds) *Images of Australia*, St Lucia: University of Queensland Press.

Walters, L. and Palmer, J. (1997) *The Ethics of Gene Therapy*, New York: Oxford University Press.

Ward, R. (1992) 'The Australian legend', in G. Whitlock and D. Carter (eds) *Images of Australia*, St Lucia: University of Queensland Press.

Webb, L., McCaughtry, N. and MacDonald, D. (2004) 'Surveillance as a technique of power in physical education', *Sport, Education and Society*, 9(2): 207–22.

Weirick, J. (1999) 'Urban design', in R. Cashman and A. Hughes (eds) *Staging the Olympics: the event and its impact*, Sydney: University of New South Wales Press.

Wheaton, B. and Beal, B. (2003) '"Keeping it real": subcultural media and the discourses of authenticity in alternative sport', *International Review for the Sociology of Sport*, 38(2): 155–76.

Wheeler, R. (1995) '"My savage", "My man": racial multiplicity in *Robinson Crusoe*', *English Literary History*, 62(4): 821–61

Whiting, F. (1998) 'Lie tests nab drug cheats', *Sunday Mail*, 11 October.

Whorton, J. C. (1982) *Crusaders for Fitness: the history of American health reformers*, Princeton: Princeton University Press.

Wigglesworth, N. (1996) *The Evolution of English Sport*, London: Routledge.

Williams, R. (2008) 'Swimmers should get new space-age swimsuits says Talbot', *Herald Sun*, 23 April.

Williams, R. and Wilson, J. (2006) 'Drug slur leaves Lenton tormented', *Herald Sun*, 5 December.

Williams, S. J. and Bendelow, G. (1998) *The Lived Body: sociological themes, embodied issues*, London: Routledge.

Wilmore, J. H. and Costill, D. L. (2004) *Physiology of Sport and Exercise*, Champaign: Human Kinetics.

Wilson, J. L. (2005) *Nostalgia: sanctuary of meaning*, Bucknell: Bucknell University Press.

Wilson, R. R. (1995) 'Cyber(body)parts: prosthetic consciousness', in M. Featherstone and R. Burrows (eds) *Cyberspace, Cyberbodies, Cyberpunk: cultures of technological embodiment*, London: Sage.

Wohl, A. S. (1983) *Endangered Lives: public health in Victorian Britain*, Cambridge: Harvard University Press.

WADA (World Anti-Doping Agency) (2007) *International Standard for Therapeutic Use Exemptions*. Available at: www.wada-ama.org/rtecontent/document/internation al_standard.pdf (accessed 15 March 2007)

180   *Bibliography*

—— (2005) *WADA Homepage*. Available at: www.wada-ama.org/en/dynamic.ch2?pageCategory.id=281 (accessed 12 December 2006).

—— (2003) *World Anti-Doping Code*, Montreal: WADA.

WHO (World Health Organization) (2007) *Basic Documents*, 46th edn. Geneva: World Health Organization.

Yesalis, C. E. and Bahrke, M. S. (2002) *Performance-Enhancing Substances in Sport and Exercise*, Champaign: Human Kinetics.

Yesalis, C. E., Kopstein, A. and Bahrke, M. S. (2001). 'Difficulties in estimating the prevalence of drug use among athletes', in W. Wilson and E. Derse (eds) *Doping in Elite Sport: the politics of drugs in the Olympic movement*, Champaign: Human Kinetics.

Young, K. (1993) 'Violence, risk and liability in male sports culture', *Sociology of Sport Journal*, 10(4): 373–96.

Index

abject 10, 40–43, 100, 103, 159
administrators 3, 6–7, 52, 54–55, 89, 109, 112, 128, 137–38, 142–43, 157
advertising 2, 18, 37, 99, 111, 145–46, 150–51, 153–54, 156
Allmark, P. 74, 77
alterity 120
amateurism 5, 16–18, 23, 40, 43, 64, 66, 116, 130, 135, 144, 157
amenorrhoea 80, 101–2
Anderson Inquiry 84
androgeny 11, 68, 103, 105–7, 115
androids 44–45, 123
anti-doping strategies 11, 19, 37, 45, 47, 55, 68, 72–73, 86–87, 89–90, 128–29, 137–38; policies 19, 37, 47, 55, 72, 81, 83, 86–87, 89–90, 128, 137, 158
Aoki, D. 102
apparel 4, 11, 16, 26, 55, 98, 110, 114, 116, 118–19, 126–27, 144, 153
appearance 31, 47–48, 73, 77, 90, 93–98, 103, 105, 107, 118, 121, 139, 154–55
Arbeit, Ekkart 138
athletics 4, 111, 124–25, 138; *see also* track and field
Athletics Australia 138
audience 10, 48, 52, 54, 57–65, 69–70, 92, 104, 114–15, 118, 147, 149–1, 156
Auslander, P. 56, 59, 121
Australia 9, 12, 18, 48, 55, 72, 83–85, 93, 96, 101, 103–4, 107, 112, 114, 120, 129–56, 162; as sports-mad 129, 131, 135, 140, 145; Aussie battler 130, 133, 141; Australianness 12, 129–30, 132, 143, 145, 150, 156; identity 9, 128–45, 147, 149–50, 156; landscape 133, 144, 145–54, 156
Australian Institute of Sport (AIS) 83–84, 136, 143

Australian Olympic Committee (AOC) 83, 85–86
Australian Senate Inquiry into Drugs in Sport 129, 137
Australian Sports Anti-Doping Agency (ASADA) 19, 55, 72, 128–29, 137
Australian Sports Commission (ASC) 18–19, 67, 84, 128, 131, 137, 143
authenticity 3, 8–10, 13, 16, 18, 23–24, 26, 29, 33, 36, 38, 51, 54–55, 58–61, 63–65, 70, 83, 96, 111, 117–18, 123, 136, 144, 152, 160–61

Bale, J. 20, 25–26, 50, 147, 152, 155
Barilan, Y.M. 3, 15, 49
Barnes, Peter 84, 142
baseball 6, 79–80
Beamish, R. 6, 66–67
Bee, P. 113
Benthien, C. 34, 111, 116–18, 154
Berlin, N. 59, 61
binary positions 3, 12–13, 38–40, 42–45, 52, 58, 87, 92–93, 97, 118, 121, 125, 130, 136–37, 141, 143–44, 151, 157–58; nature/artifice 8, 40, 43–45, 50–53, 55, 91, 94–95, 110, 112, 121, 123, 131, 136, 156, 158–59, 161–62; Self/Other 27, 39, 40–44, 52–53, 87–88, 91, 131, 140–41, 162
biomechanics 1–2, 69, 87, 112, 122
bionics 110, 120, 122–23, 126
Black, T. 28, 73, 81
blood 35, 42, 82–83, 90, 122, 148,
blood doping 8, 81–83, 90
bodily fluids 38, 41–43, 45, 52–54, 69, 83–84, 101, 155
body: as abject 10, 40–43, 100, 103, 159; as biological 15, 27, 32–37, 44, 50, 67, 84, 93–94, 103, 123, 153, 159;

182 *Index*

as fixed 5, 10, 32–35, 37, 43, 67, 93, 95–96, 107, 154, 159; as fluid 10, 13, 32–35, 41, 52, 115, 117, 159; as landscape 5, 10, 12, 33, 49–51, 117, 119, 147, 153, 155; as mechanical 10, 33–36, 159; as natural 1, 8–10, 12, 15, 25–26, 30, 33, 36–41, 43, 47, 51–53, 82, 110–11, 114, 120, 126, 135, 144–45, 147, 155, 159, 162; as text 32–33, 63, 92; grotesque 32, 95, 101, 103–5, 115, 139, 141; limits of 2, 5, 7, 10–11, 15, 20–21, 33–35, 37–39, 43, 64, 66–67, 84–85, 93–95, 98, 103, 117, 121–23, 154–55, 157, 160–61; modification of 1–3, 5, 8, 11–12, 27, 31, 35–36, 46, 49, 51, 66, 85, 87, 95, 98–99, 101–2, 107–8, 112, 114–16, 118, 126–27, 137, 146–47, 155; national 9–11, 73,76, 88–89, 131, 133–35, 143–46, 153–55; nature of 13, 31–53, 91, 111; penetration of 10–11, 82–84, 111, 135, 142–43, 154; purity of 8, 10, 11, 13, 23–24, 26, 33, 36, 38–44, 47, 50, 52–53, 64, 73, 77, 82–83, 89, 111, 123, 129–30, 135, 140–42, 144–46, 148, 152–56, 162; restoration of 2, 19, 21, 72, 74, 80, 84–87, 94–95, 101–2, 106, 110, 120, 124, 126, 147, 152, 161
bodybuilding 1, 7, 11, 97–98, 100–102, 107, 115, 117
Boorse, C. 74–75, 87
boosting 122
borders/boundaries 3, 8–11, 39, 40–42, 44–45, 52–53, 64, 73, 88, 92, 94, 96, 102, 110–11, 139, 162; bodily 10–11, 30, 33, 38–39, 41, 43–44, 50–51, 73, 82–83, 88–89, 93–94, 96, 100–103, 106–7, 111, 114, 116–17, 120, 122–24, 126–27, 130–31, 133, 135, 142, 154–55; maintenance of 9, 11; national 9–10, 33, 88–89, 129, 130–31, 133, 135, 137, 140–41, 154–55; penetration of 10–11, 84, 111, 133, 142–43, 154; transgression of 7, 9, 12, 30, 38, 45, 82–84, 95, 101, 103, 114, 155
Boultbee, John 143
Boyle, Raelene 138
Braidotti, R. 92, 99–100
Bryson, L. 19
Burstyn, V. 100
Butler, J. 56, 94–95, 115

Carlile, Forbes 105, 138
Carlson, M. 56–58, 63
character 15, 19, 54, 73, 77; national 134, 143–44
character-building 2, 9, 14, 17, 19, 29
cheating 12, 43, 48, 62, 100, 104, 130, 135, 143, 157
China 93, 96, 103–7, 126, 137–39, 141–42
Citius, Altius, Fortius 1, 8, 19, 43
class 17–18, 21–23, 32, 37, 41, 76, 116, 132
coaches 1, 6–7, 16, 37, 48, 54, 59, 62, 64, 66, 68–69, 71, 103, 105–6, 109, 112–13, 128–29, 137–39, 142
Cold War 43, 67
commercialisation 1, 15–16, 29, 40, 63, 96, 100, 128, 148, 157
Commonwealth Games 137, 142
contagion 38, 74–76, 159
contamination 10, 12, 21, 27, 32, 36, 38, 41–43, 52, 71, 76, 83–84, 86, 88–89, 111, 114, 117, 127, 133, 135, 140–41, 144–46, 148, 154–56, 159
corruption 3, 10–11, 13, 16, 18, 23, 27, 33–34, 36, 38, 40, 52, 69–70, 84, 87, 90, 107, 130, 145, 153–54, 156–60
cosmetic surgery 31, 95, 98, 102
Court of Arbitration for Sport (CAS) 126,
Crawford, R. 23, 74–78
Curry-Kenny, Lisa 138
cyborg 12, 22, 44, 110–11, 120, 122–24, 126–27, 144
cycling 6, 25, 64–65, 83–84, 111, 142

Dajka, Jobie 83–84
Davenport, Lindsay 93
Davis, L. 37
de Bruijn, Inge 97
de Coubertin, Baron Pierre 22
de la Pena, C. 4–5, 22, 34–35, 67
de Merode, Prince Alexandre 48
de Montaigne, Michel 34–35
dehumanisation 22, 32, 37
Delano, L 37
Descartes, Rene 35
diet 1, 8, 16, 31, 55, 68, 77, 98, 155
disability 41, 74, 87, 110–11, 120–26, 161–62
discipline 2–3, 5–6, 10, 14–15, 19, 26–29, 46–47, 65, 69, 92, 106, 114, 119
disease 22, 31, 41, 71–78, 84, 87–88, 111, 133, 159

Index 183

doping 8, 11, 15, 19–20, 23, 27–28, 30, 37, 40, 45, 47, 53–55, 68, 72–73, 81–87, 89–91, 109, 128–29, 137–39, 143, 146, 158; sanctions 54, 83–84, 91, 103
Douglas, Mary 41, 83
drag 115, 119
drugs 7–8, 11–12, 19, 37, 41, 45, 48, 54, 68, 72–73, 77, 81, 84, 86, 88–89, 100–101, 103, 110, 114–15, 128–44; abuse 7, 72, 81, 90, 98, 100–106, 129–30, 141–43; amphetamines 68–69; colostrum 142; creatine 81; dextropropoxyphene 103; Dianabol 68; erythropoietin 47, 68, 81–84, 90, 105, 142–43; headache tablets 86, 103–4, 142; human growth hormone 68, 83–84, 139, 143; Insulin Growth Factor-1 (IGF-1) 142; performance enhancing 10, 15, 28, 45, 68, 81, 86, 94, 109, 114–15, 126, 128–29, 141–43, 145, 153; pseudoephedrine; side effects 72, 99, 101–2, 105; somatropin 139; steroids 1, 6, 42, 48, 68–69, 83–86, 90, 96, 99–102, 105, 138, 143; testing 42, 45–48, 53–54, 69, 90, 103–4, 106, 122, 144, 153, 155; testosterone 68, 83, 101; use 7, 37, 41–43, 45, 48 102, 105, 128, 135, 141; Ventolin 81; war on 7, 12, 72, 128, 137, 143, 153; see also performance enhancing substances
Duncan, M.C. 46
Dunlap, T. 22, 148, 150
Dyer, R. 118

East Germany 138–39, 141
Eastern Bloc 135–38
efficiency 5, 26, 31, 35, 50, 56, 66, 115
Elliot, Herb 133
endurance 60, 66, 68, 82, 105, 109
enhancement 7, 9–11, 20, 28, 48, 53, 55, 65–66, 69–70, 81–82, 84–87, 107, 109, 114, 120, 122, 126–27, 143; illicit 8–9, 12–13, 15, 37, 40, 43, 47–48, 53, 69, 72, 81, 91, 93, 99, 103, 109–10, 120, 136–37, 140, 144, 154–55, 158–59; technological 6, 9, 43, 51, 64, 96
Enlightenment 5, 23, 33–34, 76
environment 12, 16, 20–22, 24–26, 29, 49–50, 76, 82, 112, 121, 133, 145–53, 155–56, 160
equipment 1, 4, 8, 16, 25, 35, 64–67, 113, 120; safety 4, 5, 16, 72, 79

Erlmann. V. 119
ethnicity 105, 118, 132
eugenics 3, 31
exercise 1–2, 22, 71, 78–79

fair play 2, 14–15, 19, 27–28, 112, 116, 147
Fairchild, D. 42, 83, 88
fairness 19, 27–28, 89, 112–13, 126
Fastskin 1, 64, 107, 109–20, 126–28
Fauquet, Claude 113
Federation Internationale de Natation (FINA) 103, 109, 139
femininity 11–12, 37, 46, 48, 90–103, 106–8, 115–16, 118, 136, 160
fitness 1, 31, 46, 71, 77, 88, 98, 140, 158
Foucault, M. 4, 46, 95
Frankenstein 3, 32, 100, 102, 123, 159
Fraser, Dawn 133

gardens 10, 25, 33, 50–51, 152, 155
Garnier, Alain 20
gender 9, 11, 32–33, 38, 90–101, 106–7, 115–18, 139
genetic technologies 3, 23, 28, 31, 49, 68, 83, 127–28,
genitalia 38, 101–2
Gilot, Fabien 113
golden age 17, 20, 40, 64, 130, 132–33
golf courses 25, 117, 155
Gould, Shane 133
government 37, 45, 67, 72–73, 76, 78–79, 89–90, 128–29, 131–32, 143, 148, 157
Graham, Sylvester 77
Griffith-Joyner, Florence 160
Grosz, E. 39, 41
Groth, P. 147
gymnastics 4, 21, 48, 80, 97
Gyulail, Istvan 125

Hackett, Grant 114
haematocrit 82, 90
Haraway, D. 22, 44, 99, 102, 123
hard work 2, 6, 26, 36, 65, 103, 106, 114
health 2, 4, 7–11, 15–16, 21–22, 25, 31, 36, 38, 43, 45, 47, 66,68, 70–90, 95, 99, 101–2, 121, 129, 133–34, 141–43, 145–46, 152, 154, 158–60, 162; restoration of 11, 22, 45, 85–87, 89, 142,
Heywood, L. 97–98
Hingis, Martina 93

184 *Index*

Hoberman, J. 5, 8, 20, 32, 37, 66–68, 161
Homebush Bay 12, 144–49, 152–53, 155–56
Hood, M. 110, 123, 125–26
hormones 11, 45, 68, 83, 98–99, 102; manipulation of 32, 102, 104–5, 107, 114, 116–17, 142
Hunter, C.J. 48
hybrid 3, 44, 123–24, 126
hygiene 16, 22–23, 38, 76–78
hyperhuman 115, 123
hypoxic chambers 6, 16, 81–82, 90

identity 9–10, 12, 33, 38–40, 52, 73–74, 77–78, 96–97, 100–101, 103, 105–6, 118, 121, 123, 139, 162; national 9, 39, 87, 129–45, 147–50, 153–54, 156, 159
ideology 2–3, 14–15, 17–18, 22, 24, 29, 32–34, 36, 38, 40, 43, 50, 52, 57, 64–65, 70, 88–89, 95, 111, 116–17, 132, 136–37, 143–44, 147–48, 153, 157–59
illness 22, 71, 74–75, 79, 87, 99, 159; headache 79, 86
Imaginary Stage 140
industrialisation 3–5, 9, 16, 18, 21–24, 27, 29, 34–36, 46, 49,56, 66, 76–77, 148, 150, 153,
injection 7, 81–84, 141–42, 155
injury 5, 11, 71–72, 74, 78–80, 84, 87–88, 100, 122, 159
Inside Sport 96, 101, 104–6, 138
integrity 2, 12–13, 36, 39, 45, 54–55, 70, 88–89, 143, 159–62; of the body 11, 30, 37–38, 82, 88, 110–11, 117, 123, 126–27, 131, 153–56, 158–59; of sport 16, 19, 29, 42, 52, 72, 112, 128–29, 137, 158–59, 162
intention 10–11, 54, 56, 70, 84–85, 87
International Association of Athletics Federations (IAAF) 124–26, 161
International Federation of Bodybuilders (IFBB) 97–98
International Olympic Committee (IOC) 18, 47–48, 54, 68, 85, 138, 143, 145, 149; IOC Medical Commission 47–48, 54, 68, 143

Johnson, Ben 1
Jones, James Earl 151
Jones, Liesel 93, 96
Jones, Marion 160

Jones, S. 101–2
Judovitz, D. 34–35

Keating, J. 26
Kellogg, John Harvey 77
Kirk, D. 46
König, E. 19
Kournikova, Anna 96
Krayzelburg, Lenny 112
Kristeva, J. 41, 52, 82–83, 103, 117

Lacan, J. 39–41, 52, 94, 139–40
landscape 5, 9–10, 20–21, 24, 26–27, 29, 33–34, 36, 49–50, 88, 119, 133, 144–51, 153, 156; national 12, 33, 144, 155; natural 12, 22, 37, 49–51, 117, 146, 148, 154, 156
Larson, J.S. 75
Le, Jingyi 91, 138
Lenton, Libby 93, 96
Leopold, Winfried 139
level playing field 15, 20, 26, 28, 85, 112–13, 115, 124, 126
Levine, B.D. 6, 16, 82
liminality 8, 10, 33, 39, 43–44, 50–51, 102–3, 123, 152, 159, 162; liminal body 8, 10, 33, 43–45, 50–51, 102–3, 123, 159; liminal space 43–45, 50, 52–53, 141, 143, 162
Locatelli, Elio 125
Lovell, N. 24, 147, 152

machines 1–5, 18, 22, 35–36, 50, 65–67, 120, 123–24
Macnaghten, P. 21, 23–24, 76
Magdalinski, T. 7, 9, 32, 43, 45, 47, 83, 89, 103, 112, 117–18, 129, 140, 142
Malson, H. 96–98
Manaudou, Laure 109
masculinity 11, 47–48, 61, 90–94, 96–103, 105–8, 115, 118–19, 136, 139; arena of 11, 92, 106, 108, 115
Mauresmo, Amelie 93
media 1, 7, 12, 38, 47–48, 53–55, 59, 62–63, 67, 69, 77, 89, 91–93, 95–96, 100, 103–4, 107, 115, 118,-19, 122, 126, 129, 131, 133, 137–41, 143, 146, 149, 151–52, 154
medication 1, 84–86, 101
Miah, A. 3, 7–8, 31, 37, 55, 68, 80, 82, 127
mirror stage 39–40, 140
Møller, V. 2, 19
Moneghetti, Steve 135

monsters 11, 91, 100–102, 107, 123, 155, 159
monstrous feminine 11, 90, 94, 100, 102–4
moral panic 43, 109, 112, 157
morality 7–9, 11, 14–18, 22–27, 44, 66,70, 72–73, 76–78, 89–90, 92, 119, 130, 137, 141, 156–60, 162
Moussambani, Eric 51, 118–20
Munthe, C. 28
muscle 7, 59, 82, 87, 91, 93, 96–98, 107, 114–15, 117; hypermuscularity 47, 98; muscularity 96–97, 100, 106; musculature 91, 97–98, 105, 117
Muscular Christianity 9, 16–17, 77

nakedness 118–19
nation 9–12, 14, 21, 32–33, 39, 47, 49, 61, 67, 72–73, 75–76, 78–79, 86–90, 103–5, 129–48, 150–57, 162
nature 3, 6, 8–10, 12, 14–16, 18, 20–30, 32, 34–38, 40, 49–53, 70, 76, 78, 85, 91, 101, 107, 111, 123, 135, 142, 145–56, 158–59, 162; as rejuvenating 16, 49, 76; performance of 12, 145–46
naturists 21
nostalgia 16, 21, 64, 130
nutrition 1, 16, 35, 52, 69, 71, 76–77, 154–55

Olympic Games 14, 18, 54, 79, 84, 87, 105, 120, 123, 125, 148–50; 'green' games 146, 148–49; 1968 Mexico 47; 1972 Munich 138; 1976 Montreal 136, 144; 1980 Moscow 139; 1988 Seoul 129, 137; 1992 Albertville 149; 1994 Lillehammer 149; 1996 Atlanta 105, 112, 139; 2000 Sydney 12, 48, 118, 126, 131, 137, 144–56; 2004 Athens 83, 119; 2008 Beijing 124–26
Olympic movement 2, 18, 22, 145, 153, 156
Olympism 21, 118, 147, 149
O'Neill, Susie 96
Orwell, George 6, 32, 89
Overton, Elli 139

panopticon 46, 53, 95–96
Pape, A. 28, 73, 81
Paralympics 87, 121–24, 126
parks 23, 25, 50, 148–49, 152, 158
Peacock, J. 57
performance 1–3, 5–10, 12–13, 15–16, 19–20, 25–29, 31–32, 35–37, 43, 45,
49, 50, 52–70, 73, 79, 85–87, 93–99, 104, 109–17, 119–22, 124, 126–27, 134, 142, 144, 146–47, 153–54, 156–58, 160–62; authenticity of 8, 29, 36, 54–55, 58–59, 61, 63–65, 70, 110, 147, 161; nature of 6, 8, 10, 13, 53–70, 160–61; performance studies 10, 55–56, 60; pure performance 26, 49–50, 64–65, 111, 126, 128, 146, 156, 161; theatrical 10, 55–56, 58, 60–63, 69–70
performance enhancement 6–13, 20, 28, 40, 48, 52, 54–55, 65, 66–69, 81, 91, 99, 103–4, 122, 136, 142–44, 160
performance enhancing substances 7–9, 11, 20, 28, 36, 38, 43, 45, 47, 52–55, 64–69, 72–73, 78, 80–86, 90, 93–95, 99, 101, 103, 107, 110, 129–31, 138, 141–43, 155, 157, 160; see also drugs
performance technology 1–13, 15, 23, 28–30, 33, 36, 39, 51, 53, 60, 63, 70, 73–74, 78, 81–82, 100, 107, 114, 128–29, 137, 140, 143, 153, 157–58, 160, 162
performativity 56, 60
Perkins, Kieren 134
pharmaceuticals 20, 28, 64, 68, 84, 86–87, 99, 104, 111
Phelps, Michael 114
phrenology 48
physical activity 2, 4–5, 7, 9, 15, 17, 22, 71, 78, 80, 102, 121, 135
physical capacity 1–2, 5–6, 15–16, 19, 21, 26–29, 31, 35–37, 42, 49, 55, 62–64, 66–67, 70, 73, 82, 87, 110, 122, 155, 160
physical education 17, 46, 71, 78
physiology 2, 5–6, 22, 34, 75, 81–83, 85–87, 112
Pistorius, Oscar 124–26, 161–62
Porritt, Sir Arthur 54
professional wrestling 60–61
professionalism 2, 11, 15–16, 40, 42–43, 72, 79, 85, 87, 135, 157,
prosthetics 12, 31, 35, 87, 107, 109–11, 120–27, 161; Cheetah blades 124–25

race 32, 37, 41–42, 48, 76, 119, 121, 132
Raducan, Andreea 48, 160
reality television 58, 61, 133
records 8, 19, 37, 43, 53–54, 60, 62, 64–65, 67, 113, 124, 126, 129, 137–38, 140, 157, 160,
rejuvenation 2, 4, 21–22

186 *Index*

religion 32–34, 41, 76, 132
reproduction 94–95, 99, 102
Riesser, Otto 20
Riley, Samantha 103–7, 142, 160
Rinehart, R. 60–62
Ritchie, I. 6, 66–67
robots 44–45, 136
Romantic era 9, 15–16, 21, 23, 27, 29, 36, 150
rules 4, 14, 23, 27, 42, 52, 55, 62, 80, 97–98, 109, 112, 121, 125, 160; changes to 26, 72, 79–80, 125, 161

Sandahl, C. 121
Sando, Brian 142
Savulescu, J. 20, 28, 66, 80, 82, 85–86, 90
Schieffelin, E. 57, 62
science fiction 32, 110, 120, 123–24
scientisation 15, 19, 104, 135, 144
scopophilia 92
Second World War 6, 67
sex testing 47
sexuality 3, 11, 32, 37, 42, 90, 92, 95–96, 98, 103, 107, 115–16, 160
shamateurism 135–36, 144
Shelley, Mary 32, 100–101
Shilling, C. 4, 33, 35–37, 65, 87, 110, 120, 122, 141
shortcut 6, 15, 36, 65,
Sibley, D. 41–42, 44, 88, 14–1
skin 10, 25, 83, 101, 109–11, 114–19, 123, 127, 154–56
Smith, Michelle (de Bruin) 97, 160
Smith, N. 23, 146
Soper, K. 24, 27
South Africa 113, 124
Speedo 109, 112–14, 118–19, 127
sport: as natural 3, 9, 27, 129, 135; essence of 2, 14–15, 17–19, 26, 36, 40, 51, 128, 137, 143, 157–58; nature of 8–10, 14–30, 40, 62, 127, 144, 160; purity of 15, 18, 32, 43, 63, 89, 125, 129, 153, 161; Soviet 67–68, 104, 135–36, 138, 144; spirit of 2–3, 6, 9, 14–17, 19–20, 23, 29, 36, 40, 51, 55, 62, 68, 70, 122, 135, 143–44, 157–58, 160
sports federations 16, 37, 42, 45, 47, 53, 67–68, 72, 79–80, 86, 89–90, 97–98, 109, 125, 127, 129
Sports Illustrated 93, 112–15
sports industry 2, 5, 15, 40, 65, 67, 72, 79, 157
sports medicine 72, 79

sports science 2, 5, 7, 19–20, 27, 32, 35–37, 59, 65–67, 69, 142, 144, 161
sportscape 9, 25, 27, 49–51, 147, 152
stereotypes 44, 52, 88, 105, 107, 136, 139, 141
strength 48, 60, 68, 75, 87, 92, 96–97, 106, 121–22, 134; national 76, 88, 134, 140, 143, 153–54
superhuman 31, 37
supplements 1, 7–8, 11, 19, 68, 101, 110, 142, 155; supplementation 7, 19, 52, 81, 99, 124, 144; vitamins 83–84
surfaces: bodily 12, 32–33, 48, 50, 53, 90, 92, 96, 107, 111, 117, 127, 147, 153–55, 159; playing 16, 59, 65
surveillance 4, 10, 45–47, 51, 53, 88, 92, 96, 141, 147, 159; CCTV 46–47
swimming 1, 12, 20, 55, 79, 90–91, 93, 96–97, 103–7, 109–16, 118–21, 126, 128, 137–39, 142
swimming pools 1, 25–26, 51, 55–56, 65, 91, 109, 112, 126, 138–39, 148
swimsuits 1, 12, 55, 64, 105, 107, 109–20, 126, 128, 138
Sydney Olympic Bid Limited (SOBL) 148–49, 152–53
Sydney Organising Committee for the Olympic Games (SOCOG) 146, 148–49, 151
Symbolic Order 44, 52, 140
symbols 22, 104, 117, 134, 144, 151–52

Talbot, Don 112–13, 139
talent 26,28, 52, 114, 158; talent identification 105, 128, 135–36
Taussig, M. 120
technologisation 2, 19, 40, 45, 66, 91–92, 116
technology 1–13, 15–16, 19–21, 23, 25, 27–28, 32, 37–38, 42, 44, 51, 53, 65, 69, 82, 87, 91, 94, 99, 107, 110, 112–15, 117–19, 123–28, 135, 154, 158–59
technophobia 3, 15, 49
tennis 4, 6, 93, 96,
Terminator 32, 110, 123
terra nullius 150
terrain 10, 12, 88, 119, 133, 144, 147, 150, 153–54
The Bionic Man 110
theatre 56, 60–64, 69; theatre studies 10, 55–56, 69
Therapeutic Use Exemption (TUE) 81, 86
Thompson, Jenny 115

Thorpe, Ian 1, 55, 114, 144
Tour de France 6, 47, 142
track and field 124–25, 135, 138, 161;
  see also athletics
training 6–8, 10, 16–17, 20, 26–27, 34,
  36, 43, 45, 51–52, 55, 59, 64–66,
  70–71, 75, 79–80, 82, 87, 90, 98, 102,
  105–7, 113, 118, 121, 135–38, 144,
  147–48, 153, 155, 158; altitude 81–82,
  90; centralised 135–36, 138, 144;
  scientific 135–37, 142, 144
Turner, B.S. 37, 77, 83, 88

UK Sport 19, 55, 89
unfair advantage 7, 15, 27–28, 54, 113,
  124, 126, 142,
uniform 105, 116, 153, 160
United States of America 19, 48, 55,
  61, 68, 71–72, 75, 77, 105, 112,
  114–15, 120, 133, 150–51
unpredictability 25–26, 29, 59, 61, 82,
urbanisation 16, 21–22, 76
Urry, J. 21, 23–24, 76

van Dijck, J. 49
Victorian era 15, 22, 29, 64, 66, 76, 78
Volkers, Scott 103, 106

Warwick, Zoe 1, 11, 101–4, 107, 115,
  160
weightlifting 48, 68, 93
Weintraub, M. 3, 15, 49
well-being 4, 8, 10–11, 15, 22, 36,
  71–73, 75–79, 88–90, 133, 143, 159
wheelchair 87, 110, 122–23
Wheeler, R. 119,
wilderness 4, 10, 21–22, 24, 33, 50–51,
  151–52
women 7, 11–12, 22, 38, 41–42, 46–48,
  72, 80, 90–107, 109, 115, 118–19,
  121, 130, 136–39, 153, 160
World Anti-Doping Agency (WADA)
  19–20, 47, 55, 81–82, 85–87; World
  Anti-Doping Code 55
World Conference on Doping 47, 85
World Health Organisation (WHO) 75
World Swimming Championships
  137–39

Yuan, Yuan 139

Zandberg, Gerhard 113
Zeigler, John 68

A library at your fingertips!

eBooks are electronic versions of printed books. You can store them on your PC/laptop or browse them online.

They have advantages for anyone needing rapid access to a wide variety of published, copyright information.

eBooks can help your research by enabling you to bookmark chapters, annotate text and use instant searches to find specific words or phrases. Several eBook files would fit on even a small laptop or PDA.

NEW: Save money by eSubscribing: cheap, online access to any eBook for as long as you need it.

Annual subscription packages

We now offer special low-cost bulk subscriptions to packages of eBooks in certain subject areas. These are available to libraries or to individuals.

For more information please contact webmaster.ebooks@tandf.co.uk

We're continually developing the eBook concept, so keep up to date by visiting the website.

www.eBookstore.tandf.co.uk